Jews and Christians on Time and Eternity
Charles Péguy's Portrait of Bernard-Lazare

Stanford Studies in Jewish History and Culture
Edited by Aron Rodrigue and Steven J. Zipperstein

Jews and Christians on Time and Eternity

Charles Péguy's Portrait
of Bernard-Lazare

Annette Aronowicz

Stanford University Press
Stanford, California 1998

Stanford University Press
Stanford, California
© 1998 by the Board of Trustees of the Leland Stanford
Junior University
Printed in the United States of America

CIP data are at the back of the book

Frontispiece: Left, Bernard-Lazare, photograph courtesy
Bibliothèque de l'Alliance Israélite Universelle (Paris), Fonds
Bernard-Lazare. *Right,* Charles Péguy, portrait by Jean-Pierre
Laurens, © Centre Charles Péguy—Orléans.

To Kees and to Pien

The reflections in this volume circle around a classical text, the portrait that Charles Péguy, a Catholic, drew in his essay "Notre jeunesse" of Lazare Marcus Manassé Bernard, a Jew, who is known to us under his nom de plume, Bernard-Lazare.[1] It might seem presumptuous to label Péguy's pages classical, ranging them with the great works of the Western tradition. "Notre jeunesse" is, after all, unknown to most English-speaking readers. It is also less than mellifluous, passages of great beauty alternating with more plodding ones. In fact, reading Péguy's portrait of Bernard-Lazare can be compared to going on a somewhat demanding hike, where the hard work is periodically interrupted by breathtaking views.

Nonetheless, one reason the portrait can be called classical is that Péguy, in these pages, addresses one of the perennial questions in Western history, the relationship between Jews and Christians. Moreover, he does so in a way that touches upon a yet broader question, that of the relation to the other, to the one who is not "us." This too is a perennial question, colored in the latter half of the twentieth century by huge migrations across continents and changing relationships of all sorts. How to locate the universally human in all this sudden mixing, but not at the expense of the particularity that makes the other other, remains the urgent modern problem.

Péguy's portrait of Bernard-Lazare is a classic, however, not only because it addresses a perennial question but also because it does so in a paradigmatic way. In many respects, it provides us with the equivalent of a mythological model. We are presented with a pattern characteristic of our relation to the one who is not "us," applicable at all times and places. This pattern, however, is conveyed to us more immediately than in a theoretical exposition. It is *embodied* in the images and rhythm of the text. I have made much of this embodiment (alternately using Péguy's own term for the same phenomenon, *incarnation*), claiming that it is integrally related to Péguy's understanding of a particular in which a universal always lies hidden.

My exposition explores this embodiment from various angles. First of all, I place Péguy's text in its historical context, one way of showing how it was itself embodied. That context—turn-of-the-century France—involved an atmosphere heavily imbued with antisemitism. On one level, Péguy's portrait is an attack on that antisemitism. I want to show, however, that that attack was not just a point-by-point rejoinder to common antisemitic arguments but stemmed from a certain theological framework buried in the fabric of his text and permeating it as a whole.

I focus in Chapter 1 on how Péguy's specific wording responds to the intellectual climate of his time, but I also at several points indicate the relevance of Péguy's discussion of Jews to our own debates about diversity and multiculturalism. Péguy's work can be used neither to embrace nor to oppose a particular side in the present-day debate. It simply deepens the question. Chapter 2 contains my translation of Péguy's portrait of Bernard-Lazare, and in Chapter 3, I align Péguy's work with that of two twentieth-century Jewish thinkers of note, Franz Rosenzweig and Emmanuel Levinas. While retaining its own import, Péguy's thought nonetheless finds parallels in that of these two authors, simply because for them too the great problem remained how to describe a universal embodied in the particular. Péguy's portrait of Bernard-Lazare, I wish to suggest, is as if an illustration of some of the philosophical insights of the two Jewish thinkers, not because he was influenced by them—his work in fact chronologically preceded theirs—but because they brought to greater theoretical articulation certain themes that already preoccupied Péguy in the early 1900's. This is not to say that Péguy himself did not articulate these themes. It is rather to say that they emerge in starker profile when juxtaposed to the work of these two Jewish authors.

In Chapter 3, too, I reflect on why the comparison yields such echoes between the Christian author and the Jewish ones. Among other possible explanations, I suggest that we have in these three authors the outlines of a certain sort of religious expression that crossed confessional lines, simply because the events of the twentieth century confronted people from both traditions with very similar dilemmas. It has been the century of the ideological crushing of the particular, eventually to death. The work of all three authors responds to this brutal reality, drawing on the resources of their respective religious traditions.

Finally, in Chapter 4, I expand indirectly on the idea that the thought of these three authors (although I continue to draw my main categories from Péguy himself) reveals the religious orientation of our times, by turning to two recent works of historiography, Jaff Schatz's *The Generation* and Philip Hallie's *Lest Innocent Blood Be Shed*. This may seem a strange place to turn, since history writers rarely display what might be considered religious sensibilities. In fact, modern historical methodology most often requires keeping such sensibilities far removed from the task of interpreting. It goes without saying, however, that writing history always involves understanding others. The tension between the difference of the people studied—their particularity—and the common human situation that their difference nonetheless reveals—the universal—lies at the heart of the discipline of historiography. The two histories I have chosen reveal this tension in ways quite reminiscent of Péguy, Levinas, and Rosenzweig.

I am not claiming that these two histories are theological or even philosophical treatises. They remain histories of particular people, of Polish Jewish communists in one case and of Huguenots in a southern French village in the other. But once we have been made more aware of the way embodiment is related to certain theological issues through reading Péguy, Levinas, and Rosenzweig, we can begin to detect certain religious hues in the details of these histories. That history writing can be a significant key to the religious temper of an epoch is an insight for which I am indebted to Péguy himself, whose most important source for evaluating the hidden theological assumptions of his time was the historiography of his contemporaries.[2]

I realize that deriving such large questions from a text as brief as Péguy's portrait of Bernard-Lazare may, at first glance, seem an improbable exercise. That too, of course, reflects the peculiar relation of particular to universal. The whole world can lie hidden in the smallest of details. But it must be added that my reflections, although centered on Péguy's portrait of Bernard-Lazare, also incorporate my knowledge of his other writings, starting with the rest of "Notre jeunesse" but including many other of his essays, which I occasionally refer to in the notes. This translation and commentary are intended to give a taste of Péguy's thought as a whole; I hope to draw the reader into a further examination of his work, while focusing on the portrait of Bernard-Lazare. Such an examination, I suggest, will enable us to approach the religious emphases of our own times from a new angle.

Three appendixes supply some other relevant short texts. Appendix A contains Péguy's meditation "The Secret of the Man of Forty," taken from his "Clio—Dialogue de l'histoire et de l'âme païenne," in which we get a further glimpse of his notion of hope. Appendix B provides the Talmudic text from which Levinas derives his interpretation of revelation, to make it easier for the reader to follow my exegesis of his work. Appendix C consists of a series of other passages from "Notre jeunesse" itself: descriptions of Bernard-Lazare that do not form part of the portrait and comments on Jews or Péguy's concepts of *mystique* and *politique*, to which I frequently refer.

I have many people to thank for the different sorts of help they extended to me while I was working on this book. For reading carefully and commenting on a manuscript from a nearly complete stranger, I want to thank Brian Fay and John A. Bernstein, each of whom I sent a penultimate version, hoping that scholars not in my immediate field would find it of interest. They responded very generously with pages of agreements and disagreements, both of which gave me the courage to plow ahead. I also want to thank Richard A. Cohen, Catherine Chalier, and Tamara Eskenazi, all of them friends of long standing, for reading the manuscript. We are laborers in parallel vineyards, if not in the identical one. I am grateful for the friendship they showed me in their critical attention to detail.

Turning to my circle at Franklin and Marshall College, I want to thank two former colleagues and current good friends, Mark Harman and Michael Steinlauf, the former for many discussions about translation and suggestions on style; the latter, also for many discussions, and for having directed me to Jaff Schatz's book on Polish Jewish communists. Still within the same circle, I want to express my gratitude to Lina Bernstein and David Kramer for many conversations, for reading me, for feeding me, for being home to me.

Nothing of this book would have reached publishable form, however, were it not for the extraordinary efforts of Tana Pratt, who in her enormously busy schedule found time to prepare the manuscript. She did so in her usual way, with great efficiency and good will. I thank both her and Scott Feifer, who briefly reassumed his old role as my assistant when he was needed in a pinch.

Finally, I want to thank Kees Bolle and Pien Pook van Baggen. Pien bought me my first collection of Péguy's writings in 1974. Kees began to talk to me about Péguy around the same time. Both have inspired and read everything I have ever published. This book is yet one more attempt to translate, however awkwardly, that inspiration.

Contents

Jews and Christians on Time and Eternity
Charles Péguy's Portrait of Bernard-Lazare

CHAPTER ONE

Speaking About the Other

It has become a tradition among recent writers on Charles Péguy to begin by stating that, up to the present work, he has been severely misunderstood.[1] This study would fit squarely within this tradition if American readers were sufficiently familiar with his thought to have misunderstood him. But since even his name remains unknown to most, the task of this translation and commentary is first of all simply to introduce him.

To introduce Péguy is to introduce an important thinker of the twentieth century. In the many works about him, he is presented as a great patriot, a pious Catholic, a fervent socialist, and a fierce polemicist, but rarely as someone who, while he might be all of the above and more, also articulated a coherent vision of the world not easily subsumed under any of these categories. Nothing if not a serious thinker, he searched all his life for the basic structures undergirding the reality he lived in. Despite the idiosyncrasies of his style,[2] he remains surprisingly readable, not least because of the contemporaneity of many of his intellectual struggles. I have chosen one of these struggles as an entryway into his thought, embodied in the portrait he drew of his friend Bernard-Lazare in his essay "Notre jeunesse."

"Notre jeunesse," one of the most beautiful pieces of writing in an oeuvre that includes not a few beautiful pieces, exhibits, like all Péguy's works, his signature: a peculiar repetitiveness and an inimitable mixture of melancholy and humor.[3] It is, however, more succinct, more compact, than many of his other essays. Its aesthetic qualities aside, "Notre jeunesse" is a good point of entry into Péguy's thought, because it addresses one of our contemporary debates, the debate about how to include "the other," how to speak about him or her. While we are busy revising the curricula of our universities and reforming our language, it seems to me that we often lack a discussion at the right level, beyond rhetoric and politics, about what the relationship to the other entails. Péguy is not the only person who can help us to find the right level and perhaps even the right direction. But he is one such person. His portrait of Bernard-Lazare is, after all, an illustration of a Christian speaking about Jews.

Someone might object that from the point of view of the current mainstream, at least in the United States, Jews are not sufficiently other.[4] In our latest parlance, they are "Anglos," in the same category as many Protestants and Catholics. Is not the real other, from the point of view of that mainstream, the Asian, the African-American, or the Hispanic? In response, it hardly needs to be recalled that Jews were the great other in European history, not least in the period in which Péguy was writing, about which I shall say more later. But, more important, the other is not just the out-group of the moment. The other is the neighbor who, despite all similarities, remains different.[5] In this sense, while there may be a group or groups much more discriminated against at a given time than, let us say, American Jews, the relationship of Jew and Christian in our culture will always be paradigmatic of an irreducible difference that refuses to go away.

Péguy's essay does not talk about the problem of the "other." It simply presents the other, in all his difference and in all his common humanity. In the essay, there are an "us" and a "them." But the line between the two is continually being effaced, leaving only a "we." The "we," on the other hand, keeps on being interrupted by the line between "us" and "them," continually reemerging. The interest of the portrait, then, lies in the tension it maintains between the universal, in which all differences disappear, and the particular, the irreducibly different.

The bulk of my commentary will attempt to illustrate this tension. Beforehand, though, I want to acquaint readers altogether unfamiliar with Péguy's life and thought with some of their salient features. Included among them will be a few words about his relationship to Bernard-Lazare and about Bernard-Lazare himself.

Péguy and Bernard-Lazare

Péguy was born in 1873 on the outskirts of the city of Orléans. His father, a carpenter, died shortly after his birth, leaving him in the company of his mother and grandmother. The former supported the family by mending chairs. Here and there throughout his writings, Péguy refers to his humble roots.[6] One of the most beautiful evocations of his background occurs in the last essay he wrote (published posthumously) before he went off to war in 1914, "Note conjointe sur M. Descartes et la philosophie cartésienne." In a long passage in it, he speaks about the illiteracy of his peasant ancestors, all Catholics, starting with the most recent, his grandmother. He contrasts it with the perennial literacy of the Jews and the 500-year literacy of the Protestants. In the following excerpt, he describes Julien Benda,[7] a Jew, and himself, a Catholic, walking the streets of Paris, talking philosophy:

> So similar, so different; such enemies, such friends; such strangers, so much penetrated one by the other; so intertwined, so allied and so loyal; so opposite and so conjoined, our two philosophers, those two accomplices, walk down the street. Another, deep, difference walks between them but does not disjoin them. It is a difference between them that goes back far, another, more subtle, difference of race, a scission from a fissure perhaps yet more disjoining. The Jew knows how to read. The Christian, the Catholic, does not know how to read.
>
> In the social category to which they belong, the Jew can go back generation upon generation and he can go back for centuries: he can always find someone who can read. If he were to trace himself back to some cattle merchant of the *pulta* plains,[8] or some horse dealer of the immensities of *tchernosium*,[9] if he were to trace himself back to some seller of matches of the late Empire or Alexandria or Byzantium or to some Bedouin in the desert, the Jew is of a race in which one always finds someone who can read. And not only that, but to read for them is not to read a book. It is to read the Book. It is to read the Book and the Law. To read is to read the word of God. The very inscription of God on the tablets and in the book. In this immense sacred apparatus, the most ancient of all, reading is the sacred performance as it is the ancient performance. All Jews are readers. All Jews are reciters. It is because of this that all Jews are visual, and visionary. And that they see everything. As if instantaneously. And at a single glance, they instantaneously run over, cover surfaces. . . . Seeing this the Catholic looks into himself. No matter which way he traces himself back, he is illiterate beyond the second generation.[10]

This is but an abbreviated taste of a meditation that goes on for many pages, whose refrain is that the Jews have been reading forever, the Protestants since Calvin, and the Catholics only since 1880. Péguy finds a virtue in illiteracy perhaps greater than that acquired through literacy. But, and this is crucial, in the passage quoted above, there is a continual movement between difference and similarity, neither winning out against the other. In this respect, it is reminiscent of the passage on tents in the desert in the portrait of Bernard-Lazare. The Jews turn all houses, even the most solid, into tents. People like Péguy turn even the flimsiest tents into houses. In both cases, there is real, irreducible difference. And, yet, the difference, as I hope to show in more detail later, does not disjoin.

Péguy himself left the tradition of illiteracy far behind, as he completed his university education in the most prestigious school in France, the École normale supérieure, the training ground for its professors. His own formation was in philosophy, and, in this area, the greatest influence upon him was Henri Bergson, whose courses he attended both at the École normale in 1896–97 and later at the Collège de France.[11] Although Péguy never passed the exams that would have entitled him to teach in a lycée or eventually at the university, and although his reputation among many is that of a great poet, he nonetheless engaged in philosophy all of his life. His reflections range widely, but, most especially, and here the influence of Bergson goes without saying, he is a philosopher of time.

Péguy's occupation, from 1900 until his death in battle in 1914, was as the editor of the journal he founded, *Les Cahiers de la Quinzaine*, which was an outgrowth of his participation in the Dreyfus Affair.[12] He had been an ardent defender of Dreyfus, inspired by socialist principles, of which the *Cahiers* was to be an embodiment, a continuation of the striving for a just society.[13] Péguy refused to accept advertisements or capitalist backing of any sort. The journal was to be funded by subscriptions only, and contributions were to appear strictly uncensored, representing all points of view, as long as they were not merely party lines. The journal was thus to reflect a freedom from tyrannies of all sorts, economic as well as political. Péguy expressed his vision of it thus: "We have . . . little by little established, without anyone's explicit commitment, an undeniably new kind of society, a kind of hearth, a society in all freedom naturally free, a sort of family of minds, without doing it on purpose, in no way *a group*, as they call it; that horror; but literally what has always been the most beautiful in the world: a *friendship* and a community [*cité*]."[14]

The *Cahiers* began mainly as a center for disseminating information on political events—socialist congresses, international trouble spots, the progress of the Dreyfus Affair itself (which was not over in 1900, when the *Cahiers* first appeared). With the years, they also became a center for literary talent. Romain Rolland's *Jean Christophe*,[15] for instance, was first published there in installments. In later years, the journal often became an exclusive mouthpiece for Péguy's own long essays and poems, although his comments had been present from the beginning.

The *Cahiers* posed Péguy many grave financial difficulties, making him particularly apt to speak, as he often did, of the economic miseries of the ordinary person.[16] They were also to lead him to such strained circumstances as to exhaust him and make him despair. The sheer burden of running the journal—whose subscribers never exceeded 1,400 and sometimes dipped to 900—and which he managed entirely by himself—from its finances to the selection of articles, to proofreading, even to selecting the type set[17]—

made him long occasionally for a teaching career.[18] It would at the very least have provided him with a steadier income. On the feeble and uncertain earnings of the *Cahiers*, he supported not only his wife and three children (a fourth was born to him shortly after he died in battle), but also his mother-in-law and his brother-in-law.[19]

It was in 1907 that Péguy first intimated to a friend that he was a Catholic again. His rediscovery of Christianity was to confuse and anger many people, given the bitter opposition between the Church and the Republic, not to say the Church and the socialists.[20] Many of his socialist friends either broke with him or remained in a state of disbelief about his return. The Catholic establishment soon found out that he was not what it had thought either. He remained loyal to the socialism of his youth, called for an economic revolution, and was a fervent republican. When the Church put Bergson's works on the Index in June 1914, it was Péguy who rose to his defense.

His return to Christianity also increased his difficulties at home. His wife, an ardent republican, whom he had married in a civil ceremony in 1897, refused both to have their union sanctified by the Church and to have the children baptized.[21] Partially as a result, he never took communion and never participated in parish life, although he did pray, go on pilgrimages, and write some famous devotional poems to the Virgin.[22]

The last years of Péguy's life were thus marked by great isolation, accompanied by ever-present financial strain. They were complicated as well by his love for a young Jewish girl, Blanche Raphaël. Péguy wrote thousands of quatrains expressing his anguish, his resolve not to betray his word, his desire.[23] Apparently, the relation remained platonic. Blanche married. At the time of his departure for the front, shortly before his death, he sent her the Latin text of three prayers—the Pater Noster, Ave Maria, and Salve Regina—and asked her to pray for him every day.

These same years of isolation and suffering of all sorts were also years of intense and voluminous productivity. His work of this period, roughly from 1909 to 1914, can be divided into two main categories—his essays on the philosophy of history, *Clio—Dialogue de l'histoire et de l'âme charnelle* and *Clio—Dialogue de l'histoire et de l'âme païenne*,[24] and his long poems on the key realities pinpointed by the Christian terms *faith*, *hope*, and *love*. It is no doubt the latter, *The Mystery of the Charity of Joan of Arc* (1910), *The Portico of the Mystery of the Second Virtue* (1911), *The Mystery of the Holy Innocents* (1912), and *Eve* (1913),[25] that have given him his reputation as a mystic. He had an extraordinary way of piercing the most ordinary experience to reveal its ineffable, transcendent dimension, all in the simplest, most prosaic language in the world.

It is not always clear, in fact, where to draw the line between prose and poetry in Péguy's work. The classic French collection of his writings, the Pléiade series, divides them neatly into separate volumes, but, as the portrait of Bernard-Lazare amply testifies, many passages are sheer poetry by reason of their rhythm, imagery, and compression of sense. His poems, on the other hand, sound like everyday spoken language, seemingly devoid of any poetic devices whatsoever, except for rhythm.

During his lifetime, Péguy was known primarily as the editor of *Les Cahiers de la Quinzaine*, but he did win momentary literary fame for his long poem *The Mystery of the Charity of Joan of Arc* and for the essay "Notre jeunesse," both published in the same year, 1910. His name was suggested for the grand prize in literature of the Académie française, and there was some talk of that august body granting him a chair. Neither of these events came to pass. His later published writings received scant attention, and a good deal of his most beautiful and important work appeared posthumously, such as his two dialogues on history, mentioned above.

Throughout his life, Péguy fought fiercely—for Dreyfus, against Jaurès, for Bergson, to name just a few of the better-known names. He took sides that did not fit party lines. After his death, his work was most often made to fit the very same party lines that he had avoided at such cost in his own lifetime. The Catholics made him into a right-thinking Catholic; the nationalists reduced him into a hero fallen for his country; the socialists focused only on his socialism, ignoring his religious reflections. The portrait of Bernard-Lazare, like all of Péguy's writings, should help us to rediscover the unclassifiability of his thought. That very unclassifiability still gives potency to his voice, long after the battle lines of his time have been redrawn.

The subject of Péguy's portrait, Bernard-Lazare, is considerably less well known than Péguy himself, whose name, if not his thought, commands instant recognition in France. Were it not for Péguy's portrait of Bernard-Lazare, it is possible that the latter might have fallen into oblivion. It long remained one of the few sources of information about him. In the several biographies of Bernard-Lazare that have appeared in the past two decades, Péguy's portrait is amply quoted.[26] These biographies, while adding many details, have corroborated many of the facts that Péguy makes available in "Notre jeunesse."

Bernard-Lazare came to Paris in 1886 from the provinces—from Nîmes, to be precise—to make a career for himself as a writer. He wrote novellas and poems in the style of the period and became a literary critic of note. He was also an ardent defender of Dreyfus (and of many others). In fact, his initial pamphlet, *A Judicial Error: The Truth About the Dreyfus Affair*, published in 1896 and sent in sealed envelopes to 3,500 people well placed in public life in France, played a crucial role in launching the affair as such.

It turned it from a court-martial that seemed sealed once and for all into a national discussion engaging people's lives, fortunes, and reputations. As Péguy also points out, Jews, especially the more affluent, abandoned Bernard-Lazare after his initial activity, embarrassed by the fact that he drew attention to himself as a Jew defending a Jew, and by his criticisms of the social structure in France and elsewhere. It is in part because of the sheer information it makes available that Péguy's portrait is often included, as preface or postscript, usually in a somewhat abbreviated form, in new editions of Bernard-Lazare's works.

Several interesting details that Péguy does not mention, no doubt because he did not intend to give an exhaustive overview of his friend's life, have emerged in recent biographies. For instance, for two or three years after arriving in Paris, Bernard-Lazare took courses on comparative religion at the École pratique des hautes études, studying Christianity, Hinduism, and Semitic and Far Eastern religions.[27] Perhaps in keeping with these studies, or perhaps not, he also wrote a book on the latest research into parapsychological phenomena, *La Télépathie et le néo-spiritualisme* (1893). To the end of his life, Bernard-Lazare was to exhibit that disdain for religion typical of the positivistic era in which he lived. Yet these protracted studies might also reveal his interest in what Péguy called spiritual jurisdictions, despite or because of his avowed positivism.

His most important book, written before the outbreak of the Dreyfus Affair, was a two-volume study of *Antisemitism: Its History and Its Causes* (1894). This work has remained controversial to this day, owing principally to Bernard-Lazare's claim that one of the permanent causes of antisemitism was the Jewish tradition itself and the way it made Jews relate to the rest of the world. "Everywhere up to our own days, the Jew [has been] an unsociable being," he asserted, in a sentence often quoted with great glee by antisemites of the period.[28] The source of this unsociability, with its concomitant exclusivism, was Jewish law, which made Jews unwilling to bend to the laws and customs of the land and kept them closed in upon themselves.

Bernard-Lazare never claimed that the Jews were solely to blame for the persecutions they had endured everywhere they settled. He detailed many reasons for the hatred they evoked, having to do with the host countries themselves, including a generalized hatred of the stranger. Nonetheless, he was bent on pointing to an empirical fact: the Jews did not have to await external persecution to develop the desire to keep their own traditions separate from those surrounding them. It was they, in fact, who asked to retain a separate status wherever they settled. This separatism, in Bernard-Lazare's mind, could not be ignored as an important source of antisemitism.

In his book, Bernard-Lazare's attitude toward Jewish particularism, the desire of Jews to remain separate and different, is ambivalent. One of his tendencies, and it is the stronger of the two, is to see it as a form of egotism and narrowness. For this, he frequently blamed the rabbinic tradition, particularly the Talmudic sages, who "had cut off Israel from the community of nations; they had made of it a sullen recluse, a rebel against all laws; foreign to all feeling of fraternity; closed to all beautiful, noble, and generous ideas; they had made of it a small and miserable nation, soured by isolation, brutalized by a narrow education, demoralized and corrupted by an unjustifiable pride."[29] This same distaste for Jewish particularism made him acclaim the assimilation of nineteenth-century Jews into European culture, not only because, to his mind, it would eliminate antisemitism, but because it would be a further triumph of the universal over narrow, sectarian loyalties.

However, in the same work, Bernard-Lazare also praises some of the consequences of Jewish particularism. He sees in the Jewish tradition a perpetual thirst for justice, a notion of equality based on the oneness of God, and a refusal to concede ultimate authority to government.[30] He also occasionally expressed praise for the rationalism of the classical rabbinic sages involved in legal discussions, rather than in establishing dogma.[31]

Bernard-Lazare's ambivalence about the rabbinic tradition is visible down to his last writings. But he entirely stopped wanting to promote the assimilation of Jews. Instead, he became an ardent defender of the right of the Jews to remain a separate people, even if this separateness were no longer based on the traditional rituals. A passage from one of his later essays underlines his defense of Jewish particularism: "People told me that by affirming the permanence and reality of a Jewish nation, I made myself the ally of the antisemites. I have reflected a great deal upon this grave complaint, and I insist upon remaining, on this point, in alliance with the antisemites. . . . I find there are not enough states within the state, that is to say, to make myself clearer, that there are not, within modern states, enough free groups bound to each other. The human ideal does not seem to me to be political and intellectual unification. Only one unification seems to me necessary: moral unification."[32]

It is difficult to say what led to Bernard-Lazare's reversal on the subject of Jewish particularism. The Dreyfus Affair is often mentioned, as it is in the case of the founder of modern Zionism, Theodor Herzl.[33] The visceral hatred expressed against the Jews in the course of those events, in France, the country considered to be the most enlightened in the world, must certainly have brought home the fact that assimilation was not as possible as either of them had initially thought. But Bernard-Lazare's work on Jewish history, and later his involvement with eastern European Jews, also perhaps made him much more keenly aware of the inner reality of the Jewish people as such.[34] In any case, whatever led to his change of position, change of position it was, entailing a defense of Jews as Jews, of their particular spirituality, of their right to exist as a people apart.[35]

This did not make Bernard-Lazare an observant Jew. As Péguy noted, he was an atheist, a positivist, a scientist. In his will, he even requested that no religious ceremony be performed at his funeral. (The request was not honored. He was given a Jewish burial.) Whatever he might have meant in his disclaimer, also in his will, that *Antisemitism: Its History and Its Causes* could be republished, but only with a statement declaring that the author had changed his mind on many a point, it was certainly not that he had become a practicing Jew. He was raised in a Sephardic family with a modicum of ritual and remained secularized to the end of his days. One interesting detail deserves to be mentioned, however. His wife, a childhood friend, was observant. In fact, they renewed their acquaintance as a result of a Yom Kippur service they both attended when Bernard-Lazare came home to visit his family. Detached from traditional Jewish observances though he was, Bernard-Lazare was not quite as remote from them as we might think.

This detail might shed some light on a puzzle mentioned by several commentators. Péguy was surrounded by Jewish friends, who were almost all nonobservant, removed from their tradition.[36] Yet he was able to see how they remained Jews, not in their ethnic mannerisms, but in their spirit. This might strike us as either uncanny or preposterous if we did not pay some attention to the fact that assimilation, even at its nineteenth-century height in western Europe, was not always as complete as the term implies.

Péguy's friendship with Bernard-Lazare was not of many years' duration. It probably did not date back much before 1899, which would mean a close contact of no more than four years, since Bernard-Lazare died in 1903.[37] Nonetheless, Bernard-Lazare's influence on Péguy is apparent in the many statements Péguy makes about Jews in "Notre jeunesse," which seem to echo themes to be found in Bernard-Lazare's own writings. To name just a few such echoes, Bernard-Lazare speaks of the Jewish desire for peace, for being left alone, for not stirring up any trouble, in terms very similar to Péguy's.[38] He speaks of Jewish neurosis, manifested as if physically, as a grazing upon the skin, in language very similar to that of Péguy's, when he describes the black and blue marks upon the Jewish body.[39] He speaks of a tendency to agitation and revolution among Jews with an approval we also see in Péguy.[40] And, he insists, as does Péguy, that the vast majority of Jews are poor, that at best the antisemites know only rich Jews, and, perhaps more strongly than Péguy, that antisemitism is a struggle between the owners of capital.[41]

These echoes, and there are more, need to be qualified by at least two remarks. The first is that some of these themes were simply part of the reper-toire of images about Jews used by a wide number of people. For example, it was commonplace to think of Jews as neurotic and as sources of disorder. Nonetheless, there is a similarity of tone and phrase between Bernard-Lazare and Péguy, suggesting a more direct influence. Secondly, while Péguy refers to many of the same motifs about Jews as Bernard-Lazare, this does not mean that they do not derive new meaning when transposed into Péguy's framework. Péguy, in speaking about Jews, does so self-consciously as a Christian.[42] This in itself changes the context.

The same dependence on and yet independence of the influence of others can be noted in Péguy's focus on the Jews as a people of prophets. In stressing this, he is in complete continuity with the emphasis of many thinkers of the nineteenth century and even the eighteenth.[43] For in-stance, the great French historian Ernest Renan, whose influence is visible through the efforts Péguy made to distance himself from him,[44] claimed that prophecy was at the heart of the religion of Israel, and that as such the Jews were contributors of the moral ideas of justice and the universal to subsequent world history.[45] James Darmesteter, a Jewish scholar whom Péguy mentions in "Notre jeunesse," wrote a book, *Les Prophètes d'Israël*, in which he made essentially the same claim, seeing the universalism and messianism of ancient Jewish prophecy being realized in modern science and in the modern Church.[46] Péguy's linking of the Jews and prophecy is thus not in the least original. What he meant by it, however, and how he situates himself vis-à-vis the Jews as a Christian, remains to be seen. It is not the way of either Renan or Darmesteter.

Jewish commentators have often remarked, mostly in gratitude, that Péguy's portrait of the Jews in "Notre jeunesse" differs significantly from those drawn by his contemporaries. The great Jewish historian Gershom Scholem, in his essay on German-Jewish relations, pointed out that unlike German writers, who at most rose to praising a Jew because of his univer-sally human qualities, Péguy in "Notre jeunesse" praised the Jew in his dif-ference as a Jew.[47] Alain Finkielkraut, in a recent study of Péguy, *Le Mé-contemporain*, makes essentially the same point. Péguy allows the Jewish difference to remain.[48]

Some commentators go further and see in Péguy's portrait of Bernard-Lazare, as well as in his other writings, not only praise for the Jews in their particularity as Jews, but a kind of Jewish quality itself. In an interview given to Wladimir Rabi many decades after Péguy's death, Edmond-Maurice Lévy, one of Péguy's few Jewish friends who was observant, states: "There is in Péguy a Jewish resonance absolutely unique in French literature."[49] This last theme also appears in one of Péguy's Catholic interpreters, Pie

Duployé, who claims that Péguy is a prophet whom the force of circumstances made into a Jewish prophet.[50]

In this last comment, we have the blurring of a difference Péguy himself took a great deal of trouble to maintain. He did not seek in his portrait to blend Judaism and Christianity or Judaism and anything else. He differs from other commentators about Jews precisely in that he did not want to do away with Jewish difference, either through assimilation or conversion. In whatever way his portrait expresses a relation between Jews and Christians, it is not a matter of a hyphenated tradition, Judeo-Christianity. He resolves the tension between the particular and the universal another way.

The sympathy Péguy expresses for the Jews as Jews in his portrait of Bernard-Lazare should not be mistaken for mere sentimentalism.[51] Péguy does not wish to preserve Jewish difference because he had many Jewish friends, although he did and no doubt this influenced his tone. His desire to preserve particularity was the direct result of a theology and philosophy of history that, although focused on the Jews in "Notre jeunesse," also implies the proper relation to the other, the irreducibly different as such.

"Notre jeunesse" is one of the few of Péguy's prose writings that has been translated into English.[52] One of the curiosities of this translation is that the portrait of Bernard-Lazare has been left out. Alexander Dru, the translator, explains in the preface that he felt the essay had a greater harmony without it, as it is mainly about Christianity.[53] If my understanding of Péguy's theology is correct, it is through the portrait of Bernard-Lazare that one gets the best glimpse of Christianity at work, the way Péguy understood it. It is this that I seek to demonstrate in what follows.

Péguy and Antisemitism

I have claimed that Péguy's portrait of Bernard-Lazare maintains a certain tension between the particular and the universal. It does not explicitly investigate this topic, however. Rather, the tension emerges in the interstices of historical discussions—about the meaning of the Dreyfus Affair, about the viability of the republican form of government, about the role of the Church in modern times. One of these discussions—the central one in the portrait of Bernard-Lazare—regards the role of the Jews, both in the Affair and in history as a whole. It is by first turning to this discussion that we may eventually discern the tension between the particular and the universal.

Even a cursory reading of Péguy's portrait of Bernard-Lazare reveals that it is, despite some harsh criticisms, a very sympathetic description of Jews. One needs to know a bit about the literature of the period about Jews, though, to realize the extent of its polemical edge. Almost every line can be read as a rebuttal of some commonly held antisemitic, or sometimes, philo-semitic, assumption. (They were not always so different from each other, as some of what follows will illustrate.) This polemic might not have been Péguy's first intention, but in the context in which he wrote, his observations inevitably took on this meaning. The social and political role of the Jews was not a neutral topic in the France of 1910.

We can detect the polemical thrust in the very first two sentences of the portrait: "The Dreyfus Affair was the culmination, the point of intersection of three mystiques. In the first place, it crossed paths with the Jewish mystique." In proclaiming the existence of a Jewish mystique, Péguy, whether he wanted to or not, from the start crossed swords with the antisemites. In order to grasp what was at stake, we first need to examine what Péguy intended when he used the terms *mystique* and *politique* in "Notre jeunesse."

The meaning of these words is not as immediately accessible as one might wish, because, while both antedate Péguy's usage of them by far, he uses them in his own idiosyncratic way, playing with the commonly accepted connotations, and modifying them significantly in the process.[54] Also, and we shall have cause to come back to this point, he never, except on nearly the last page, defines them, expecting the reader to derive their sense from the multiple specific passages in which they are found in the text. Readers, as a result, have often differed in their interpretations of the terms. Nonetheless, two ways of understanding the word *mystique* are fairly common, and, it seems to me, do much to obscure Péguy's use of it.

In the first place, *mystique* has often been associated with an idealism preoccupied solely with the purity of its principles, either unconcerned with action or unconcerned with effective action.[55] While mystique does have to do with the purity of principles, it is, in Péguy's sense, very much engaged in action. Péguy often, in fact, speaks of "action mystique." It is not a spiritual attitude uncompromised by the tug and pull of getting things accomplished. In an earlier version of the portrait, Péguy refers to Bernard-Lazare as a man who had a genius for action, a man of action par excellence.[56] In the portrait in "Notre jeunesse,"[57] it is clear that Bernard-Lazare engaged in unceasing activity, on behalf of Dreyfus, Romanian Jews, Armenians, and French Catholics. If he were not a man of action, stirring others into action as well, there would have been no reason to ostracize him, dissociate oneself from him. He was, in fact, too effective in drawing attention to certain problems. The term *mystique* in "Notre jeunesse," then, refers neither to a contemplative attitude nor to an idealism unwilling to sully itself through political activity. It refers to an action that does not confuse the truth it is serving with the quest for power of the party it might be associated with.

Secondly, *mystique* has frequently been understood to mean that Péguy favored an irrational attachment over rational deliberation.[58] While it is true that a person who acts according to a mystique, as "Notre jeunesse" describes it, is committed to a truth or a good arrived at otherwise than through logical syllogisms, this commitment prior to reason is never presented as opposed to rational deliberation at all levels. In the following passage, as in several others, Péguy signals the key role of critical reflection in the very maintaining of the purity of a mystique. There always comes a point at which one needs to turn back because a mystique has changed into politique.

At the point of turning back, nothing of the old analysis, of the old idea, of habit, should be kept. One must be ready to start over, to start the analysis all over again from scratch. . . .

Above all and before everything else, one must mistrust, be wary of oneself, of one's own judgment, of one's own knowingness [*connaissement*]. Most of all, one must keep oneself from continuing. Continuing, persevering, in this sense, is that which is most dangerous for justice, for understanding itself. To buy a ticket from the start, in a party, in a faction, and never again look at how the train is rolling along, and, above all, over what the train is rolling along, is, for a man, to place himself resolutely in the best conditions for becoming a criminal.[59]

Following a mystique, the above passage makes clear, is not the same as following a party line. In fact, Péguy says, nothing is more dangerous to a mystique than to give up one's intellectual autonomy in such a way. The only thing that ensures the purity of a mystique, prevents it from turning into politique, is perpetual rethinking, in the face of specific events. Politiques come into being not only because of people's thirst for power but because of intellectual laziness. It is so much easier to think along fixed ideological lines, to be consistently anti-Catholic, for instance, than to evaluate, at each point, whether the Catholics should be opposed or not. It is stopping that inertia that the intellect is called upon to do. It is crucial in keeping people from merely rolling along.

People who act according to a mystique, then, are, in fact, in the public arena, not contemplative souls or mere idealists. And their actions are governed neither by party politics nor by the desire for power or glory accompanying party politics. A mystique is not only a disinterested action but an action that does not lock the world into fixed opposing camps.[60]

Having established this, we can now return to Péguy's claim that the Dreyfus Affair was the culmination of Jewish mystique. It immediately opposes one of the most common antisemitic assumptions, that Jews were inherently incapable of rising above their self-interest. That is, Jews could never act disinterestedly. A caricatural expression of this position can be found in the infamous antisemitic work *La France juive*, whose author Edouard Drumont contrasts the Semitic and Aryan temperaments thus:

"The Semite is mercantile, avaricious, intriguing, subtle, crafty; the Aryan is enthusiastic, heroic, chivalrous, disinterested, honest, trusting to the point of naïveté. The Semite is a terrestrial being, not seeing beyond this life; the Aryan is a son of Heaven, endlessly preoccupied with superior aspirations."[61] Similar statements can be found in less concentrated form in the philosemitic work of Anatole Leroy-Beaulieu, who claims that Jews have a warped conscience and no sense of honor.[62] To state, as Péguy did, that they had a mystique was thus to refute Drumont's and Leroy-Beaulieu's contentions. Jews, Péguy was asserting, could act from motives other than self-interest, for the sake of truth or justice alone.

Péguy does not deny that the Jews also have a politique, a strategy meant to promote their self-interest as a group. But in describing this politique, Péguy once again butts against a common antisemitic assumption. People like Drumont and Charles Maurras, the head of the ultrarightist organization Action française, claimed that the Jews had plotted the Dreyfus Affair as a way of destroying the French state by weakening one of its bulwarks, the Army, with the intent of profiting from the disarray.[63] Péguy shows the maneuvering of Jews to promote their own self-interest in quite a different light. The Jews' basic policy was to lie low, to wait until the crisis had passed, to remain as unnoticeable as possible. Thus, in the Dreyfus Affair, far from raising a hue and a cry against the Army in order to sow dissension in France, Jews were actually the most difficult to persuade to participate in the protest. They were afraid to stand up for a Jew publicly for fear of reviving the oft-repeated accusation that their loyalties were with other Jews rather than with the French. They sensed trouble, and only after a good while did they finally come to Dreyfus's defense. Jewish support of Dreyfus, then, far from being evidence of a Jewish urge for power (politique), was evidence of its very opposite, the capacity of Jews to sacrifice their perceived self-interest as a group for the sake of justice (mystique).

Both of these thrusts against antisemitic views occur within the first two paragraphs of Péguy's portrait of Bernard-Lazare. But other thrusts occur throughout the portrait, lodged in this or that detail, seemingly neutral, and yet latent with a polemical intent, once the context is known. For instance, the following partial sentence might appear to be only another example of Péguy's passion for exactitude. Indeed it is, but for reasons other than pedantry. It refers to how Romanian Jews viewed Bernard-Lazare, who exerted himself mightily to draw attention to their plight. "Some destitute foreign Jews, I mean foreign to French nationality, for there was not a single Romanian Jew, I mean a Jew from Romania, who did not know that he [Bernard-Lazare] was a prophet, who did not consider him to be a true prophet."[64]

Péguy is seeking to point out that Jews are not foreigners as such, the claim of the antisemites. Romanian Jews are indeed foreign, but only in the sense that they do not hold French nationality, not intrinsically. In Péguy's distinction between Romanian Jews and Jews from Romania, there is, then, an implicit comparison between the situation of Jews in France and those of Romania. Jews of French nationality are French Jews, whereas the Jews of Romania can never be Romanian Jews because they have not been granted civil rights in that country. Thus Romanian Jews remain foreigners in Romania, while French Jews are not foreigners in France. They are fully French. Péguy, in fact, does not just evoke Bernard-Lazare's Jewish qualities; he also refers to some of his French ones—the clarity of his style, for instance.[65] The Dreyfus Affair, it must be remembered, was the meeting point of three mystiques, the Jewish, the Christian, and the French. Both the Jewish and Christian mystiques intersected with the French one.

This acceptance of French Jews as French makes Péguy's text singularly devoid of any reference to "the Jewish question," the phrase used to indicate the difficulty of assimilating Jews as a foreign element into the national unit. For Péguy, Jews were different, but their difference did not place them outside the community of citizens, make them foreigners. There was no need to do away with their difference as a prerequisite to their acceptance into the social body.[66] In fact, one of the complaints he brings against antisemitism in a later part of "Notre jeunesse" is that it does not merely want to reform the Jews: "At bottom, you don't want them to be who they are. You want them to cease to exist."[67]

A last example of a detail taking on additional meaning within the context of antisemitism is Péguy's description of Bernard-Lazare himself. His focus on his rare capacity for friendship, for loyalty, is obviously at odds with the antisemitic commonplace of the Jews as Judases, as betrayers. But even Péguy's reference to Bernard-Lazare's eyes, so frequent in the portrait, takes on a polemical hue when seen against the background of descriptions such as Drumont's: "The chief signs by which a Jew can be recognized remain as follows: that famous hooked nose, blinking eyes, teeth tightly drawn together, protruding ears, square nails. . . . The torso too long, flat feet, round knees, ankles extraordinarily turned outward, the melting and slippery hand of the hypocrite and the traitor. They rather often have one arm shorter than the other."[68] Against this backdrop, the goodness of Bernard-Lazare's eyes takes on another layer of meaning. I am saying neither that this layer is the most profound nor that Péguy deliberately described Bernard-Lazare's eyes this way to counter antisemitic physiology. I am saying, rather, that given the intellectual climate at the time the portrait was written, this layer of meaning must have suggested itself to contemporaries.

The sheer frequency of Péguy's thrusts against antisemitism in the portrait—and I have given only a few examples—speaks of the pervasiveness of antisemitism in turn-of-the-century France. In fact, all of Péguy's life is marked by its presence, starting with his first public combat, in defense of Dreyfus, a Jew, and ending with his last public combat in defense of Bergson, a Jew,[69] whom Péguy referred to as such. In his thrusts against antisemitism, he did not have far to go to seek it out. Given the atmosphere of the times, it was practically impossible to take a public stand without eventually bumping into one antisemitic expression or another. A few facts about this period should make plain how little out of one's way one needed to go to encounter antisemitism.

It is telling, for instance, that two of the largest newspapers of the day, in an era of journalistic expansion, were both antisemitic, *La Croix*, a publication of the Catholic Assumptionist Order, and *Libre Parole*. The latter, founded in 1892 by Edouard Drumont, had as its sole purpose exposing the machinations of the Jews, its subtitle being *La France aux Français*. To say that these two newspapers were antisemitic is not to say that many others were not. It is simply that these two were more centrally preoccupied with making accusations against Jews. At their height, in the 1890's, *Libre Parole* claimed 500,000 subscribers, and *La Croix* 165,000–170,000. Two decades later, on the eve of World War I, the daily *Action Française*, whose nationalist ideology was antisemitic through and through, could boast between 200,000 and 300,000 subscribers. It is also telling that the national bestseller in 1886, running to 100,000 copies, was Drumont's *La France juive*, a book of nearly 1,300 pages, analyzing the differences between Jews and Aryans and describing the efforts of the Jews to take over France. This book was to go through 201 editions in 25 years.

While violent verbal expressions of hate appeared in these and other publications, Jews in France proper during the decades around the turn of the century were rarely exposed to physical violence.[70] There were occasional threats to expel them from France, boycotts of their businesses, demands to exclude them from state service. There were also episodes revealing intense hostility, such as the contest Drumont organized through *Libre Parole* to propose a solution to the "Jewish question."[71] The prize went to two priests who suggested that Jewish wealth should be confiscated and redistributed. Another instance of hostility was the violence done to the statue of Bernard-Lazare erected in 1908 in Nîmes, his native city, through the efforts of his friends. The Camelots du Roi, a militant rightist organization associated with Action française, defaced it by chopping off its nose, and every year, on the anniversary of its unveiling, they would vandalize it by spilling ink on it.[72] In 1940, the statue was finally destroyed. These are but a few examples of incidents that fall short of violence to persons but reveal a climate pregnant with its possibility.[73]

One of the most astonishing aspects of the antisemitism of this period, from the vantage point of our own time, is the degree to which it had legitimacy as an outlook. Today, in the United States, no one but a member of the lunatic fringe would publicly call himself an antisemite. Politicians against whom the charge is made are eager to clear their names of it.[74] In turn-of-the-century France, however, one could wear one's antisemitism openly and even flaunt it as a badge of honor. Even politicians who defended Dreyfus, whose agendas did not justify themselves through antisemitism, were liable to make antisemitic remarks in speeches, almost as an aside.[75] Even if one were not oneself of the antisemitic persuasion, one might still see some merit in it, as Daniel Halévy makes clear in his essay *Apologie pour notre passé*: "Antisemitism is a very plausible opinion, and to a certain degree prudent; but it is a passion that can blind to the point of committing a crime and that must be watched over."[76] At the height of the Dreyfus Affair, antisemitism was, in fact, so much a viable political position that 23 antisemitic deputies were elected to the Chamber of Deputies.

The legitimacy or, perhaps more precisely, the taken-for-grantedness of antisemitism can be detected in the statements of people who declared themselves to be defenders of the Jews. While arguing for the preservation of Jews' civil rights or their positive attributes, they often protested that this defense did not mean that they liked the Jews personally; on the contrary. Léon Bloy's book *Le Salut par les Juifs* begins, for example, by claiming to defend the Jews against their detractors, who seemed to have forgotten the point of the title—that the Jews held the key to the spiritual salvation of all mankind. Bloy nonetheless asserts (and it is among the milder of his comments): "From both the moral and the physical point-of-view, the modern kike [*youpin*] seems the point of confluence of all that is ugly in the world."[77] "Where does this persistent and involuntary antipathy to Jews come from?" asks Anatole Leroy-Beaulieu, who includes himself among those who feel it, although his book in defense of Jews, *Israel Among the Nations*, exhibits none of Bloy's vulgarity.[78] This, then, was one aspect of the atmosphere in which Péguy wrote his portrait of Bernard-Lazare. He attempted to free himself from its grip by combating many of the assumptions antisemites generally held about Jews.

In the process, however, a curious phenomenon occurs. Péguy makes many statements that, by their very nature as generalizations, are potential stereotypes, even negative stereotypes, unwittingly joining the ranks of those he is combating. For instance, could not his claim about the nature of Jewish politique, which is to remain as invisible as possible, although meant to defend the Jews against the charge that they had plotted the Dreyfus Affair for their own gain, be used to attack them as cowards? Here we encounter a dilemma well expressed by the Polish poet and essayist Czesław Miłosz.

In his autobiography *Native Realm*, Miłosz muses about the national passion of both Poles and Russians for generalizing about each other, usually in a derogatory manner. He proceeds to demonstrate how he, as a Pole, would characterize Russians.[79] We have become justifiably wary of such generalizations, he observes, given the horrific ends they have been made to serve in our century, but he cannot help regretting the concomitant loss of our articulateness about ourselves and other people. People confront inexplicable differences in their neighbors—expressed in the shape of their plows, the slant of their roofs. History is made of such confrontations. Miłosz yearns for the day when it will once again become possible to speak about the other, even negatively, because such speech is an acknowledgment of linked destinies.[80]

Since Miłosz wrote these words, our wariness of generalizations has, if anything, increased, one consequence of this being our inability to speak either about the other or about ourselves. We sometimes don't even seem to know what to call groups for fear of offending. Are whites whites? Are African-Americans blacks? Are blacks African-Americans? When we do manage to stutter something, it is considered either racist or politically correct. The dilemma, then, is that if we speak about other people, we run the risk of doing violence to them, but if we don't speak about them, we fail to acknowledge the link between us.

Péguy's essay, written before some of the bloody events that have led to our great nervousness, might seem at first glance to exhibit a naïve unawareness of the dangers lurking in generalizing about a group.[81] His portrait of Bernard-Lazare is, after all, replete with generalizations. He describes how the Jews act when they are following their mystique, and how they act when they are following their politique. He describes their psychology, their tendency to neurosis, their love of being elsewhere. He distinguishes their behavior along class lines.

Yet, while it is clear that he does not share the depth of our contemporary anxiety about making generalizations, his essay demonstrates a consistent concern to temper generalization once it is made, to provide a brake against it. This is fighting antisemitism on another ground than the content of its doctrines, in its very mode of thinking. It is in this brake upon generalization that we can catch our first glimpse of the tension between the particular and the universal.

The first corrective or brake upon generalization noticeable in the portrait occurs at its very beginning. After claiming that there is a Jewish politique, Péguy immediately adds: "It is stupid, *like all politiques*. It is pretentious, *like all politiques*. It encroaches on everything *like all politiques*" (emphasis added). In other words, he immediately places the Jews within the common run of humanity. This does not deny their difference. Their politique, in its specifics, remains different from that of the French republican politique he cites shortly thereafter. The Jews prefer to lie low. Yet within this tactic he locates a common element. The difference between us and them created by the statement that the Jews have a politique is simultaneously erased and kept in place.

This is especially visible in the next long segment (going on, typically, without a paragraph break for nearly three pages), in which Péguy delineates the specific characteristics of the Jewish politique. The first set of sentences seems designed to make antisemites happy, or, if not them, at least those who claim that, despite everything, Péguy is antisemitic, because it brings to the fore a common antisemitic motif: that of the Jews as betrayers of the innocent.[82]

Politicians, rabbis, Jewish communities, during century upon century of persecutions and trials, had only too much taken the political habit, the bent, of sacrificing a few of their members to have peace, the peace of the political household, the peace of kings and the great, the peace of their debtors, the peace of the masses and of princes, the peace of antisemites. They only asked to start again. They only asked to continue doing it. They would have been perfectly happy to sacrifice Dreyfus to conjure the storm.

There is no mistaking the sense of the generalization. The Jews have a tendency to betray one of their own in order to stave off persecution. But the very next sentence removes the safe distance between us and them. "The vast majority of Jews is like the vast majority of (other) voters. It fears war. It fears turmoil. It fears agitation." We find out that the Jews are motivated by exactly the same fears as all other peoples. The difference remains, because Péguy does not say that all peoples have a history of compromising in this particular manner. Nonetheless, the difference lives within a similarity. All people would rather avoid trouble if they could, in whatever way.

The passage continues at exactly this rhythm, the Jewish difference shading into similarity, reemerging as difference, dissolving again into similarity. One of its strongest sentences, "To hand over innocent blood, it knows what that is," is followed, a few lines down, with, "Still, in ordinary times, the people of Israel is like all peoples—all it asks is not to enter into extraordinary times." At the very end of this section, when Péguy brings up another motif commonly associated with antisemitic generalizations, the Jews' preoccupation with making money, he immediately finds the common dimension once again. The Jews' focus on business is similar to all people's attempts to avoid confronting their destiny. "How about [the Jews are speaking] doing business, good business. Let us not feel victorious, let us not feel victorious over them. How many Christians have been forced unto the path of salvation through lashings. It is always the same. They are afraid of blows. All human beings in general are afraid of blows."[83]

What emerges from this portrait is that the Jews have a peculiar historical destiny, their prophetic calling, which brings troubles of all sorts upon them. They try to avoid this destiny at all costs, often by giving up one of their own in return for peace, or by engaging in business and avoiding the public limelight. Other peoples have neither a prophetic calling nor, as a consequence, a similar history of perpetual troubles and perpetual attempts to avoid trouble. Nonetheless, in the desire for tranquillity, for order, in the fear of suffering, all human beings are the same.

We can see from the above that not only does Péguy not hesitate to make generalizations about another group but also that he does not hesitate to make negative generalizations. In some cases, he does not hesitate to make the very generalizations that an antisemite might make. The difference between his and those of the antisemites, though, is that his are always checked by the point in common, by the point of universal humanity.

I want to give one last example of this capacity to locate the universal without denying the particular. It does not come directly from "Notre jeunesse" but from a letter Péguy addressed to the French Jewish poet André Spire: "It is not the Jews who have crucified Jesus Christ, but the sins of us all; and the Jews, who were merely the means, share like all the others in the fountain of salvation."[84] Here Péguy is not denying the historical role of the Jews, specific to them, as his tradition sees it. Yet within this specificity, he discovers a universal human feature, sinfulness, which the Jews do not have in any more abundance than anyone else, and for which they cannot be blamed more than others. Echoes of this same theme reverberate in Péguy's portrait when he accuses the Jews of having betrayed Bernard-Lazare. He accuses them of ingratitude but immediately adds that it is a common ingratitude, that of Jews toward their prophets, of Christians toward their saints.

In a much later section of "Notre jeunesse," outside the purview of his portrait of Bernard-Lazare proper, Péguy makes clear that his effort to keep in sight our common humanity is indeed deliberate. One could hardly imagine otherwise, given the construction of the text. Nonetheless, it is still surprising to what degree Péguy was conscious of the need for vigilance when making generalizations about another group, in this case, the Jews. In this section, he mentions a mental exercise he finds most salutary in combating antisemitism. That he needs to come up with such an exercise at all testifies, again, to the pervasiveness of antisemitism in the atmosphere of his day. Even those who, like himself, were opposed to it on principle had to remain constantly on their guard to make sure that it did not invade their outlook unaware.[85] He describes the mental exercise as follows:

> To rediscover justice and accuracy, there is a healthy exercise, excellent for justice, for accuracy, for intellectual and moral hygiene, a beneficial exercise, a sort of Swedish exercise routine for the spirit, a mental *Müller*.[86] It consists in creating the best of proofs, the proof through arguing the reverse. . . . The results are always marvelous. It consists in arguing the reverse. It is a marvelous exercise for increasing flexibility and improving posture. It consists in paying attention to certain events as they happen and to say to oneself, to ask oneself about the protagonist what we have already asked ourselves: *What would people say if he were Jewish?* Not only does this exercise pay off but it is surprising how much it pays off, how much it corrects one's vision. *How much* it is worth it. One quickly sees, then, one quickly determines that the biggest and most numerous scandals are not Jewish scandals. By far not.[87]

One of the most humorous and pointed examples of this exercise in practice is the response Péguy makes to someone he characterizes as a cheerful young antisemite, who had complained that Jewish finance is not French: "And French finance, my friend, *is* it French? Is there any finance that is French?"[88] We see that the proof through arguing the reverse is precisely an exercise to locate the point in common, across differences. Jewish finance might not have the interests of France in mind. But does any finance have any interest other than that of finance in mind?

It is interesting to note that this very ability to detect commonality and to insist on it was one of the features Péguy admired most in Bernard-Lazare himself. In quoting the latter on the prohibition by the government of Émile Combes of assemblies of Church members,[89] he points out that Bernard-Lazare wanted Catholics treated like everyone else ("that same word, that same expression, *like everyone else*, which he always used, which he used specifically in the case of Dreyfus"). Later, Péguy continues: "A generally applied law *for* Dreyfus, a generally applied law *against* the congregations: It doesn't look like much but it can have great consequences. It brought him [Bernard-Lazare] to the point of isolation in death." The insistence on a law applied universally presupposes, of course, a common humanity. Yet Bernard-Lazare is also the man whom Péguy presents as completely devoted to his own people. The tension between the universal and the particular comes back.

This tension is not always expressed in the same way. That is, sometimes a declaration of difference is not tempered by an accompanying statement of similarity at all. One such example occurs when Péguy speaks of the Jews' being elsewhere, simultaneously their vice and their virtue, explicitly contrasting it to a "we" (the French who aren't Jewish) who remain rooted in a specific environment.

He emphatically stresses difference in this passage. For the Jews, every house, even the most solid, becomes a tent in the desert. For "us," every tent becomes a house. They, the Jews, love speed, modern transportation, travel. We are not so enchanted with such things, for they transport us too fast. The difference is accentuated through repetition. No explicit statement pinpoints the similarity within the difference. It is allowed to stand starkly. It is no wonder that Charles Maurras praised this section of "Notre jeunesse" for describing the Jews correctly.[90] In his estimation, the Jews were indeed elsewhere, incapable of being attached to any one country, permanent foreigners eroding the organic fabric of society through their very foreignness.

Yet something happens in the course of the passage Maurras so admired, muting the difference he so clearly saw, by putting it in tension, once again, with a universal image of the human being.

A peculiar people. How often have I not thought about it. For whom the most estatelike homes will never be more than tents. And we on the contrary who have really slept in tents, in real tents, how often did I not think of you, [Edmond-Maurice] Lévy, who have never slept in a tent, otherwise than in the Bible, at the end of a few hours, these tents at the camp of Cercottes were already our homes. *"How fair are your tents, O Jacob; your encampments, O Israel!"*[91] How often have I not thought about it, how often have I not thought of you, how often did not these words come back to me mutely, through a glory going back 50 centuries, like a great secret joy of glory, with which I mutely burst through a sacred reremembering, when we would come back to the camp, my dear Claude [Casimir-Périer], during those harsh May nights. A people for whom the stones of houses will always be the canvas of tents. And for us, on the contrary, it is the canvas of tents that already was, that always will be the stone of our houses.

The passage begins and ends with a contrast between us and them. But, in the middle, it is interrupted by Péguy's address to Lévy, his observant Jewish friend, a librarian upon whom he often relied for information of all kinds, including information on the Jewish tradition.[92] This interruption is precisely what distinguishes Péguy's intention from that of both antisemites and philosemites. Both of these groups talked about Jews without ever imagining that they were speaking *to* them at the same time.

Leroy-Beaulieu, for instance, who was renowned as a philosemite, expresses puzzlement in his *Israel Among the Nations* that some Jews disagree with his descriptions of them: "I have endeavored to describe the physiology and the psychology of the Jew. The task is not an easy one. The picture which I have drawn has not satisfied all Israelites. Some have thought it their duty to answer me."[93] In a later passage, Leroy-Beaulieu makes an analogy between his own descriptions and those of a natural scientist, classifying and labeling living beings.[94] Perhaps therein lies the source of his bemusement. The Jews, beings in the process of being classified and labeled, seem to be refusing their status as objects of empirical investigation by insisting on their simultaneous status as subjects.

In this mode of viewing Jews as objects only, Leroy-Beaulieu's approach parallels that of his antisemitic opponent, Drumont, whom he is often at great pains to refute. Drumont, much more than Leroy-Beaulieu, saw himself as a scientist informing the public about empirical data: "Let us start our work with the ethnographic, physiological, and psychological comparison of the Semite and the Aryan."[95] A bit later, when he tries to distinguish among Jews based upon the twelve tribes of Israel, he admits that he cannot go further into the subject because insufficient scientific data are as yet available.[96] In *La France juive*, there are no interlocutors. The observer has before him a more or less transparent object.

Péguy never appeals to scientific objectivity in his portrait of the Jews. Even as he speaks about them, he also speaks to them. There is a common enterprise. Witness the number of times Péguy refers to something Bernard-Lazare himself said. ("One always comes back to something Bernard-Lazare said.")[97] The passage addressing Lévy, previously quoted, reveals an attitude characterizing the entire essay. The Jews, in the process of being described, remain *within* the conversation about them. They retain their subjectivity, have voices outside the generalizations made about them.

It is this preservation of the subjectivity of the Jews that mutes the difference between "them" and "us," introducing a common bond. Listening or responding to someone else, rather than merely describing him or her, creates common references or, better yet, assumes common references. Péguy's passage on tents points out these common references, there before actual speech begins, and yet, made visible through speech as well, on several levels at once. He quotes Numbers 24:5: "How fair are your tents, O Jacob; your encampments, O Israel."

On one level, of course, by citing this biblical text, he is pointing to the common legacy he, a Catholic, and Lévy, a Jew, share, despite their differences. But, on another level, since he and Lévy do not experience tents the same way, do not situate themselves the same way in space, the biblical text serves as a reminder of their difference, but also of a common language they can refer to at the same time that they recognize their difference. Isn't all speech addressed to another just that, the forging of a common vocabulary within which difference can be maintained? Péguy thinks of his friend, addresses him, at the very moment he experiences the discrepancy in their orientation. Speech joins them and disjoins them. On this level, the biblical verse functions not so much as a specific content but as speech par excellence, preserving similarity and difference simultaneously.[98] Péguy, in this passage as elsewhere, does not allow the reader to favor one moment over the other. The point in common and the point of difference alternate.

We see, from the foregoing, that Péguy's fight against antisemitism occurs on at least two levels. On the first level, he refutes antisemitic generalizations with generalizations of his own, meant to correct misperception or outright fabrication. On the second level, he counters antisemitism by imposing brakes on generalization itself. The difference between us and them that generalizing about another group causes to appear never stands unqualified. Always it is placed within a common humanity, both negating and preserving the difference.

But the brakes Péguy imposes on generalization are not at the deepest level of the tension between the universal and the particular. In fact, the very impetus to impose those brakes stems from a more underlying concern, which they symbolize: Péguy's philosophy of history. Beyond and beneath the arguments against antisemitism, although nonetheless intimately related to them, the portrait of Bernard-Lazare forms part of Péguy's continuing meditation on the human being's position in time. The fact that there is this deeper layer prevents his ways of defending Jews—the Müller exercise, addressing them—from turning into mere gimmicks. The proper relation to the other person cannot be guaranteed by turns of phrase. These turns of phrase must be based on something other than rhetoric. It is to this something other—Péguy's philosophy of time—that I now turn. The dialectic between the particular and the universal has its source there.

Péguy's Philosophy of Time

Upon first reading Péguy's portrait of Bernard-Lazare, the overwhelming impression one may come away with is the sense of man's defeat. The march of time deprives man of all that is most precious, destroying, or simply transforming, what he once held dear. Small details strewn throughout the essay set this tone. For instance, when Péguy describes the Paris neighborhood in which Bernard-Lazare used to live, he cannot quite remember the number of his friend's house, although he had gone there so often. Time has passed, and his recollection has dimmed. That number, like events and people themselves, has faded from center stage, without any intention on anyone's part. Péguy's continuing meditation about how unrecognizable that neighborhood has become underlines the same loss. The people who once lived there have moved away, many of them into death.

These details weave an atmosphere of melancholy,[99] serving as a backdrop to the articulated theme of the essay: "Everything begins in mystique and ends in politique."[100] Again and again, Péguy illustrates how time works to undermine a disinterested pursuit. Always a struggle for truth or justice settles into a struggle for power or riches or glory. This, of course, is Péguy's understanding of the Dreyfus Affair. Initially a struggle to exonerate an innocent man, it ended as a struggle to enthrone a political party, the Socialist Party, even if this enthronement meant perpetrating injustice against other innocent people.

Péguy, it must be emphasized, did not think a transformation of a mystique into a politique occurred only in the Dreyfus Affair. On the contrary, the latter was simply an eminent illustration of the general rule prevailing in human affairs. "It had to be this way, so that the great work of our misery could be completed, so that bitterness could be drunk to the dregs, so that ingratitude could be truly crowned, so that the disillusionment could be fulfilled," Péguy says of the betrayal of the Dreyfusards by the politique stemming from their mystique, suggesting that it was inevitable. Given the recognizable resonances, he seems to be suggesting that the betrayal of those who held on to the Dreyfusard mystique has its model in the betrayal of Christ. Put another way, the betrayal of Christ by his followers is paradigmatic of the human condition, revealing man's infirmity, his inability to remain faithful, to bring truth to fruition in time.

Yet, just as the echo of Christ's crucifixion immediately, to a Christian ear, brings to mind the Resurrection, so Péguy accompanies his emphasis on defeat with another emphasis altogether, the emphasis on the utter invincibility of a mystique. Bernard-Lazare, in fact, is his chief example of a mystique defeated and yet invincible.

Here, too, one might first notice only the defeat. After all, so many details surrounding Bernard-Lazare are melancholy. He died an abandoned man, without resources, in obscurity. As we know, Péguy presents him as a victim of the Jewish politique, the Jewish way of assuring its position as a group, which is to avoid trouble at all costs. Bernard-Lazare, being too visible, was simply quietly allowed to disappear from the front lines, deprived of a forum and even of a livelihood.

Péguy elaborates on Bernard-Lazare's defeat, on his apartment, too large for his means, in which he had hoped to work but in which he ended up dying an agonizing early death instead. Everyone always dies from something or another, Péguy muses, but the immediate cause of Bernard-Lazare's death—probably colon cancer—only concealed longer-term causes: a life of overwork, of enormous strain on behalf of others, repaid only with ingratitude. If the focus of Péguy's portrait of Bernard-Lazare is on his death, this is not only because the two of them became close in the last years of the latter's life, when he was already sick, but also because that lonely, premature end so poignantly underlines time's destructive power.

Yet Bernard-Lazare's invincibility is as present as his defeat, accompanying it throughout the portrait. One need only turn to the recurring motif of Bernard-Lazare's eyes: "I still have upon me, in my eyes, the eternal goodness of that infinitely gentle gaze, that goodness that did not hurl itself out but was poised, informed. Infinitely disabused; infinitely informed; itself undefeatable." Passages like this occur countless times. Always, as in these lines, Péguy insists that Bernard-Lazare's goodness stemmed from a complete loss of illusion about human beings. It was not a naïve trust preceding bitter experience but rather coincided with a full recognition of others' capacity for betrayal. He himself had been betrayed by the people he had helped most. Yet this betrayal, although leading to the defeat of his vision of justice, was nonetheless incapable of stemming the flow of his goodness. His responsibility for others and to others remained untouched. He could not be made to swerve, remaining loyal to his mystique, presented here not as a set of principles but as a way of acting toward others, as a goodness.

He manifests the same invincibility in the face of the ultimate defeat, death. In Péguy's anecdote about one of their last discussions, regarding Romain Rolland's *Jean Christophe*, we see Bernard-Lazare lying immobile, in the bed he will die in shortly.[101] During their exchange, he observes that the Greek soul and the Jewish soul are two key aspects of the universal soul. Péguy marvels at this comment:

I showed nothing; because I have said that when one visits the sick, one is determined to show nothing. One is therefore protected by an invincible armor, by an impenetrable mask. But I was struck, I felt pierced to my very vertebrae. For I had come to see, I had been expecting to see, the inroads of death. And that is already a lot. And I suddenly saw the inroads of beyond death.

In his last moments, Bernard-Lazare does not dwell on his own mortality or immortality. In the face of death, he affirms the existence of something beyond it, unaffected by time. It is this same ability to perceive something outside time and to remain faithful to it that Péguy so admired in Bernard-Lazare's political activities. Temporal authority, the authority of those in power, was insignificant to him in the light of truth, always outside time. Neither his defeat nor victory in the temporal realm affected his discernment of truth as truth.

The invincibility of a mystique, however, does not have to do only with the inability to destroy it in the hearts and behavior of those individuals who are prevented from embodying it in human institutions. It has to do also with its capacity to resurge on a wide scale, even after a period of suppression. A politique can stop a mystique for a time but it cannot permanently do away with it as a historical force. For instance, Péguy claims that both the republican and the Christian mystiques, currently defeated by the self-interested machinations of those who claim to be acting in their names, will eventually rise again to become the moving spirit of people's lives, if not in the generation of his children, then in that of his children's children.[102]

Contrary to what most people, especially politicians, think, he maintains, politiques do not cause fundamental change in society. What drives fundamental change is always a mystique. Only it has the power to inspire people to take risks, to break with habit, to act, in short. The movement to free Dreyfus did not derive its impetus from a politique but from a mystique, from several mystiques acting jointly. The politiques that grew out of these mystiques were dependent upon them for their very existence. Their very struggle for power clothed itself in the vocabulary of the mystiques they resorted to in order to legitimate themselves. It is true, of course, that the politiques, despite this vocabulary, quickly neutralized, if not negated, the mystiques from which they stemmed. But the brief moment of the mystique's appearance was the moment that fructified activity and that continues to fructify activity. Bernard-Lazare might be dead, his way of proceeding rejected, but whatever had any impact on the Dreyfus Affair had come from him and people like him and would continue to do so.

It was no doubt to make the latter point that Péguy wrote "Notre jeunesse." At least in part, it is a rebuttal of Daniel Halévy's "Apologie pour notre passé," an essay published in Péguy's *Cahiers* not long before.[103] Halévy, a comrade-in-arms during the Dreyfus Affair, and a friend, seemed to conclude, upon looking back, that the Dreyfusards had been somewhat naïve in their enthusiasm for justice. Péguy balks at this reduction of the Dreyfusards' passion to a youthful enthusiasm unaware of political realities. That thirst for justice was precisely what made them significant historical actors. They might have been defeated, their intentions distorted by others in political machinations for control of the state, but their defeat should not obscure the fact that they had set the Dreyfus Affair in motion. To have done so was not merely to create disorder but to have struggled to determine the very spirit in which France would continue its life as a nation. This was not naïve enthusiasm but the most necessary and penetrating of political combats.

The very writing of "Notre jeunesse" can, in fact, be viewed as Péguy's contribution to the eventual resurgence of the Dreyfusard mystique. For those who might have forgotten it or who were too young to have participated in it, he makes understandable the impetus behind the defense of Dreyfus. The essay can thus be read as a kind of incubator of that mystique, or as a message sealed in a bottle, eventually to surface when the time is ripe, when the right people are there to find it. As such, it is a declaration of invincibility within the very acknowledgment of defeat.

Péguy's philosophy of time, then, seems to involve an affirmation of human beings' ability to defeat time's power at the very same moment that they are defeated by it. His analysis makes no appeal to any authority other than common human experience to justify his conclusions. Yet the combination of uncombinable things he speaks of—defeat and nonetheless invincibility, invincibility yet nonetheless defeat—brings to mind a Christian theological term: *hope*. Nowhere in the essay does Péguy mention hope. That is, the term as such does not appear. Yet in another essay, parts of which were written during the same period as "Notre jeunesse," he does name this peculiar uncombinable combination by its theological name.

The fact that Péguy does not so much as mention hope in "Notre jeunesse" deserves further consideration, and I shall return to it later. Meanwhile, I would like to reflect a bit on one of the passages in which hope is explicitly labeled as such.[104] It occurs in the very long meditation "Clio—Dialogue de l'histoire et de l'âme païenne," which Péguy scholars often refer to as Clio 2.[105] Here Péguy muses for a few pages on what he calls the secret of the man of 40.[106]

He goes on at some length about the knowledge only a man of 40 can acquire, hermetically sealed from anyone who is not near that age. What is the great secret? "He knows that *one* is not happy. He knows that ever since there has been man no man has ever been happy."[107] The mystery is that this very same person who knows so intimately that no one in the whole history of the world has ever been happy immediately turns around and with an obsession so pervasive that he need not even be conscious of it wants nothing so much than that his son should be happy. Not only that. But that his son should prove him right despite his defeat. He looks anxiously into the eyes of his son to detect the latter's judgment of him. Péguy concludes by saying that "nothing is as moving as this perpetual, as this eternal, as this eternally reborn inconsistency; and that nothing can disarm God more, and that is the common miracle of your young Hope."[108]

Péguy capitalizes *Hope* here, as the theological virtue necessary for salvation. The phenomenon it encompasses resembles in its structure the combination of defeat and invincibility pervading "Notre jeunesse." The man of 40 is defeated. He knows that he will never reach fulfillment in time. Everything he loves will either be taken away or remain unattainable. He also knows this is true for all human beings. Yet at the same time he persists in working for the happiness of his son; he persists in thinking that although he himself has been defeated, his son will affirm him, will vindicate him in a future time. Is knowing that no one has ever been happy and yet yearning for the happiness of one's son not like Bernard-Lazare's stance? His loss of illusion about the possibility of success cannot divert him from his responsibility to others. Is admission of defeat and yet the searching for vindication in the eyes of one's children not like Péguy's own stance? He writes "Notre jeunesse" as an affirmation that the Dreyfusard mystique, although defeated, will resurge in the future, in his children or in his children's children. In the case of both the man of 40 and of Bernard-Lazare and Péguy, time defeats and does not defeat. Something in human beings continually rises above time at the very moment in which they acknowledge its power.

There is another dimension to Péguy's meditation on time, permeating the entire essay. It is his insistence on embodiment. That is, time is filled, in specific places, with the eternal, and, conversely, the eternal is paradoxically subject to the temporal, can make its way only by passing through specific times and places. The Christian theological term for this mode of entry of the eternal is *incarnation*.[109] Not surprisingly (once we understand a bit better what Péguy intends by it), hardly any discussion of incarnation as such occurs within the essay, just as there is no discussion of hope. Nor, once again, does Péguy rely on any authority other than that of human experience when he claims that time embodies something beyond it, although the reality he describes throughout "Notre jeunesse" is most easily understood as incarnation. Nonetheless, some points of the essay are relatively more explicit than others about it. We shall start with these and gradually move to more implicit references.

Perhaps the most explicit discussion of the relation of time to eternity occurs in Péguy's discussion of the Church in the modern world. He notes that it has lost its spiritual power, its capacity to move the vast majority of people. Both the Church and its opponents claim this is so because science has destroyed many principles hitherto adhered to by the faithful. Péguy disagrees. What has weakened the Church in the modern world, according to him, is its lack of charity.[110] That is, what has weakened it is its unwillingness to act compassionately toward those most in need. The Church hierarchy has consistently sided with the bourgeoisie, refusing to correct the plight of people caught in unending economic misery. Scattered acts of charity to individuals are not enough to stem this misery. Only a structural economic reform, a revolution in the workplace, will do: "The only ones who will scoff at this are those who do not want to see that Christianity itself, which is the religion of eternal salvation, is bogged down in that mire, in that mire of bad economic, industrial mores; that it will itself not rise out of it, get out of it without an economic, industrial revolution."[111]

Péguy's emphasis in this analysis is twofold. On the one hand, ideas or beliefs, by themselves, are not enough to transform reality. Scientific ideas, by themselves, cannot defeat religious orientations. Religious ideas, by themselves, do not make for the spiritual power of a tradition. Spiritual power manifests itself only through action, action that penetrates the public realm and that is defined as action by the fact that it is done at some cost to the actor. This is how spirit becomes incarnated in matter, the eternal in time. The social, the economic, the political count as vehicles. Without action in the public realm—always requiring sacrifice—the spiritual fails to take on reality.

> Such is eternally, temporally (eternally temporally, and temporally eternally), the mysterious subjugation of even the eternal to the temporal. Such is the proper inscription of the eternal itself within the temporal. One must pay the economic costs, the social costs, the temporal costs. None can escape it, not even the eternal, not even the spiritual, not even the inner life. That is why our socialism was not so stupid and why it was profoundly Christian.[112]

The other way to articulate the same point is to say that human beings cannot reach the eternal unless the temporal realm is shaped in a particular way. Péguy claims that the contemporary workplace is sure terrain for perdition. Perhaps he is saying that when human beings are forced to degrade themselves and others in order simply to have enough to eat, the theological virtues necessary for salvation—hope, faith, charity—fail to become embodied. In other words, the eternal needs to fill time in order to become accessible to human beings, but in order for that to occur, human beings need to fashion time in such a way that the eternal finds a passage.

The concerns expressed in this discussion of the Church find numerous echoes throughout "Notre jeunesse." Ideas unexpressed in public action do not have bite, do not penetrate reality. The social, the economic, the political are the central roadways of the spiritual, without which its entry into the world is blocked. An illustration of both these propositions occurs in Péguy's discussion of the socialists' defense of Dreyfus. He claims that their activity ultimately stemmed from a Christian source, embodying as it did a charity that Dreyfus's opponents, many of them Catholic, did not demonstrate.

This line of reasoning often shocks Péguy readers who think he is trying to reconcile his present Catholicism with his former socialism, at some cost to the truth.[113] Was he not an avowed atheist at the time of the Dreyfus Affair? But this is precisely where Péguy's stress on embodiment comes into play. Ideas, beliefs by themselves, do not give access to the deepest realities. Only action in the public realm does so. The socialist Dreyfusards, risking as they did their reputations, their livelihoods, their family ties, for the sake of a man unjustly condemned, did more to manifest the Christian spiritual realities—hope, love—than did their religious opponents, who engaged in disquisitions about the dangers posed to the state or about the place of the Church but failed to reach out to a suffering human being:

And I do not want to reopen an old debate today, now in the past, but in our enemies, on the side of our enemies, on the side of our then adversaries, historical like us, who have become historical, I see much intelligence, even much lucidity, much sharpness: what strikes me most is surely a certain lack of charity. . . . It is unquestionable that there was infinitely more Christianity in all our socialism than in all of [the Paris churches] St. Madeleine, St. Pierre de Chaillot, St. Philippe du Roule, and St. Honoré d'Eylau put together.[114]

In both these examples, that of the Church's failure to risk an economic revolution and that of the socialists' being more Christian than the self-acknowledged Christians, the stress on the importance of embodiment is fairly explicit. It becomes less so at several other junctures, although it is just as much there. In fact, embodiment is central to Péguy's depiction of the Jews in his portrait of Bernard-Lazare.

As mentioned previously, it was a commonplace of nineteenth-century thought to identify the Jews with prophecy. Generally, what was meant was that the Jews, at least in their most illustrious representatives, the prophets, adhered to certain ideas—one God, a universal morality. Their function in world history had been precisely to propagate those ideas. For most nineteenth-century thinkers, including many Jewish ones, this function had been accomplished, making the Jews, in their separateness, superfluous.

While Péguy, too, sees the great contributions of the Jews as their prophets, prophecy, for him, is neither a matter of ideas alone nor a function already surpassed. After all, he stresses several times that Bernard-Lazare, his quintessential example of a prophet, was an atheist, a positivist, someone who thought the Jews would be most easy to convert to free-thinking because they least believed in God. It is difficult to ignore Péguy's striking characterization of him as "that atheist dripping with the word of God." Given this phrasing, it is obvious that prophecy, for Péguy, did not have to do with belief or ideas alone. It is the way that Bernard-Lazare behaves that makes him, atheist that he is, a speaker of the word of God.

At the center of Bernard-Lazare's activity is his opposition to the powers that be. Their authority, as Péguy puts it, does not weigh an ounce against the authority of conscience. Bernard-Lazare enacted this opposition in his public stands against Jaurès, against the Combes government, and previous to that, against the entire apparatus of the state, at the beginning of the Dreyfus Affair.[115] Each of these stands was an act in Péguy's sense of the word. They cost Bernard-Lazare a good deal. Given the example of Bernard-Lazare, the importance of the Jews, then, is not that they once produced prophets whose ideas have since been universally disseminated.

It is that they continue to produce individuals who defy the power of the state, of the wealthy, making present another authority altogether.

But Péguy goes further, for he claims that the Jews not only produce a few outstanding individuals from time to time, the prophets, but that they are themselves as a people, a prophet, or prophetic. As unwilling as they are to follow their prophets, they eventually always do. That is, as a group, they end up defying the authorities of the time, abiding by an authority that is not that of a government. They do not do so only when they join in a political movement, as they eventually did in the Dreyfus Affair. They do so also through their position within the social body. Their very "being elsewhere," their outsideness, makes them pointers to another authority than the one accepted by everyone else at the time. Thus, the Jews continue to exercise a spiritual function, to be the carnal body and the carnal voice of God, not because of what they believe but because, through their place and activity within the social body, they point beyond the powers that be, beyond the times.

The stress on embodiment also marks Péguy's defense of the Jews against the antisemites' charge that they had planned the Dreyfus Affair from scratch. He calls this the intellectuals' fallacy,[116] which is always to imagine that once one knows the outcome of an event, one can logically reconstruct all the steps that led to that outcome. Thus the antisemites saw that Dreyfus had been exonerated, and that the Army had lost prestige, and surmised that the Jews had arranged for the arrest of Dreyfus and for all that followed in order to sow dissension among the French.

The flaw here is that the antisemites attribute too much power to the intellect as a mover or predictor of reality. One can scarcely plan the activities of even one day, let alone the activities of twelve years (the time span of the Dreyfus Affair).[117] The most unexpected of all remains the actual occurrence.[118] It has a way of unfolding in defiance of the best-laid plans. Real events cannot be ordered or managed beyond a very rudimentary stage. The antisemites' intellectual fallacy is thus twofold. They assume that events submit to logic, in that a plan formulated beforehand can direct their course, and they assume that events can be understood through a logic formulated after the fact. In this, they fail to pay attention to what in events does not conform to expectation. That is, they fail to pay attention to reality itself. Péguy is not arguing that events are not subject to intellectual grasp, but that the intellect has a tendency to grasp, not what actually happened, but what it has preestablished should have happened.

It might seem more difficult in this discussion about the antisemites' intellectualizing to establish the connection with incarnation. Yet we can detect what we have already detected in previous discussions: Péguy's extreme wariness of abstractions, of treating ideas and logic as if by themselves they were sufficient pointers to reality. Reality reveals itself in the thickness of specific acts. The first rule of the intellect is to beware of its own tendencies to bypass them.

The above are only a few examples, at different levels of explicitness, of how Péguy's insistence on embodiment, or incarnation, structures the content of "Notre jeunesse." But this same insistence also structures its form. Perhaps the most striking illustration of this is the way he eludes defining his central terms.[119] We are never told in so many words, for instance, that *prophet* means this or that. The word appears repeatedly but without an accompanying list of features clarifying Péguy's usage. Neither are *mystique* or *politique* defined, with one exception to which I shall turn shortly. One could even go further and say that the most important structural elements of the essay are not only not defined but do not appear at all.

I would like to suggest that Péguy's avoidance of definition transposes his concern for embodiment from the realm of action to the realm of thought. It might have appeared from the previous examples that thinking can never by itself be an illustration of embodiment, since embodiment always involves action. But there is a mode of thinking, for Péguy, analogous to action. It occurs when an idea is so deeply implanted that it influences the very form in which it is expressed.[120] Rather than being accessible merely through its overt expression, it is accessible through all the details that go into making the expression in the first place: the tone, the rhythm, the juxtapositions, the echoes of one part with another, in short, the texture, what Péguy often called the tissue. To operate with definitions whose meaning does not pervade the text beyond the definitions themselves would thus be analogous to disembodiment, to mere ideas that do not really bite into reality. On the other hand, to incorporate meaning into the tissue, even without any explicit definitions, would be analogous to that action manifesting the real, in which meaning is buried.

That Péguy quite deliberately avoided defining his central terms, in this case *mystique* and *politique*, becomes clear at the very end of "Notre jeunesse," two pages from its conclusion, in fact: "And you, sir, who ask that I define a bit through demonstrative reasoning, through reasoning of ratiocinating reason what is mystique and what is politique, *quid sit mysticum, et quid politicum*, the republican mystique was when one died for the Republic; the republican politique is now that one lives off of it. You do understand, don't you?"[121]

The placement of this definition, so close to the end of the essay, extending to almost 160 pages (in the extremely small print of the new Pléiade edition), and the irony of Péguy's tone as he responds to the imaginary interlocutor who demands it of him reveal both his reluctance to operate with explicit definitions and his impatience with people who think meaning can be conveyed only through demonstrative reasoning.

The content of the definition reinforces this latter point. Mystiques are not distinguishable from politiques by their ideologies, by the system of beliefs they represent. They are distinguishable by the manner in which their ideologies are embodied in action. A mystique is recognizable by the fact that people risk their lives for it. The same ideas, without the attendant willingness to risk one's life, no longer qualify as mystique.

Some commentators, writing in the latter half of our century, having witnessed the willingness for self-sacrifice in movements such as Nazism, recoil before this definition, some even seeing in Péguy's approval of mystique so defined a fascist element in his thought.[122] While the willingness to risk even death is obviously part of Péguy's understanding of mystique, one must also note the peremptory nature of the definition, a brief sentence in such a lengthy essay. By the time this definition appears, the terms *mystique* and *politique* already carry an array of associations, none contradicting the definition, but many adding to it in significant ways. For instance, we know from an earlier passage that the first rule of a mystique that does not wish to turn into politique is to avoid buying a ticket at the start in some party or faction and never looking at what the train one is on is rolling over. We also know from Péguy's descriptions of Bernard-Lazare, his great example of a mystique in action, that temporal authority, most especially that of the state, did not weigh one ounce in the face of a movement of conscience. Given these and other contexts for the word *mystique*, it would be difficult to take the explicit definition as the sole indicator of Péguy's meaning. Those who take it that way unwittingly prove his point about the inadequacy of definitions.

We find a similar eschewing or qualifying of definition regarding the term *prophet*. Rather than stating precisely what he means by the term, he gives the reader many examples, chiefly of Bernard-Lazare. The following is one such example:

It must be realized that this was a man, I said very specifically a prophet for whom the entire apparatus, the reason of state, temporal powers, political powers, authorities of all sorts—political, intellectual, even mental—weighed not an ounce in the face of a revolt, of a movement of conscience itself. One cannot even begin to conceive it. The rest of us cannot even imagine it. When we revolt against an authority, when we march against the authorities, at the very least we lift them off ourselves. We feel their weight, in short. At least within us. At the very least we need to lift them off ourselves. We know, we feel that we are marching against them and that we are lifting them off. For him they did not exist. Less than what I am telling you. I do not even know how to convey to what degree he dismissed temporal authorities, to what degree he dismissed the powers that be. I have no idea how to convey it. It was not even that he had dismissed them. He ignored them, and even beyond that.

In a way, there is a definition of what a prophet is in this passage, since it emphasizes the ability to oppose temporal power, the power instituted in government and the mighty of this world, with an authority over which they have no jurisdiction. But the interesting fact about these lines is the degree to which the definition is tied to the person of Bernard-Lazare. Péguy does not say: here is what a prophet does, and Bernard-Lazare does this too. He simply presents Bernard-Lazare's attitude, in all its idiosyncrasy. Within the idiosyncrasy, nonetheless, the prophetic features manifest themselves.

As if afraid, however, that even this description is too abstract, too devoid of flesh, Péguy immediately follows it with an anecdote illustrating the ease with which Bernard-Lazare shook off temporal authority. He tells of the time the Court of Appeals ruled in a manner opposed to Bernard-Lazare's own position on Waldeck-Rousseau's law and Combes's decree about the right of Church members to free association.[123] A friend came to see him to exclaim triumphantly that the Court of Appeals had ruled against his position, implying that the authority to determine the truth lay with the Court of Appeals. Bernard-Lazare responded that, on the contrary, he had ruled against the Court of Appeals. In other words, in matters of truth, the state could not overrule an individual conscience. On the contrary, an individual conscience always stood beyond the authority of the state. This anecdote embeds the struggle between two different sorts of authority, characteristic of prophecy, in a concrete event, burying it within its details, incarnating it.

In the cases of both *mystique/politique* and of *prophet*, it is as though Péguy thickens the meaning of the terms, either by avoiding definitions that are not immediately given body through example or, more commonly, by avoiding definitions altogether, leaving the readers only with a series of different passages all sharing the same term. But, as hinted previously, embodiment or incarnation is given expression in the essay in a yet more hidden—perhaps one could say more embodied—way. In the case of the terms just mentioned, at least they themselves appear in the text, even if their definitions do not. But, as I have already indicated, the terms *hope* and *incarnation* do not even appear. Yet it is possible to see the entire essay as organized by precisely these two realities. Péguy often speaks of this hiddenness or secrecy of that which is most present—too present in fact to receive separate expression.[124] One such reflection occurs in Clio 2, regarding the classical Greeks.[125]

Péguy observes that if one reads Homer, for instance, or Sophocles, one is struck by the contempt the Greeks had for their gods. They might envy them their immortality, their feasting, their lovemaking, their strengths, but the gods could never be great, because they never had to confront the three miseries through which greatness comes—destitution, risk, and death. "They lack falling short." ("Ils manquent de manquer.")[126] The important point for our present discussion is Péguy's continual reiteration, over ten pages of text, that this was an unacknowledged, perhaps even un-conscious, contempt on the part of the Greeks. It was so basic that it was not overtly stated.

Hope and incarnation, then, might be understood as those things that Péguy so internalized that they are the window through which he sees rather than the objects of his seeing. In an earlier essay, "Zangwill," he had called that level of thought the idea behind the head.[127] All expression exhibits this idea behind the head, invisible on the surface but nonetheless detectable in the body.[128] It is the level upon which the guiding meta-physic of an author operates, even if he himself is unaware of it.

Péguy's insistence on embodiment, or incarnation, has consequences for interpretation. Neither "Notre jeunesse" as a whole nor the portrait of Bernard-Lazare within it is constructed as a developing argument. There is no logic to reconstruct.[129] Rather, we are presented with a number of repetitions of themes, each adding a nuance of meaning to the whole. We are also presented with juxtapositions and echoes suggesting a connection not made explicit by Péguy himself. In other words, the reader must plunge into the body of the text, pay attention to the way it is structured. The conclusions derived from such a method are never as evident as those released by demonstrative reasoning. Interpretation, too, then, is forced to become an act, a risk taken.

While the foregoing discussion of hope and incarnation as structural elements in the essay is no doubt already ample evidence of the risk this sort of interpretation requires, I would like to add one more example of this mode of proceeding. It involves unpacking the meaning of one of Péguy's terms by noticing, not explicit logical argument, but significant juxtaposition:

I still see him in his bed. That atheist, that professional atheist, that official atheist, in whom resounded, with unbelievable power, with unbelievable gentleness, the eternal word; with eternal power, with eternal gentleness; whose equal I have never found anywhere. I still have upon me, in my eyes, the eternal goodness of that infinitely gentle gaze, that goodness that did not hurl itself out, but was poised, in-formed; infinitely disabused; infinitely informed; itself undefeatable. I still see him in his bed, that atheist dripping with the word of God. Even in death, the whole weight of his people bore down on his shoulders. He could not be told that he was not responsible for them. I have never seen a man burdened in such a way, so bur-dened with a task, with an eternal responsibility. As we are, as we feel responsible for our children, for our own children in our own family, just as much, exactly as much, exactly thus did he feel responsible for his people. In the most atrocious of his sufferings, he had only one concern: that *his* Jews from Romania not slyly be left out.

In this passage, parts of which I have referred to elsewhere, Péguy tells us that Bernard-Lazare, atheist that he was, nonetheless spoke the word of

God, more than that, sweated it out from his very body. What does Péguy mean, though, by the expression "speaking the word of God"? Certainly, it could not mean speech with a religious content, in the way we generally understand it, since we are told that Bernard-Lazare is an atheist, a positivist, and so forth. The flow of the passage may in itself provide a clue.

Immediately after the often-quoted line, we have a reference to Bernard-Lazare's responsibility for his people. Even at the point of dying, he felt their burdens as his own, acted on their behalf, drawing attention, for instance, to the plight of Romanian Jews. He could not be persuaded that he was not responsible for them. Given this juxtaposition, it would seem that speaking the word of God is not a matter of speech as such but a way of *behaving*. The word of God is revealed in the responsibility one person bears for others, a responsibility as unshakable, as deeply anchored, as the responsibility of a parent for his children. We come back to the theme of action in the public realm as revealer of truth. The word of God is not a statement. It is a deed.

Nothing forces the reader to make this association between the word of God and responsibility to others. Péguy certainly never explicitly says what I just did in the above paragraph. The obvious discordance, however, between the atheism he repeatedly points out and what we expect the word of God to mean impels the reader to search for the sense of the latter expression. Should not the placement of the two themes, so immediately juxtaposed, be an indication that Péguy meant his comments on Bernard-Lazare's sense of responsibility to clarify his comments on his speaking the word of God? Even if readers find fault with this interpretation, they will have to adopt similar techniques when formulating their own. That is, the alternate reading will have to work with echoes, suggestions, and juxtapositions, for nowhere does the text make clear the meaning through demonstrative reasoning. To understand what Péguy intended by "speaking the word of God," the reader is forced willy-nilly into the tissue, seeking thought beyond the surface connections, since often the surface connections are not there.

Just as the notion of hope, then, crisscrosses Péguy's portrait of Bernard-Lazare in invisible yet visible ways, so does the notion of incarnation, shaping both content and form and even the interpretive mode of the reader. Hope, in Péguy's usage, is the individual's affirmation of eternity, something beyond time. But, and this is the crucial emphasis in his work, this affirmation occurs through the way a person continues to work for the sake of another, despite all the signs, in his own time, that the goal is unattainable or the cause lost. Thus, the father, in Péguy's reflections on the secret of the man of 40, continues to work for the happiness of his son, even though he knows that no one has ever been happy, and continues to hope that his son will exonerate his stand in the future, despite the failure of his enterprise in the present. Similarly, Bernard-Lazare, defeated in his public battles, nonetheless continues the fight to redress injustices against his people. He does this, not out of stubbornness, but out of a commitment to others that temporal setbacks cannot erase. The affirmation of something beyond time thus has an unmistakably ethical twist. It is not ideology as such the person who hopes holds on to despite everything. It is the relation to the other that cannot be severed, despite everything.

I would claim that incarnation functions in a very similar way as well in Péguy's thought. On one level, it would simply mean going beyond abstractions, to a fleshier reality. But the fleshier reality is always interhuman relations, action on behalf of others in the public realm. The eternal reveals itself precisely in this nexus, or fails to reveal itself.

Hope and incarnation, then, function very closely together in Péguy's thought. While each directs us to a different aspect of human activity, both draw attention to how this human activity points to something beyond itself. Hope directs us to human beings' encounters with defeat. Incarnation directs us to human beings' uses of their intellect. Both relocate the eternal on earth, in the least "spiritualized" of our activities, in our political, social, and economic relations.

Conclusion: Of Hope, Incarnation, and Justice to the Other

In the course of this commentary on Péguy's portrait of Bernard-Lazare I have made several claims to which I would like to return. Most recently, I suggested that his philosophy of time is at the source of the tension between universal and particular characterizing the essay. Earlier, I stated that the portrait addresses, although not explicitly, a problem confronting us today: the proper relation to the other person. I also claimed that the portrait embodies Péguy's understanding of Christianity.

While all three of these claims are interrelated, I would like to start with the first. How does Péguy's philosophy of time reflect the tension between the universal and the particular? On the one hand, the notion of hope functions to erase differences among people, for the combination of defeat and invincibility Péguy depicts is not the property of any one group or any one individual. It is simply the fully human way of being. The term *hope*, while Christian, does not indicate people affiliated with the Church. After all, Bernard-Lazare is most emphatically Jewish. Christianity, then, the way Péguy understands it, provides a language to describe the deepest level of humanity, perhaps making possible distinctions between people who have attained it and people who have not. But this distinction never coincides with the national, ethnic, gender, or religious differences with which we normally divide the world. In fact, hope, as the essay presents it, effaces all these divisions by pointing to the common trait we share beyond it.

On the other hand, the concept of incarnation stresses the particular, the different, the unique with full force, since the eternal always lodges itself in time, in specific moments, in specific actions of specific people. This means that the divisions hope effaces reemerge through incarnation. People are always Jewish or Christian, men or women, black or white, German or French, rich or poor. Their particularity is tied to these distinctions. Thus, Bernard-Lazare is Jewish, from the first to the last line of the portrait. His defeat is through the Jewish politique. His invincibility is that of a Jewish mystique.

Péguy's opposition to antisemitism in the portrait, then, is based on a desire to defend particularity as such, not as the sign of an unbridgeable difference but as the very avenue to a universal hidden within it. His techniques for locating this universal are not mere techniques. Ultimately, they are the expression of hope.

Péguy's portrait of Bernard-Lazare sends us in the direction of discovering and deepening our own image of who the human being is. His source was the Christian tradition. It goes without saying that this need not be our own. But I do think Péguy's work stimulates our imagination regarding religious traditions, helping us see them not just as compilations of practices and beliefs, but as repositories of a way of discovering the human face in all its specific guises. His way of approaching his own tradition should encourage similar approaches to traditions not his own. Our problematic relations with others will not suddenly be made unproblematic. But in the world we live in, which is as polemicized, politicized, and ideologized as the world Péguy lived in, although across different lines, the ability to see beyond the divisions while recognizing their reality is *the* worthy struggle.

CHAPTER TWO

Péguy's Portrait
of Bernard-Lazare

A Word on This Translation

In translating Péguy's portrait of Bernard-Lazare, I feel the most important choice I made was to reproduce the rhythm and repetitions characteristic of his style, despite occasional losses in readability. The rhythm, in its alternations of very long sentences with very short ones, in all its lengths and pauses, conveys, more than any third party can say, the moods of the essay—its melancholy interspersed with unexpected points of humor. It is very much the body through which meaning is conveyed, although that meaning also pierces through in other ways.

The repetitions convey nuances, of course, but they do more than that. They are also the visible representation of a person speaking rather than writing, searching for words. I am not claiming that Péguy wrote without stylizing. It is clear that he did. But the style he chose aims at a certain intimacy, most readily available in direct speech. That this style takes some getting used to I am far from denying. When one gets used to it, however, it provides a pleasure all its own.

Neither Péguy's rhythm, especially the great length of many of his sentences, nor his repetitions are particularly French. Neither is his punctuation or lack thereof. I do not, therefore, feel that in reproducing all these features I am abiding by Franz Rosenzweig's theory of translation, in which the foreign language should inflect the structure of the home language in new ways. I am not trying to convey the modes of the French language here. I am merely trying to convey Péguy. Occasionally, though, I have resisted. Either I have not been able to find a word in English adequately duplicating Péguy's French, or the sentence reads so poorly in English that I felt something had to be done to save either its common sense or its thrust. In that case I have either broken it down into smaller sentences or punctuated differently from Péguy. Such instances are rare.

They reveal, however, that I am not wedded to reproducing Péguy's rhythm or repetitions at all costs. In general, readability remains a most important goal. By readability, though, I do not mean providing a text that poses no obstacles, because it conforms to our habitual expository prose. I mean providing a text whose ordinary sense comes through, despite the fact that readers may have to bend to a style unlike the ones most in currency. The plain meaning of Péguy's sentences in his portrait of Bernard-Lazare is completely within reach of its general French reader. As a result, no sentence should be reproduced in English in such a way that the syntax makes that plain meaning inaccessible. I am not talking here of the philosophical meaning of the portrait but of the logic of individual sentences.

Now, as to certain special problems: the key one has to do with the mystique-politique opposition, the leitmotif of the essay. I first tried to find English equivalents, translating them variously in different contexts. In the end, I decided to stick to the French terms throughout. The reason is that although the resonances of these words in English are misleading—*mystique*, for instance, does not refer either to charisma or to mysticism as it is generally understood and neither does *politique* refer to politics as action in the public realm as such—the problem the English-speaking reader faces when he sees these words is not that different from the French reader's. Péguy is not using them in their conventional French connotations either. He is, in fact, playing against some of those connotations. As a result, the distance between Péguy's usage and the accustomed meaning of these words occurs in both languages. The only way either the French or the English speaker has access to Péguy's sense of them is by paying attention to the many contexts in which they occur. By leaving them untranslated, then, I think I have more closely reproduced the relation of the reader to the original text than if I had tried to find unequivocal translations at every point. In any case, in my commentary, I give several successive interpretations of the sense of these words.

The other difficulty, especially for a translator of prose, is that some passages in the portrait have a density characteristic of poetry. I think, for instance, of the following sentences about Bernard-Lazare: "Il était comme sacré. L'honneur d'avoir fait l'affaire Dreyfus lui collait aux épaules comme une chape inexpiable." This imagery contains so many senses at once that even if one manages to convey some of them in English, the speed and power of the original escape. "Inexpiable" refers to something that cannot be forgiven. More figuratively, it means irremovable, unrelenting. Thus I have translated the sentences as: "He was as if sacred. The honor of having made the Dreyfus Affair stuck to him like an irremovable mantle of guilt." This might convey that he was trapped in his sacred status, made guilty in the eyes of others by the very same deed that they also recognized as saintly. But only some of the associations come through in the English, without the economy of the original, which makes for its power. This example only points to the inevitable losses of sense facing all translators of poetic imagery.

Not that all of Péguy's portrait of Bernard-Lazare is poetry. There are passages on current political developments that are nothing but passages on current political developments. Nothing could be more proselike, if not prosaic. I sometimes debated as to whether they should not be left out, since they make for slow reading, partially owing to the reader's unfamiliarity with the context. However, those passages provide background important for understanding Péguy's admiration for Bernard-Lazare and his usage of the terms *mystique* and *politique*. Besides, although most readers will not be experts in the various policy shifts of the Third Republic at the turn of the twentieth century, Péguy's main points remain well within reach, especially aided by a few strategically placed notes. In the vast majority of cases, I have decided to retain these passages.

There has been one prior translation of the portrait into English, by Harry Lorin Binsse, which serves as an introduction to Bernard-Lazare, placed before some of his writings on Jews, in a book entitled *Job's Dungheap*, with a preface by Hannah Arendt. Binsse's translation is quite good. I have nonetheless often made different choices from his. In the first place, as explained above, I have left the terms *mystique* and *politique* untranslated, while he translates them as "mysticism" and "politics." Secondly, I have kept many passages that he elected not to translate. On this latter point, the reader must be made aware that there are no fixed limits to what constitutes the portrait of Bernard-Lazare in "Notre jeunesse." Roughly speaking, Péguy spends the central third of the essay focusing almost exclusively on his friend, but within that third, there are occasional interruptions, in which he seems to be speaking about other topics. In addition, there are two short passages in the latter third of the essay directly describing Bernard-Lazare yet again. As these passages occur in contexts different from the central 50 pages, I have included them in Appendix C.

Péguy's Portrait of Bernard-Lazare

The Dreyfus Affair was the point of intersection, the culmination of at least three mystiques. In the first place, it crossed paths with the Jewish mystique. Why deny it? To say the contrary, on the contrary, would be suspect. There is a Jewish politique. Why deny it? To say the contrary, on the contrary, would be suspect. This politique is stupid, like all politiques. It is pretentious, like all politiques. It encroaches on everything, like all politiques. It is sterile, like all politiques. It advances the affairs of the Jews the way republican politicians advance the affairs of the Republic. It is most of all busy, like all politiques, snuffing out, devouring, abolishing its own mystique, the mystique from which it emerged. And it succeeds in nothing but this.

Far, then, from considering the Dreyfus Affair as a scheme, a maneuver, an operation of Jewish politique, it must on the contrary, be viewed as an operation, a deed, an explosion of Jewish mystique. Politicians, rabbis, Jewish communities—during century upon century of persecutions and hardship—had only too well acquired the political habit, the bent, of sacrificing a few of their members to have peace, the peace of the political household, the peace of kings and the great, the peace of their debtors, the peace of the masses and of princes, the peace of antisemites. They were perfectly willing to do it again. They were perfectly willing to continue. They were perfectly willing to sacrifice Dreyfus in order to ward off the storm. The vast majority of Jews is like the vast majority of (other) voters. It fears war. It fears turmoil. It fears agitation. Above all, perhaps, it fears, it dreads disorder itself. It would prefer silence, a shameful calm. If only one could come to some arrangement, by agreeing to be quiet; buy peace through handing over the scapegoat, buy a precious peace through some handing over, some betrayal, some shamefulness. To hand over innocent blood, it knows what that is. In times of peace, it fears war. It is afraid of blows. It fears conflicts. It is forced to rise to its true height. It meets its great, painful destiny only because it is forced to do so by a handful of rebels, an active minority, a small band of enthusiasts and fanatics, a small band of the driven, grouping themselves around a few chiefs who are none other than the prophets of Israel. Israel has provided innumerable prophets, heroes, martyrs, countless warriors. Still, in ordinary times, the people of Israel is like all peoples. All it asks is not to enter into extraordinary times. When it is in a period, it is like all peoples. All it asks is not to enter into an epoch. When it is in a period, all it asks is not to enter into a crisis. When it is on a good plain, thick with grass, where the streams of milk and honey flow, all it asks is not to go back up the mountain, even if that mountain is Moses' mountain. Israel has provided innumerable prophets; more than that, it is itself a prophet, it is itself the prophetic race. All together, in one body, a single prophet. But in the end it wants only this: not to give the prophets cause to exert themselves. It knows what it costs. Instinctively, historically, organically, so to speak, it knows what it costs. Its memory, its instinct, its very organism, its temporal body, its history, its entire memory tell it. Its entire memory is filled with it. Twenty, forty, fifty centuries of ordeals tell it. Innumerable wars, murders, deserts, captures of cities, exiles, foreign wars, civil wars, innumerable captivities. Fifty centuries of misery, sometimes gilded. Like modern misery. Fifty centuries of anguish, sometimes anarchic, sometimes masked by pleasures, sometimes masked, covered with the makeup of sensuality. Fifty centuries, perhaps, of neurosis.

Fifty centuries of wounds and scars, of spots that always hurt, the Pyramids and the Champs-Élysées, the kings of Egypt and the kings of the Orient, the whip of the eunuchs and the Roman spear, the Temple destroyed and not rebuilt, an unrelenting dispersion, have told them the cost for all their time to come. They know what it costs to be the carnal voice and the temporal body.[1] They know what it costs to bear God and his agents the prophets. His prophets the prophets. So, dimly, they would prefer it not to start over again. They are afraid of blows. They have had to take so many. They would prefer it not to be talked about. So many times they have paid both for themselves and for others. Why cannot one talk of something else? They have paid so many times for the world, for us. How about not talking about anything at all? How about doing business, good business? Let us not feel victorious. Let us not feel victorious over them. How many Christians have been forced onto the path of salvation through lashings. It is always the same. They are afraid of blows. All human beings are, in general, afraid of blows. At least beforehand. And afterward. Luckily, they are not always afraid of blows at the moment itself. Were not the most wonderful soldiers of the great Napoleon, those of the end, those who usually came from the small bands of deserters and insubordinates that the imperial police had handcuffed, pushed, driven back like a flock of sheep until that island of Walcheren? From there, however, came Lützen, Bautzen, the Berezina, the glorious Walcheren Infantry, the 131st regiment.[2]

They have fled so often, so often and in such a way, that they know the value of not fleeing. Having entered the modern nations, camping in their midst, they would so like to feel at ease there. Israel's entire politique is not to make any noise, in the world (there has been enough of it), to buy peace through a prudent silence. With the exception of a few pretentious scatterbrains, whom everyone denounces, it wants to let itself be forgotten. So many of its wounds are still bleeding. But the whole mystique of Israel is to pursue its resounding and painful mission in the world. Which leads to unbelievable splits, the most painful internal antagonisms that there have perhaps ever been between a mystique and a politique. A people of merchants. The same people a people of prophets. The ones know for the others what calamities are.

The ones know for the others what ruins are; always and, once again, ruins; a piling up of ruins; to live, to pass in a people of ruins, in a city of ruins.

I know this people well. It does not have a spot on its skin that isn't painful, upon which there is not an old black-and-blue mark, an old contusion, a dull pain, the memory of a dull pain, a scar, a wound, a bruise of the East or the West. They have their own, and all those of everyone else. For example, when Alsace and Lorraine were annexed [by Germany in 1871], all the Jews there were wounded *as Frenchmen*.[3]

It is to know Jewish politique quite poorly, at the very moment one is talking about it, to suppose that it is Jewish politique or the Jewish party that ever got an affair like the Dreyfus Affair going. On the contrary. They are never the ones to start any commotion. They want, they seek only silence. They want only to let themselves be forgotten. Apart from a few scatterbrains, they seek only obscurity and silence.

In fact, in this specific case, it is not to know a thing about the Dreyfus Affair and about Dreyfusism, and especially about how it started, to believe, to imagine that it is some sort of invention, fabrication, contrivance of the Jewish politique, that the Jewish party watched its outbreak with pleasure. It is very precisely the opposite. They did not quite know, but they were on their guard. They were right to be on their guard. From the point of view of their interests. This affair, all things taken into consideration, beneath apparent victories, beneath aspects of conquest(s), beneath surfaces of triumph, did them (much) more harm than good.

Given how low the curve of the history of this affair has fallen on the graph today, we can in fact now say that the first time we won against the anti-Dreyfusist anti-Dreyfusists; that the second time we lost against the anti-Dreyfusist Dreyfusists;[4] and that today finally we are in the process of losing to both of them at once.

They were on their guard. Did they foresee this enormous uproar, this enormous shake-up? One never foresees everything. In any case, they don't like causing uproars.

When, therefore, M. Dreyfus's family, in order to obtain individual reparation, considered a total upheaval of France, of Israel,[5] of all Christendom, not only was it going against French politique but also it was going at least as much against Jewish politique as it was going against clerical politique. A mystique can go against all politiques *at once*. Those who learn history elsewhere than in polemical debates, those who try to follow it in events, in reality itself, know that it is within Israel that the Dreyfus family, that the nascent Dreyfus Affair, that nascent Dreyfusism first ran against the greatest obstacles. Wisdom is also a virtue of Israel. Besides the Prophets, there is also Ecclesiastes. Many were saying, "*What for?*" The wise saw that most of all it would start a commotion, launch a beginning whose end one might never see, the nature of whose end, especially, one did not see. Within families, within the intimacy of families, this attempt was commonly considered madness. Once again madness would carry the day, in this chosen race of restlessness. Later, soon thereafter, all, or nearly all, would go along because when a prophet has spoken in Israel, all hate him, all admire him, all follow him. Fifty centuries of a sword at their back forces them to go along.

They recognize the test with an admirable instinct, with an instinct fifty centuries old. They recognize, they greet the blow. It is yet again a blow from God. The city will be taken again, the Temple destroyed, the women taken away. A captivity comes, after so many captivities. Long convoys will drag along in the desert. Their corpses will mark the routes of Asia. Very well, they know what they're in for. They gird their loins for this new departure. Since it must be, they will go through it again. God is harsh, but he is God. He punishes, and he upholds. He leads. They who with impunity have obeyed so many external masters, finally bow to the master requiring the most rigorous servitude, the Prophet, the inner master.

The prophet, in this great crisis of Israel and of the world, was Bernard-Lazare. Let us honor here one of the greatest names of modern times, and after Darmesteter,[6] one of the greatest among the prophets of Israel. As for me, if I am granted the time, I would consider it one of the greatest rewards of my old age finally to be able to establish, to restore, the portrait of this extraordinary man.

I had started to write a *portrait of Bernard-Lazare*.[7] But for those human beings who are 50 centuries old, one may well need a distance of 50 years. An enormous number of fools, both among Jews and among Christians, still believe that Bernard-Lazare was a young man, a youthful man, it isn't quite clear, a young writer, who had come to Paris like so many others, to make his way, make his fortune, in letters, as they used to say then, in the theater, in short stories, in novellas, in the anthology, in the tale, in the jumble, in the newspapers, in politics, in the whole of temporal misery, coming to the Latin Quarter, as all the young people from those parts, a young Jew from the South, from Avignon and from Vaucluse, or from the Bouches-du-Rhône, or rather from Gard and Hérault. A young Jew from Nîmes or Montpellier. I would not be surprised, I'm even sure, that the young Bernard-Lazare thought this himself. The prophet at first does not know himself. One could still find people who would do entire studies of Bernard-Lazare, the symbolist or young poet, or the friend of the symbolists or the enemy of the symbolists. One no longer knows which. And in the Dreyfus Affair itself, I wouldn't be surprised if the Dreyfusist General Staff, the circle around Dreyfus, Dreyfus's family, and Dreyfus himself always considered Bernard-Lazare as an agent whom one pays, a sort of juridical, or judicial counsel, but not only for judicial matters, or a maker of memoranda, on the payroll, a pamphleteer, working for wages, a polemicist and a polemic maker, a journalist without a newspaper, a semi-official attorney, respected the way a semi-official, nonlitigating attorney is respected. A maker, a founder of memoranda and files, a sort of legal consultant in juridical matters and above all in political matters, in short, a hack journalist. A professional writer. As a result, a man for whom one has contempt. As for a man who works, who writes on a subject. That was given to him, that had been given to him. A man who earned his living, who earned what he could, who earned what he earned. As a result, a man one held in contempt. A man on the lookout for something. Maybe an agent who executes orders. Israel passes by the Just and has contempt for him. Israel passes by the Prophet, follows him, and does not see him.

The way the Jews fail to recognize their prophets, and nonetheless the leadership of the Jews by the prophets, is the whole history of the Jews.

The way the sinners fail to recognize the saints, and nonetheless the salvation of the sinners by the saints, is the whole of Christian history.

The way the Jews fail to recognize the prophets is, while quite different, equal, comparable only, to the way sinners fail to recognize the saints.

One could even say that the Jews' failure to recognize the prophets is a *figure* for the sinners' failure to recognize the saints.

When the prophet comes by, the Jews think he is a publicist. Who knows, maybe a sociologist.

If only we could find him a position at the Sorbonne. Or rather in the École *pratique* (?)(!) des hautes études.[8] Fourth section. Or Fifth. Or Third. The *religious* SCIENCES, in short. In the Sorbonne, *at the end of the gallery of Sciences*, staircase E, on the first floor. We could do it. We are so powerful in the French state.

One of the most frightening records of human ingratitude (here it was especially Jewish ingratitude, but it was also generally, the ingratitude of so many others, with the exception of ourselves, a common ingratitude) was the position into which Bernard-Lazare was put immediately after the launching and apparent victory, the false victory of the Dreyfus Affair. The total lack of recognition, even ignorance, the solitude, the contempt, the oblivion into which he was allowed to fall, into which he was made to fall, into which he was made to perish. Into which he was made to die.

"It is his fault too that he died," they say in their unbelievable, in their inveterate vileness, in their vulgar, revolting promiscuity. "One should never die. It is always wrong to die."—It must therefore be said, it must therefore be written, it must therefore be made public that just as he had lived for them, he literally died because of them and for them. Yes, yes, I know. He died of this. And of that. One always dies of something. But the terrible disease from which he died would have given him a reprieve, 10, 15, 20 years' respite, if it had not been for the dreadful overload he took upon himself to save Dreyfus. A frightful nervous tension, which lasted for years. A frightful overload of both body and mind. An overload of the heart, the worst of all. An overload of everything.

One always dies of some injury(ies).

I will paint the portrait of Bernard-Lazare. He had, undeniably, something of the saint, of sanctity, about him. And when I speak of saints, I am not under suspicion of speaking metaphorically. He had a gentleness, a goodness, a mystical tenderness, an even-temperedness, an experience of disappointment and ingratitude, a kind of goodness that could not be outdone, a kind of goodness perfectly informed and perfectly learned, of unbelievable depth. As if he had goodness to spare. He lived and died for them like a martyr. He was a prophet. It was therefore proper that he be prematurely buried in silence and oblivion. In a fabricated silence. In a concerted oblivion.

His death should not be charged against him. His very death was for them. He should not be blamed for his death.

Most of all it was held against him, most of all the Jews held it against him, had contempt for him that he was not rich. I even think he was considered a spender. This meant he was no longer needed or that it was thought he was no longer needed. Maybe he did cost them some; he should have cost them more. He was a generous man.

Only it should perhaps be considered that he was invaluable.

For he was dead before having died. Once again, Israel was pursuing its temporally eternal destiny. It is extremely noteworthy that the only newspaper in which our friend was ever worthily treated, I mean, according to his worth, according to his greatness, at the proper scale, in his order of greatness was *La Libre Parole* and the only man who spoke of him this way was M. Edouard Drumont. In this newspaper, he was, of course, treated like an enemy, violently, harshly, like an enemy, but nonetheless in a manner corresponding to his greatness, at his scale. There, in enemy terms, it was nonetheless said how much he loved Israel and how great he was. It is our shame that the name of Bernard-Lazare, in the five, seven years he has been dead, has appeared only in an enemy newspaper. I am not speaking of the *Cahiers*, whose intimate friend, whose secret inspirer, whose patron I would be quite willing to say, and very literally, he has remained. Outside us, I mean this very limitedly, as they say in the law, outside us of the *Cahiers*, there is only M. Edouard Drumont who knew how to speak of Bernard-Lazare, who wanted to speak of him, who gave him his due.

The others, those on our side, kept quiet even before his death, and have kept quiet since with shameful care, perfectly, patiently, with extraordinary success.

And he was dead before having died.

They were as if ashamed of him. But really it was they who were ashamed of themselves before him.

It was the politicians, it was politique itself that was ashamed of itself before a mystique.

How many times have I not gone up that rue de Florence. Not only do all the neighborhoods of Paris have an established personality, but that personality has a history like we do. It has not been long and yet everything speaks of another time. Already. History is this very change, this *generation and corruption*,[9] this constant abolition, this perpetual revolution. This death. It has only been a few years, eight or ten, and already how unrecognizable, how unrecognizable the buildings are.

> Old Paris is no more (the shape of a city
> Changes faster, alas, than the heart of a mortal);[10]

At the time people lived in that upper part of Paris where no one lives any more today. So many houses were built everywhere, boulevard Raspail. M. Salomon Reinach was probably still living at 36 or 38 rue de Lisbonne.[11] Or at another number. But the point is that Bernard-Lazare could drop in, could drop in like a neighbor on his way. The quartier Saint-Lazare. Rue de Rome and rue de Constantinople. All the quartier de l'Europe. All of l'Europe. Sounds of names that secretly fed their need to travel, their ease in traveling, their European residency. A neighborhood around a train station, which fed their need for railroads, their taste for railroads, their ease on railroads. Everyone has moved. A few into death. And even many. Zola used to live on rue de Bruxelles, 81 or 81*b* or 83 rue de Bruxelles. *First ses-*

sion of the court.—Session of February 7th.—Your name is Émile Zola?—Yes, sir.—What is your profession?—Writer.—What is your age?—Fifty-eight. —Where do you live?—81 bis rue de Bruxelles.[12] Didn't M. Ludovic Halévy live on rue de Douai, which must be in the same neighborhood, 22 rue de Douai, and still today at 62 rue de Rome, 155 boulevard Haussmann.[13] Those were the addresses of those days. Dreyfus himself was from this neighborhood. Only [Fernand] Labori still lives at 41 or 45 rue Condorcet.[14] I've been told he has just moved to 12 rue Pigalle, Paris IX[e]. A whole population, an entire people lived in this manner on the heights of Paris, in the flanks of the heights of Paris, on those crowded Paris heights, an entire people, friends, enemies, who knew each other, who didn't know each other, but who sensed, who knew that they were country neighbors in that immense Paris.

How many times did I not go, during the painful days, up to that rue de Florence. Painful days for him and for me, for both equally, for we both felt, equally, that all was lost, that a politique, our politique (I mean the politique of those on our side) was beginning to eat up our mystique. He felt it, if you will, in a more experienced way. I felt it in a more innocent way. But he still had a disarming innocence. And I already had a good deal of experience.

I can say, so that there be no misunderstanding, I must say, that during those last years during this last period of his life, I was his only friend. His last and only friend. At the time it was to me alone that he would say what he thought, what he felt, what he knew, in short. I will convey it some day.

I am forced to insist that I was his only friend and his only confidant. I insist because certain contraband friends he had, or rather that he had had, literary friends, in a word, engaged in making themselves believe and to make the world believe, that they had remained his friends, even after they had sabotaged, perverted, failed to recognize, failed to know, politiqued his mystique.

Friends from the Latin Quarter, in short, old friends from student days, maybe from the Sorbonne. Friends that use the informal mode of address.[15]

And he was so good that through this unshakable, through this inexhaustible goodness, he let them believe it as well, and he let the world believe it. But he spoke of it altogether otherwise to me, because I was his sole confidant, because he entrusted me with all the secrets, all the hidden side, of his thought.

Of friendship he had not only a mystical idea but also a mystical feeling, an experience of incredible depth, a mystical experience, a mystical knowledge. He had that mystical attachment to faithfulness that is at the heart of friendship. He practiced mystically that faithfulness that is the heart of friendship. Thus between him and us was born that friendship that no death would sever, that perfectly reciprocated friendship, perfectly mutual, perfectly complete, nourished by the loss of illusion about all the others, by the disabuse about all the unfaithfulnesses.

That friendship that no death will sever.

He had to the highest, most profound degree that morality of the small group of friends, which is perhaps the only morality there is.

For his mystique itself he had that mystical faithfulness, that mystical friendship.

That friendship, that morality of the small group of friends.

He had that faithfulness to himself that in the end is what matters. Many can betray you. But it is a great deal, it is already much not to betray yourself. Many politiques can betray, can devour, can consume many mystiques. It is a great deal that the mystiques do not betray themselves.

Many marshals were able to betray Napoleon. But at least Napoleon did not betray himself. Napoleon the marshal did not betray Napoleon the emperor.

It can be said that his last pleasures, as long as he was able to walk, as long as he was able to keep going, were to come as if to warm himself up among us on the Thursdays of the *Cahiers*, or, to speak more precisely, on Thursday at the *Cahiers*.[16] He much liked to chat with M. [Georges] Sorel.[17] I must say that their discussion was usually marked by a great loss of illusion.

He had a secret affinity, very pronounced, very profound, and almost very violent, for M. Sorel. A common affinity for disabuse; for people you couldn't fool. When they laughed together, when they burst out, at the same moment, for both had a gushing laugh, it was with an incredible depth of agreement, an incredible complicity. This striking accord of the mind, of laughter, which does not wait, which does not calculate, which in one stroke reaches the deepest, last point, bursts out and reveals. Which in one word reaches the final word. Everything that M. Sorel said impressed him so much that he would still be talking to me about it all the other mornings of the week. They were like two great accomplices. Two great mischief makers. Two great child accomplices who had known human beings very well.

The friendship he had for these nascent *Cahiers*, for me, had something disarming in it. It was all the care, all the tenderness, all the experience, all the cautioning of an older brother who had gone through much.

Who had been much tested by life. By existence.

Henceforth he was suspect. Henceforth he was isolated. The honor of having made the Dreyfus Affair stuck to his shoulders like an irremovable ecclesiastical mantle of guilt. Suspect everywhere, alone above all in his own party. Not a single newspaper, not a single journal would accept, would tolerate his signature. In the last resort, some of his copy might have been accepted, if it were beautified, diluted, sweetened. Above all, if that devil of a signature were taken off, erased. He came back naturally toward us. It was only at the *Cahiers* that he could talk, write, publish—even chat. When negotiations were in progress to create a big daily newspaper (at the time negotiations were always in progress to create a big daily newspaper) and when the Jews were asked for money (they gave it then; they let much too much of it be pulled out of them, M. Jaurès knows something about that),[18] Jewish capitalists, Jewish financiers did it under one condition only: it was that Bernard-Lazare would not write for it.

From all directions, everything was organized quite well so that he should very quietly die of hunger.

He came back to us as if by his natural inclination. He was as if sacred, that is to say that he was seen for what he was, measured at his measure, valued at his value, and at the same time and above all no one wanted to hear anymore about him. Everyone kept quiet about him. Those he had saved were quiet more obstinately, more silently than everybody else, buried him in a more mute, more obstinate silence. Some, in the criminal half shadow of the back of their minds, were beginning to let it be thought inside them that perhaps he had been fortunate, that perhaps he had died just in time for his glory. Some may have thought it, some certainly thought it. The fact is, he must at least be given credit for dying at an opportune moment, convenient for many people. For almost everybody. Some people that he had made subscribe to the *Cahiers* during the crisis of the Dreyfus Affair waited impatiently for him to die to send us their cancellation, to get rid of this enormous tribute of 20 francs a year he had imposed on them *during the Dreyfus Affair*, as it was already being called.

We received the cancellation of M. Louis Louis-Dreyfus[19] within two weeks or a month, maybe even within a week of Bernard-Lazare's death.

Those he had saved were the most in a hurry. He himself knew it very well. It does not matter whether, in addition, one knows this is the rule. Each time it is always new. And it is always hard to swallow.

He himself had no illusions about the men he had defended. Everywhere he saw politiques, politiquing men arrive, devour everything, devour, dishonor his work. I will tell all he told me. He would reach, he would accede to a depth of feeling(s), an incredible depth of regret, he would arrive at incredible depths of gentle goodness that can exist only on the basis of a complete loss of illusions.

A small minority, a small group, an immense majority of poor Jews (there are many), of the destitute (there are many), remained faithful to him, were attached to him with a fanatical attachment, a fanatical love, exacerbated daily by the inroads of death. Those people loved him. We loved him. The rich no longer loved him.

I will tell, then, what his funeral was like.

I will tell what his end was like in its entirety.

I will tell how much he suffered.

I will tell, in these Confessions, how much he kept quiet.

I still see upon me his nearsighted gaze, so intelligent and so good all at once, with so invincible, so intelligent, so enlightened, so enlightening, so luminous a kindness, with so untiring, so experienced, so enlightened, so disabused, so incurable a goodness. Because a man wears a pince-nez firmly settled on top of a fleshy nose, fencing in, framing two large, good, nearsighted eyes, modern man is incapable of recognizing, is incapable of seeing the look, the fire lit 50 centuries ago. But I did come near him. I alone lived as his intimate, in his confidence. You had to listen, you had to see, you had to have seen this man who naturally thought of himself as a modern. You had to see that look, you had to hear that voice. Naturally, he was very sincerely an atheist. At the time, it was not only the predominant metaphysic, but it was the going metaphysic, the one one breathed, a sort of climatological, atmospheric metaphysic; which was taken completely for granted, like having good manners; and, on top of that, it was understood, positively, scientifically, triumphantly, that it was not a metaphysic; he was a positivist, a scientificist, a modern intellectual, the whole package; above all, he did not want to hear of metaphysics. One of his favorite reasonings, the one he always served me, was that since the Jews were of all peoples the one who believed least in God, they were clearly the ones it would be easiest to rid of old superstitions; and thus they were the ones who would show others the way. According to him, the excellence of the Jews came from the fact that they were as if ahead of time the freest thinkers. Even with a hyphen. And beneath this, and within this a heart that beat to all the echoes in the world, a man who would leap on a newspaper and who in its four, six, eight, in its twelve pages, with a single look like lightning would seize upon a sentence and in that sentence there was the word *Jew*, a being who flushed, paled, an old-timer of a journalist, an old hand of journalism, who would pale because of a news item that he would find in this newspaper, because of a section of an article, because of a slender caption, because in that dispatch there was the word *Jew*; a heart that bled in all the ghettoes of the world, and perhaps yet more in the broken-up ghettoes, in the diffused ghettoes, like Paris, than in the enclosed ghettoes, in the foreclosed ghettoes; a heart that bled in Romania and in Turkey, in Russia and in Algeria, in America and in Hungary, everywhere the Jew is persecuted, which is to say, in a certain sense, everywhere; a heart that bled both in the East and in the West, in Islam and in Christendom, a heart that bled even in Judea, and at the same time, a man who made fun of the Zionists; such is the Jew; a tremor of anger, and it was for some injury suffered in the Dnieper Valley. So what our Powers did not want to know, that he was the prophet, the Jew, the leader—the lowliest Jewish peddler, the most destitute Jew of Romania knew, saw. A perpetual tremor, a perpetual vibration. All that is needed to die at 40. Not a muscle, not a nerve that was not tensed for a secret mission, that was not perpetually vibrating for the mission. Never had anyone held himself to such a degree the leader of his race and of his people, responsible for his race and his people. A being perpetually tensed. A relentless pre-tension and subtension. Not a feeling, not a thought, not the shadow of a passion that was not tensed, that was not commanded by a commandment 50 centuries old, by the commandment hurled down 50 centuries ago; an entire race, an entire people on his shoulders, a race, a people 50 centuries old on his stooped shoulders; on his rounded shoulders, on his weighed-down shoulders; a heart consumed by fire, the fire of his race, consumed by the fire of his people; fire in the heart, a head on fire, and *the burning coal on the prophetic lip*.[20]

When I come into contact with one of our old enemies (it is an increasingly frequent phenomenon unavoidable, desirable even, for a people must make itself anew, and make itself anew with all its might), I start by saying to him: You do not know us. You have the right not to know us. Our politicians masqueraded publicly so much that you could not tell what was going on beneath. Our politicians did not merely consume, absorb our mystique.

They masked it completely, at least before the public, what is referred to as the general public. You did not subscribe to the *Cahiers*. That's perfectly natural. You had other things to do. You did not read our issues. But this mystique of which we speak, we are not inventing it today to serve the cause, we are not making it up on the spot today. It was for ten and fifteen years the very mystique of these *Cahiers*, in all its subject matter, and we have shown it often enough. The only difference there was is that masqued by our politicians, our issues did not reach the general public, and that today, because of the politicians' confusion, and no doubt for another reason, and for at least two reasons even, they do reach it.

The only difference is that we were not read; and that we are beginning to be read.

And, besides, it is certain that we are the only ones, that we are the only ones who for fifteen years have rigorously, impeccably, unfailingly upheld this mystique. Therein lay our strength. And today, obscure with us, ignored with us, preserved with us, through our care, today through our care, with us, this mystique naturally makes its appearance.

It was our strength, we the weak, we the poor. A mystique is the invincible strength of the weak.

But all the difference is that it was unknown; and that today, with us, through us, it is known.

Because of this, I don't mind if there is *an apology for our past*,[21] and that I find it very well made, if only it is understood that it is not talking about *our* past but of the past of others. My past needs no apology. Otherwise, there would be, there would occur, an optical illusion, extremely harmful to us; and unjust; and stupid. A certain number, a small number of Dreyfusards, the top layer, made, experienced demagogies, a whole demagogy, a whole Dreyfusist *politique*. A certain number, a very great number of others, us, the layers beneath, the insides, the fools, did everything, risked everything in order to remain faithful to our mystique, in order to oppose the establishment of the domination of that politique. We are the ones who count. We are the ones who represent. We are the ones who witness. We are the evidence. We don't mind if others make defenses and apologies, express remorse, regrets, worries, repent and make penitences, ask and obtain lay, civic, civil and obligatory absolutions. We shall even provide them with the set phrases. But we ask that they do not ask and do not obtain them for us; that they do not practice them for us; and secondly that they do not ask and do not obtain and do not practice them for the Dreyfus Affair itself and for Dreyfusism. I do not want an *apology for Péguy* nor for

Péguy's past, nor *an apology for the Cahiers*. I do not want to be defended.
I do not need to be defended. I am accused of nothing.

I fear nothing as much as this: to be defended.
Here is all the disowning that I have the courage to inflict upon myself.

I am not accused. *We* are not accused. *Our* Dreyfus Affair is not accused.
Under that common name of Dreyfus Affair, as it happens so often in history, under that almost generic name, there were at least, in reality, two
perfectly distinct, extremely different affairs. Two affairs ran, pursued their
course, followed their destiny. Made their way. Ours has nothing with
which to reproach itself. There were pure Dreyfusards and impure Dreyfusards. It is how human beings break down. There was a pure Dreyfus
Affair and an impure Dreyfus Affair. It is how events break down. We will
not allow that the first make excuses, practice penitences for the second.
Or, if one prefers, that the second make and practice them for the first.
With the first. Together. We have nothing for which to seek forgiveness.
We will not allow that those who do have to seek forgiveness, or who have
a taste for asking for forgiveness, ask forgiveness for us as well, together
with them.
    We do not at all want to be forgiven.
    We who have sacrificed everything, especially to oppose the Combist
demagogy[22] derived from our Dreyfusism, a politique derived from our
mystique, are not in Dreyfusism a negligible quantity that must or could
be ignored in the accounts, that could be eliminated and dismissed in and
for the working of history. It is we, on the contrary who are the center and
the heart of Dreyfusism, who have remained thus, it is we who are the soul.
The axis passes through us. It is by our watch that time will have to be read.
    There has been, there is a Dreyfusist honor. Those who have not been
faithful to this honor are not to ask forgiveness for those who did follow it,
who are following it.

When, at rare intervals, I come into contact with one of these former enemies, I say to him: You do not know us. You may not even have any inkling
of us. You have that right. So many of ours do not know us. Our politicians did everything to hide us from you, to mask us from you, to disavow
us, to deny us, to betray us, both our mystique and ourselves. It is altogether natural that placed before them in battle you saw only the top layer,
the politique, which was visible and that you did not see us, that you did
not see what was underneath, the insides, which nourished. You saw what
was manifest and while we were obeying the rules of our honor, you did
not see the troops. It is the very law of combat. Today you cannot read

everything. In reverse, going back. You cannot know us in our entirety. One cannot catch up, one cannot make oneself over, one does not overcome ten, twelve, or fifteen years. Take merely this. And then I give or send them a copy of *Cahiers* 3, no. 21, Jean Deck's "For Finland,"[23] not only so that they should read this thick and beautiful work of our contributor at the very moment when Finland, which had, despite everything, managed to resist pure autocracy, bureaucratic autocracy to some extent, could no longer resist parliamentary bureaucracy, could no longer defend itself against a disguised autocratic bureaucracy, masked by a vaguely parliamentary machinery, but also because at the end of that issue, in that disastrous month of August of 1902 we had, amid the failure and defeat of our efforts, in mourning for our defeat, hastily assembled, at the end of that issue, everything Dreyfusist we had been able hastily to assemble, everything we had been able to gather against the politique, against the demagogy of the *law of assemblies*.[24] Just read, I tell him, at the end of the issue, that *dossier* of 30 or 40 pages *for and against assemblies*. Just read, at the end of this dossier, the *opinion* of Bernard-Lazare, dated August 6, 1902, entitled "The Law and the Assemblies." Twenty-five pages. Really the last he submitted. A year later he was dead or dying.

It must be conceded to them that they usually leave this reading amazed. They had no inkling of who we were. And above all they had no inkling that this is who we were from the beginning. That this is who we had been for so long, since the beginning. They had no inkling of this long, this initial, this impeccable fidelity. This fidelity of a whole lifetime. Especially, most strikingly, they had no inkling of what kind of human being Bernard-Lazare was.

It must be realized that in that *dossier*, in that *opinion*, which is must reading, which is not only an admirable, but also an unforgettable memorial, Bernard-Lazare opposed with all his remaining strength the degeneration, the deviation of Dreyfusism into politique, into a Combist demagogy. Let those who succumbed, who gave in, no matter how little, to the worst of all demagogies, to the Combist demagogy, make *apologies*, or let others make them on their behalf.[25] But for those who did not budge, for those who did not give an inch, please, let none be made. When one rereads that admirable report of Bernard-Lazare, one is as if shocked, one begins to get red in the face at the very idea that it might be possible to think that such a human being would be included, could be thoughtlessly included by third parties, by the public, by the ignorant, within the forgiven, within the beneficiaries of an apology.

Operating, working the same matter, developing in the same matter, there were at least two Dreyfus affairs, shaping the matter of the same history. That of Bernard-Lazare, ours, was innocent and does not need to be defended. And in yet another sense there were very noticeably two Dreyfus affairs, the one that issued from Bernard-Lazare, and the one that issued from Colonel Picquart.[26] The one that issued from Colonel Picquart was a very good one. The one that issued from Bernard-Lazare was infinite.

It must be realized that, especially in that *opinion*, which was literally his mystical testament, he not only opposed Combism, which was the misuse, the demagogy, of the system. He had no less strongly opposed Waldeckism, which was ostensibly the norm and regular use of the system. He went not only to the misuse, but also back to the very root of how it functioned. He went back, he retraced his way to the root. As a matter of course, in a natural movement, requiring this naturally, like any human being who thinks deeply. He had discerned the effect in the cause, the abuse in the norm. It must therefore be realized that he had opposed with all his strength, with what remaining strength he had, not only the development and the potential for development, but the origin itself, the principle of Dreyfusist *politique*. One must reread that opinion, that dossier, that eloquent call to Jaurès, almost a summons, certainly already a threat.

It must be realized that this was a man, I said very specifically a prophet, for whom the entire apparatus of power, the reason of state, temporal powers, political powers, authorities of all sorts—political, intellectual, even mental—weighed not an ounce in the face of a revolt, of a movement of conscience itself. One cannot even begin to conceive it. The rest of us cannot even imagine it. When we revolt against an authority, when we march against the authorities, at the very least we lift them off ourselves. We feel their weight, in short. At least within us. At the very least we need to lift them off ourselves. We know, we feel that we are marching against them and that we are lifting them off. For him they did not exist. Less than what I am telling you. I don't even know how to convey to what degree he dismissed temporal authorities, to what degree he dismissed the powers that be; I have no idea how to convey it. It was not even that he dismissed them. He ignored them, and even beyond that. He didn't see them, he didn't take them into account. He was nearsighted. They didn't exist for him. They were not of his rank, of his order of greatness, of his dimension. They were completely foreign to him. They were less than nothing for him, equal to zero. They were like ladies who were not received in his living room. He had such a hatred, such an aversion, such a constant animosity against authority, against ruling power, against government, against temporal power, against the state, against the reason of state, that this hatred annulled them, that they did not enter, did not have the honor of entering into his reasoning. In that affair of the assemblies, of the law of assemblies, or rather of these successive laws and of the application of this law, where it was so clear that the government of the Republic, under the name of the Combes government, had failed all commitments it had undertaken under the name of the Waldeck government, in that affair, the other affair, the new affair, in which it was so evident that the government betrayed the word of a government and, consequently, of the government, betrayed the word of the state, if it is permissible to juxtapose such words, Bernard-Lazare had naturally judged that the word of the Republic must be honored. He had judged that the Republic had to keep its word. He had judged that the law must be applied, interpreted as the government, the two chambers, in short, the state had promised to apply it, as they themselves had committed themselves to applying, interpreting it. As they promised, it would be applied. It was as clear as daylight for him. The Court of Appeals,²⁷ just as naturally, did not hesitate to agree (with these gentlemen) of the government. I mean to say of the second government. A friend (as they say) came to tell him, triumphantly: *You see, dear friend, the Court of Appeals has decided against you.* The Dreyfusards turned Combists were already bursting with arrogance, with bragging, with the politicians' corruption. You should have seen his eyes, sparkling with mischief, gentle mischief, and with experience. Whoever has not seen his black eyes, his nearsighted eyes, has seen nothing; and the fold of his lips. A bit heavy.—*My dear friend*, he answered softly, *you are mistaken. It is I who have decided differently from the Court of Appeals.* The idea that the Court of Appeals, all chambers in session, could, for even an instant, be compared to him, Bernard-Lazare, seemed comical to him. Since the other seemed nonetheless somewhat shocked—*But my good fellow*, he said very gently, *the Court of Appeals is made up of human beings.* He had that sovereign way of speaking very softly, very gently as if to a dumb grammar school student. Who had not understood. Recall that this was the time when every politicking Dreyfusard hobnobbed with the Court of Appeals, would puff up his cheeks when he said *the Court of Appeals*, bursting with pride that he had been historically, juridically authenticated, justified by the Court of Appeals, rolled his eyes, assured himself deep inside on the basis of the Court of Appeals that Dreyfus was indeed innocent. He had stayed boyish, with that unconquerable boyishness, with that boyishness that is the very mark of greatness, with that noble boyishness, with that easy boyishness that is the mark of being at ease in greatness. And above all with an adult boyishness that is strictly reserved to those who are pure of heart. No, never have I seen such a sovereign being-at-ease. Never have I seen someone spiritual dismiss so sovereignly, so healthily, so freely, so evenly a temporal association. Never have I seen someone spiritual annul a temporal body in such a way. You could feel very well that for him the Court of Appeals did not impress him at all, that for him these were old fools, that the idea of contrasting them with him, Bernard-Lazare, as judicial authorities was simply baroque, burlesque, that he Bernard-Lazare was a judicial, and political, and everything else authority of a totally different kind. That he had a totally different domain, a totally different jurisdiction, that he pronounced a totally different law. That he saw them completely and constantly divested of their office, shorn of all their trappings, and even of their robes, which conceal the human being from view. That he could not see them in any other way. Even when he tried in good faith, in all good faith. Because he was good. Even were he to try hard. That he could not even conceive that they could be seen in any other way. That he himself could see them only as old, completely naked monkeys. Not at all, as one might have at first thought, as a first, superficial, hasty evaluation could at first let it be supposed, as old monkeys covered by robes and ermine. You could feel so well that he knew that he Bernard-Lazare had made these people march, and they would again be made to march, but that he Bernard-Lazare could not be made to march, that these people especially could not make him march. That he had made everyone march temporally, and that the whole world could not make him march spiritually. For him, it would never be the highest authority of the kingdom, the highest judicial authority, the highest jurisdiction of the kingdom, the highest official of the Republic. They were old judges. And he knew well what an old judge was. You could feel so well that he knew that he had made these people march but that they would never make him march. When the other left: *You saw him*, he laughed. *He was funny with* HIS *Court of Appeals*. Note that he was, and very deliberately, against the Waldeck laws themselves. Against the Waldeck law. But, in the end, since there was a Waldeck law, he wanted it to be juridically and even loyally upheld, applied and interpreted as it was. He did not like the state. But since in the end there was a state, and since it couldn't be otherwise, he at least wanted the same state that passed a law also to be the one to apply it. That the state should not shirk its responsibilities by changing names and status between the two; that it should not do something under one name and undo it under another name. He wanted at the very least that the state should at least for a few years remain in continuity with itself. The other obviously wanted to say that it was very valuable, of the highest value, of supreme court value, that the Court of Appeals had declared Dreyfus innocent.[28] For him, it had no value. He considered that sort of juridical consecration as a purely judicial one, and only a temporal victory, above all undoubtedly a victory of Bernard-Lazare over the Court of Appeals. It did not occur to him that a Court of Appeals could make or not make Dreyfus's innocence. But he sensed, he knew perfectly well that it was he Bernard-Lazare that made the authority of the Court of Appeals, that made or did not make a Court of Appeals itself, because he was its nourishment and matter, and that thus and on top of everything else, he was its very form. That in a sense, in that sense, he was its judicial body. It was not the Court of Appeals that deigned to honor him. It was he who deigned to honor the Court of Appeals. Never have I seen a human being believe, know to this degree that the greatest temporal powers, that the greatest governmental bodies go on, exist only because of inner spiritual powers. It is well enough known that he was opposed to manipulating Article 445 the way it was manipulated ([Georges] Clemenceau also was opposed to it),[29] and all the difficulties we have had as a result of the manipulation of this article, the insurmountable problems that occurred, that resulted from the manipulation of this article, or rather, from that manipulation of this article, would have been avoided if he had been allowed to take charge of the matter. There is no doubt whatsoever that he considered that manipulation to be a betrayal, an abuse, a use of force by the judiciary, an illegality. In addition, with his clear common sense, very French, this Jew who was altogether a Parisian, with his clear juridical eye, foresaw the inextricable difficulties that we would confront, that it would eternally reopen the affair or rather, that it would eternally prevent the affair from closing. He would say to me: *Dreyfus will be tried before 50 military tribunals if necessary*, or another time: *Dreyfus will be tried by military tribunals all his life. But he must be acquitted the same way as everyone else.* At bottom, his thought was that Dreyfus was quite foolish to go to so much trouble as to have his innocence sanctioned by the established authorities; that these people added nothing to the business; since he had been rescued from unjust persecution, the main thing had been accomplished; that the trappings of authority, judicial sanctionings are quite superfluous, do not exist, come from negligible bodies; that it is to do too much honor to these gentlemen; that one is very good, when one is innocent, to have it established to boot. That one thus gives to these authorities an authority of which they are much in need. But then, on another level, if one did have recourse to them, one had to have recourse to them honestly, without detours, one should not cheat, *above all, no doubt, because it would give the appearance, and maybe the reality, of bowing before them, of fearing them.* Since one resorted to them, since one made use of them, one should make use of them, resort to them honestly. It was still a way of ruling over them. If it was politics, it should at least be honest. He had an incredible taste for honesty, especially in what he didn't like, in politics and in the judicial system. He thus made up in a manner of speaking, for resorting to them despite himself, by being honest despite them. I have never seen anyone know so well how to keep his distance, be so distant, so gently, so expertly, so, so to speak, horizontally. I have never seen a spiritual power, someone who feels himself, knows himself to be a spiritual power keep his, so to speak, horizontal distance, be so to speak, so dismissive of temporal powers, in such an internal way. And therefore he had a secret affection, a friendship, a profound affinity with other spiritual powers, even with the Catholics, against whom he fought resolutely. But he wanted to fight against them only with spiritual arms in spiritual battles. His profound inner and manifest opposition to Waldeckism itself had two origins. In the first place, by a kind of political evenness, balance, fairness, equality, justice, health, equitable distribution, he did not want done to others what the others had done to you, but that you did not want them to do to you. *The clerics bothered us for years,* he would say, and still more forcefully, *the point is not now to bother the Catholics.* One has never seen a less partisan Jew, one who thought less, who conceived less of talion. He didn't precisely want to give good back for evil, but very certainly the just for the unjust. He also had this notion that it was not very clever, that one must not be feeling strong to resort to such powers. He, on the other hand, felt strong. That one must not have any self-confidence. He, on the other hand, had self-confidence. Like all those who are truly strong. Like all those who are really strong, he didn't like to use cheap weapons, to have cheap successes, diminished, degraded successes, successes that were not on the same scale of greatness as the battles he wanted to wage.

Secondly, he assuredly had a secret sympathy, an inner understanding with other spiritual powers. His hatred of the state, of the temporal, revealed itself there in its entirety. *One cannot prosecute,* he would say, *through laws, people who gather to pray together. Even if there were to be 500,000 of them. If it is considered that they are dangerous, that they have too much money, they should be prosecuted, they should be affected by general measures, like everyone else* (that same word, that same expression, *like everyone else,* which he always used, which he used specifically for Dreyfus), *by general economic laws that prosecute, that affect all those who are as dangerous as they are, who have money as they have.* He didn't like political parties, the state, the chambers, the government to take away from him the glory of the battle he wanted to wage, to dishonor his battle in advance.

In general, he didn't like, he couldn't bear the temporal to interfere in the spiritual. All those temporal mechanisms, all those organs, all those machines designed to lift heavy objects seemed infinitely too crude to him to have the right to put their crude claws not only in matters concerning spiritual rights, but also in matters concerning spiritual interests. That organs as crude as the government, the chamber, the state, the senate, so foreign to everything spiritual, should stick their fingers into the spiritual was for him not only a crude profanation but, even more, an exercise in bad taste, an abuse, the exercise, the abuse of a peculiar incompetence. He felt, on the contrary, a secret, peculiar complicity in spiritual competence, if need be, with the pope.

Never have I seen a man, I am not saying believe, I am saying know, to such a degree, I am not saying only that a conscience is above all jurisdictions, but that it is, that it itself operates as a jurisdiction in reality, that it is the supreme jurisdiction, the only one.

If he had been followed, if at least his teaching and his example had been followed, if his general direction had been followed, if only the respect owed to his memory had been followed, today the very revision of the Dreyfus trial would not be endangered, *as it is*. It would not be exposed, as it is.

We have seen his funeral. I will tell about his funeral. Who we were, how few, in that procession, in that convoy, in that faithful gray retinue, going down and crossing through Paris. In the middle of the vacation season. In that month of August or rather in that beginning of the month of September. A few, the same driven ones, the same fanatics, Jews and Christians, a few rich Jews, very few, a few rich Christians, very few, poor and destitute Jews and Christians, themselves rather few in number. A small troop, in short, a very small troop. Like some sort of reduced military unit crossing through Paris. Some destitute foreign Jews, I mean foreign to French citizenship, for there was not a single Romanian Jew, I mean a Jew from Romania, who did not know he was a prophet, who did not consider him to be a true prophet. He was for all these destitute people, for all these persecuted people, a flash of light again, a rekindling of the torch whose light eternally will not go out. Temporally eternally. And since even these signs bear a family resemblance, since everything that is of Israel is of the same species, since these matters remain in families, how is one not to recall, how not to see that previous funeral, at which there were so few people, a few weeks ago, his mother's funeral. Relatively few people. Yet they knew many people. I will tell of his death and of his long and cruel illness, and of the slow and yet so swift approach of his death. That sort of ferocious illness. As if obsessed. As if fanatical. As if itself driven. Like him. Like us. I know nothing as poignant, as gripping, I know nothing as tragic as this man who, stiffening himself with whatever strength he had left, pitted himself against his victorious party. Who in a desperate effort, in which he himself was broken, tried, attempted to go against this momentum, the unstoppable momentum of victory and abuses, of the abuse of victory. The only momentum that cannot be reversed. The unstoppable momentum of acquired victory. Of victory in the hand. Of the enthusiasm of vic-

tory. The unstoppable, mechanical, automatic momentum arising from
the very mechanism of victory. I still see him in his bed. That atheist, that
professional atheist, that official atheist, in whom resounded, with unbelievable force, with unbelievable gentleness, the eternal word; with eternal
power, with eternal gentleness; whose equal I have never found anywhere.
I still have upon me, in my eyes, the eternal goodness of that infinitely
gentle gaze, that goodness that did not hurl itself out but was poised, informed. Infinitely disabused; infinitely informed; itself undefeatable. I still
see him in his bed, that atheist dripping with the word of God. Even in
death, the whole weight of his people bore down on his shoulders. He
could not be told that he was not responsible for them. I have never seen
a man burdened in such a way, so burdened with a task, with an eternal responsibility. As we are, as we feel responsible for our children, for our own
children in our own family, just as much, exactly as much, exactly thus did
he feel responsible for his people. In the most atrocious of his suffering, he
had only one concern: that *his* Jews from Romania not *slyly* be left out for
the sake of the success of a movement, the movement of protest that a few
European publicists were undertaking then against the excesses of Eastern
persecutions.[30] I see him in his bed. One would come up to that rue
de Florence; so Right Bank, for us, so far from the Latin Quarter. There
were no buses yet. One would go up through rue de Rome, or through
rue d'Amsterdam, cour de Rome or cour d'Amsterdam, I can't remember
which is called which, up until that crossroads on the incline I still see.
That house, expensive for the time, in which he lived a poor man. He
would apologize for his rent, saying: "I'm saddled with an enormous lease.
I don't know whether I shall be able to sublease as I would like. When I
took this apartment, I thought I would launch a big newspaper and that
we would work here. I had plans." He was far indeed from launching a
big newspaper. The newspapers of others were launched, on the condition, even, that he would not be included. I still see that large room, rue
de Florence, 5 (or 7) rue de Florence, the room with the bed, the room of
suffering, the bedroom, the room of heroism (the room of holiness), the
chamber of death. The room with the bed from which he did not get up
again. Have I myself so forgotten it that this 5 (or this 7) no longer responds mechanically to the call of my memory, that this 5 and this 7 fight
like ragpickers in the storehouse of my memory, that each contests the
other, presents its claims. And yet I went there. And we would say infor-
mally among ourselves: Have you been up rue de Florence? In that large
rectangular room, I see the large rectangular bed. One, or two, or three
large rectangular windows would give much oblique rectangular daylight
from the left; hitting, falling slowly, slowly inclining. The bed came out
from the rear, not the rear opposed to the windows, where the doors were,
and, I think, the hallways, but from the rear one faced if the windows were

to one's left. From that rear the bed came at least to the middle of the room, very squarely, the head to the rear, against the wall, the legs toward the middle of the room. He himself in the very middle of his bed, on his back, symmetrical, like the axis of his bed, like an axis of equity. His two arms straight to the left and to the right. This was in the last days. The illness was reaching its end. A deep, a vigilant brotherly affection, the diligence of a fraternal affection was already thinking to make for him, to prepare for him a death that would not be the culmination of this cruelty, which would be gentler, softened a little, which would not have all the cruelty, all the barbarity of that unrelenting disease. That would not be the crowning moment of this cruelty. He had been told all kinds of lies about his illness, lie upon lie. How much did he believe them? Like everyone else, he pretended to believe them. How much did he believe them, that is the secret of the dead. *Morientium ac mortuorum*.[31] In that incurable cowardice of the modern world, in which we dare to tell a human being everything except what concerns him, in which we do not dare to tell a human being the greatest news, the news of the only great deadline, we have ourselves lied so many times, we have lied so often to so many dying people, and to so many dead ones, that it is to be hoped that when it is our turn that we ourselves will not altogether believe the lies told to us. He therefore pretended to believe them. But in his beautiful gentle eyes, in his large and round clear eyes, it was impossible to read. They were too good. They were too gentle. They were too beautiful. *They were too clear*. It was impossible to know whether it was through a miracle of (temporal) hope (and perhaps beyond) that he still hoped or whether it was through a miracle of charity, for us, that he pretended to hope. His eye itself, his clear eye, limpid like a child's, was like the lens of a pince-nez, like a second lens, like a second glass window, like a second pince-nez of gentleness and goodness, of light, of clarity. Impenetrable. Because one read in it what one wanted. These were the last days. Few people were still allowed to see him, even relatives. But he cared so much for me that he kept me on the final lists. I would sit at his bedside, to the left, at the foot of the bed. To his right, then. He talked about everything as though he were going to live to be 100. He asked me how I got there. He told me, with much childlike pride, that the Amsterdam metro station had opened. Or some other one. He was naïvely enthused by all that was means and modes of communications. All that was goings and comings—geographic, topographic, telegraphic, telephonic, one-way and round-trip, circulations, displacements, replacements, trips, exoduses, and deuteronomies—caused him to accumulate an endless supply of childlike joy. The metro in particular was a personal victory for him. All that was speed, acceleration, fever of communication, moving about, rapid circulation filled him with a childlike joy, with the old joy, the joy 50 centuries old. It was his very business.

To be elsewhere: the great vice of this race, its great secret virtue; the great vocation of this people. A history of 50 centuries made it so that each train trip turned into some caravan from 50 centuries ago. Each crossing is for them the crossing of the desert. The most comfortable homes, the most established, with free stones as large as the columns of the temple, the most landed estates, the most real estate, the most overwhelming estates are never more to them than tents in the desert. *Granite took the place of the tent with canvas walls.*[32] What do these free stones larger than the columns of the temple matter. They are always on camels' backs. A peculiar people. How often have I not thought about it. For whom the most estatelike homes will never be more than tents. And we, on the contrary, who have really slept in tents, in real tents, how often did I not think of you, [Edmond-Maurice] Lévy,[33] who have never slept in a tent, otherwise than in the Bible, at the end of a few hours those tents at the camp of Cercottes[34] were already our homes. *How fair are your tents, O Jacob; your encampments, O Israel.*[35] How often have I not thought about it, how often have I not thought of you, how often did not these words come back to me mutely through a glory going back 50 centuries, like a great secret joy of glory, with which I mutely burst through a sacred reremembering when we would come back to the camp, my dear Claude [Casimir-Périer],[36] during those harsh May nights. A people for whom the stones of houses will always be the canvas of tents. And for us, on the contrary, it is the canvas of tents that already was, that always will be the stone of our houses. Not only did he therefore not have that aversion, that distance toward the metro, which deep inside we still feel toward it, even when it serves us very well, *because it transports us too fast*, and, deep inside, because it serves us too well, but on the contrary, he had a special affection for it, filled with pride, like an author's pride. It was still being constructed; only the number 1 line, I think, was in use. He had a local pride, a neighborhood pride, that it had reached, already, to him, one of the first, that it had been extended up to him, that it had begun to climb toward those heights. He told me of it, some months earlier, when people had tried to send him, like everyone else, to recuperate in the south. He went from hotel to hotel. He was as happy as a child. Until he found some sort of small peasant house; that he presented to me in a letter as if it were the fulfillment of paradise. And from where, naturally he came back quickly, returned to Paris. He had told me of it then, in one of those expressions that reveal a man, a people, a race. *You see, Péguy*, he would say to me, *I only begin to feel I am at home when I arrive at a hotel.* He would laugh as he said it, but it was true nonetheless.

To sum up, in the realm of action, of politics, since it is necessarily there, since it is necessary to stoop to it, he was in favor of generally applied law.

A generally applied law in the Dreyfus Affair, a generally applied law in the affair of the assemblies. A generally applied law *for* Dreyfus, a generally applied law *against* the congregations. It doesn't look like much, but it can have great consequences. It brought him to the point of isolation in death.

Essentially, he was for justice, for equity, for equality (naturally, not in the democratic sense of the word, but in the sense of perfect balance, perfect horizontality, in justice). He was against the exception, against the law of exception, against the measure of exception, whether it was for or against, persecution or grace. He was for the *evenness* of justice.

I was looking at him, then, that morning, 7 rue de Florence. And I listened to him. I was sitting at the foot of his bed to the left like a faithful disciple. So much gentleness, so much generosity in so cruel a situation disarmed me, was beyond me. So much as if ineradicable goodness. I listened in pious, respectful, affectionate half-silence, providing him only with the exchange he needed to keep going. Romain Rolland's *Beethoven* had just come out.[37] Our subscribers still recall what a sudden revelation that issue was, what excitement it stirred everywhere, how it spread suddenly, like a wave, as if coming from below, as if instantaneously, how it was suddenly, instantaneously, in a revelation, in the eyes of everyone, in a sudden concord, in a common agreement, not only the beginning of the literary fortune of Romain Rolland, and of the literary fortune of the *Cahiers*, but infinitely more than the beginning of a literary fortune, a sudden moral revelation, a premonition unveiled, revealed, the revelation, the explosion, the sudden explosion of a great moral fortune. But that entire movement was still swelling, had not yet had the time to manifest itself. The issue, I repeat had just come out. Bernard-Lazare said to me: *Ah, I read your Romain Rolland issue. It is really very beautiful. It must be admitted that the Jewish soul and the Hellenic soul have been two large chunks of the universal soul.* I showed nothing, because I have said that when one visits the sick one is determined to show nothing. One is therefore protected by an invincible armor, by an impenetrable mask. But I was struck, I felt pierced to my very vertebrae. For I had come to see, I had been expecting to see, the inroads of death. And that is already a lot. And I suddenly saw the inroads of beyond death. To evaluate the depth, the novelty of words such as *eternal soul*, and even *Jewish soul*, and *Hellenic soul*, one must know to what degree, with what religious care these men, the men of that generation avoided using a single word of mystical jargon. People spoke at the time of *starting* the Dreyfus Affair *again, of taking up* the Dreyfus Affair *again*. One must recall that between the Dreyfus Affair itself and the second Dreyfus Affair there was a long period of flat calm, of silence, of total solitude.[38] During that whole time, it wasn't known at all if the affair would begin again; ever. It would have been better if it hadn't started over. We would not have been acquitted by the Court of Appeals.[39] But we would have remained what we were, we would have remained pure before the country, and before history. But still all heated up from this great affair, from that first great story, still sweating, and boiling from the battle, altogether disconcerted by the rest, the calm, the flatness, the hollow peace, the suspect rest, the suspect treaty, the inaction, the peace of dupes, altogether anxious that we had not obtained, attained all the temporal results that we had hoped for, that we had awaited, that we had counted on, altogether anxious that we had not realized the kingdom of justice and the kingdom of truth on earth, altogether anxious to see our mystique getting away from us, in the secret of our hearts we thought only of starting the affair over again, of what we called among ourselves, like conspirators, the *resumption*. We did not, alas, foresee, that this resumption would only be its worst degradation, a total vulgar twisting of a mystique into a politique. We would talk about it. He, in his bed, would speak to me of it gently. I quickly saw that he spoke to me of it as of a conspiracy, but as a foreign conspiracy, to which he remained a stranger. Voluntarily, involuntarily? I asked him: "But in the end what will they do? They haven't asked you your advice then?" He answered me gently: "*They preferred turning to Jaurès.* THEY ARE SO HAPPY TO BE DOING SOMETHING WITHOUT ME."

They, those were all the others, it was Dreyfus whom he loved liked a younger brother.[40]

What could be more poignant than that testimony, than that adjuration of Bernard-Lazare condemned, of Bernard-Lazare fated, what could be more terrifying, fear-inducing, than this testimony, fear-inducing in its very moderation. *When Jaurès*, wrote Bernard-Lazare, *presents himself before us to support a deed he approves of, to which he wants to contribute, he must, because he is Jaurès, because he has been our companion in a battle that is not over, give us reasons other than theological ones.* (He very clearly saw how much vulgar theology there was in Jaurès, in that entire modern *mentality*, in that political and parliamentary radicalism, in that pseudometaphysics, in that pseudophilosophy, in that sociology.) *And it is to give us a theological reason to say* (Here I warn that it is Jaurès speaking, cited by Bernard-Lazare): "*There are political and social crimes that have to be paid for, and the great collective crime committed by the Church against truth, against humanity, against law and against the Republic, will finally receive its just due. It did not revolt consciences through its complicity with the false, with perjury and betrayal in vain.*" (End of Jaurès, of Jaurès's quotation.) Bernard-Lazare said more simply: *You can't bother people because they're saying their prayers.* He had them, that one, the habits of freedom. He had freedom in his skin; in his marrow and in his blood; in his vertebrae. Not an intellectual and conceptual freedom, a bookish freedom, a ready-made freedom, a library freedom. A freedom for the records. But a freedom, from the source, an entirely organic and living freedom. I have never seen a man believe, to that degree, have to that degree the certainty, be aware to that degree that the conscience of a human being is an absolute, something invincible, eternal, free, that it victoriously opposed, eternally triumphed over all the powers of the earth. *Such justifications should not be accepted*, wrote Bernard-Lazare again, *even and especially when they are given by Jaurès, for, below him, others are ready to interpret them in a worse way, to draw for them consequences* FRIGHTENING FOR FREEDOM. He enumerated, in a few examples, in a striking style, cutting, brief, a few of these antinomies, the chief ones, a few of these antagonisms. He foresaw you, [Edmond] Bernus,[41] *and the resistance of the Polish people to the demands of Prussian germanization.* Already then he, in fact, wrote and these words are clear, fundamental, they are as current as when they were written: *If we are not careful, tomorrow we will be put into the position of applauding the French policeman who will take a child by the arm in order to force him to enter a secular school, while we must oppose the Prussian policeman forcing the Polish student of Wreschen.* This is the man, this is the friend we lost. He also wrote, and his words are to be pondered, they are to be meditated upon today the same as yesterday, today the same as then, they are to be meditated upon always, for they come from a perspective of height and have an incalculable import: "*Let us be presented tomorrow with ways to resolve the problem of education and we shall discuss them. Already today, it can be said that a university monopoly is not the solution.* WE SHALL REFUSE TO ACCEPT THE DOGMAS FORMULATED BY THE TEACHING STATE AS MUCH AS WE REFUSE THOSE FORMULATED BY THE CHURCH. WE HAVE NO MORE TRUST IN THE UNIVERSITY THAN WE HAVE IN THE RELIGIOUS ASSEMBLY." But I have to stop quoting. I cannot cite that whole admirable report, quote an entire issue in an issue, remake issues in issues, put all of [*Cahiers*] volume 3, no. 21 in volume 11, no. 12.[42]

This was the man, this was the friend we lost. For such a man, we will never make an apology, we will never allow that one be made.

Those are the human beings who count, and they are the only ones who count. We are the ones who count, the only ones. Not only should the others not speak for us. But it is we who should be speaking, for everything.

He was a hero, and, besides, had large parts of holiness. And with him we were, obscurely, heroes.

How not to notice in the few words we have cited, in only those few sentences we have quoted, not only that sense for freedom, but that being-at-ease in freedom, in the handling of freedom, but also that much more curious, much more unexpected, apparently more unexpected sense for theology, that taking note of theology. Instantaneously, he saw it surfacing everywhere it in fact surfaces, itself or some imitation, some copy, itself or some counterfeit.

How also not to notice his exact, his perfect, his real internationalism, Israel aside, the exactness, the at-easeness, the naturalness of his internationalism, which was much too simple, much too taken for granted, not at all learned, not at all, forced, not at all bookish, way too at ease, way too taken for granted ever to be an antinationalism. When he spoke of Poles in place of Bretons, it was not an amusement, a clever association. It was not a witticism, in order to play a good joke on someone. It was that he naturally saw Bretons as on the same level as Poles. He really saw Christianity in the same way as Islam, something none of us, even those who would most want to, could achieve. Because he was very really equally outside both. A perspective, an angle of vision none of us can achieve. At the time that all that was humanly possible was done, even and especially around him, to eject his Jews of Romania, through politiquing so as not to endanger, so as not to overload the Armenian movement, and that he saw very clearly into that muting, an old friend from the Latin Quarter had just left him. He told me gently, gently shrugging his shoulders, the way he used to do, as if indicating him to me with his shoulders, beyond the top of his shoulders: *He still wants to trick me with his Armenians. It is always the same thing. They take on the Great Turk because he is a Turk and they don't want a word to be said against the king of Romania because he is Christian. Always it is the collusion of Christianity.*

How not to notice, finally, how well written it is, how poised, measured, clear, noble, *French. Such justifications should not be accepted.* A certain proposition, a certain resolution. A certain deliberatedness. A certain tone, a certain Cartesian resonance itself.

A Brief Sketch of the Dreyfus Affair

The Dreyfus Affair was extraordinarily complicated, involving many participants over a period of twelve years (1894–1906). Although various notes to the text supply information about specific people and events, the brief

sketch that follows should enable the reader to fit together Péguy's frequent but discontinuous references to the affair.

Alfred Dreyfus (1859–1935), a captain of artillery, was one of the few
Jewish officers in the French Army of his time. He came from a wealthy
family, originally from Alsace. On October 15, 1894, he was arrested and
imprisoned on the charge of treason, accused of selling French military secrets to the Germans. The only piece of evidence adduced against him was
a *bordereau*, or note, found inside the wastebasket of the German military
attaché in Paris by a cleaning woman in the pay of the French Intelligence
Service, which indicated that classified information about French weapons
and installations was being leaked to the Germans. The General Staff accused Dreyfus on the basis of the handwriting in the note, which it claimed
was identical to his. During his court-martial, the General Staff made available to the military tribunal additional documents, beyond the bordereau,
meant to point to Dreyfus's guilt. They made them available in secret, without informing the defense, which never had an opportunity to refute them.
This illegality was compounded by the fact that these documents turned
out to be forgeries. On the basis of this secret evidence, on December 22,
1894, Dreyfus was found guilty and condemned to life imprisonment on
Devil's Island, the French penal colony off the coast of Guyana.

On January 5, 1895, Dreyfus was publicly stripped of his military insignia
in the courtyard of the Military School in Paris, before huge crowds hurl-
ing insults at him and at Jews in general. On April 14, 1895, he left France
for the penal colony, where he would spend nearly five years in increasingly harsh physical conditions. (He was chained to his bed a good part of
the time because an escape attempt had been rumored.)

Alfred Dreyfus's brother, Matthieu, sought redress for his brother. In
the initial stages of the process, he contacted Bernard-Lazare, a well-known
journalist and polemicist, convinced him of Dreyfus's innocence, and engaged him to write a pamphlet establishing the facts. In this pamphlet,
completed in 1895, Bernard-Lazare brought to light the illegalities of the
trial and the machinations of the Army. Because Matthieu Dreyfus wanted
it to have maximum effect, he delayed publication of Bernard-Lazare's essay
for a year, waiting for a propitious moment. He finally allowed it to be
published in October 1896, in Brussels and then sent it in sealed envelopes
to 3,500 people prominent in French affairs. It was republished in France
with revisions, including new information, in November 1896. At the point
of the dissemination of this pamphlet, entitled *Une Erreur judicière: La
Vérité sur l'affaire Dreyfus* (A Judicial Error: The Truth About the Dreyfus
Affair), few people outside the Dreyfus family itself were involved in trying
to clear Dreyfus's name. The Dreyfus case had not yet become the Dreyfus Affair. Bernard-Lazare was thus one of the first to perceive, not only

what really happened, but the true dimensions of the affair for the country as a whole. That is, he saw that antisemitism was at the heart of the matter.

Meanwhile, other developments pointing to Dreyfus's innocence were occurring within the French Army itself. Lieutenant Colonel Georges Picquart became head of military intelligence in 1895. In 1896, he discovered that a French officer was still selling military secrets to the Germans. All the evidence pointed to Count Charles Walsin-Esterhazy, an infantry commander of Hungarian origin naturalized as a French citizen. Esterhazy was a Catholic aristocrat, like most officers in the French Army. When Picquart told his superiors that the handwriting of the traitor matched Esterhazy's, and that, furthermore, it was identical to that of the original note attributed to Dreyfus, he was told not to conflate the two cases, removed from his post in Paris, and sent to Tunisia. He did not make the information about Esterhazy public until 1897, feeling constrained to obey his supervisors. When he finally did reveal it, more and more people had begun to doubt that Dreyfus was the guilty party. In January 1898, Esterhazy was court-martialed and, despite all the evidence against him, was found innocent.

In response to Esterhazy's trial, the renowned French novelist Émile Zola published an article in the newspaper *L'Aurore* on January 13, 1898, addressed to the president of the Republic. This was the famous "J'accuse," in which Zola lists various army generals by name, accusing them of covering up Esterhazy's guilt and of conspiring to frame Dreyfus. The letter had an enormous impact. Much of the information in it came from Bernard-Lazare's *Une Erreur judicière*, but the timing of its appearance and Zola's name made a difference. As a result of these developments, there was a growing call on the part of a wider public for a retrial in which Dreyfus's innocence might be established.

The War Ministry proceeded to sue Zola for libel. One of his lawyers was Fernand Labori, who also represented Dreyfus. During the proceedings (February 7–23, 1898), much of the secret documentation originally fabricated to accuse Dreyfus was made public. It thus became a contest between those who wanted a retrial for Dreyfus and those opposed to the idea. Zola was eventually condemned to one year in prison and fled to England, where he remained in exile for eleven months. Jean Jaurès, the great leader of the Socialist Party, who had initially held back, now joined the battle and wrote many articles demonstrating Dreyfus's innocence.

One of the most dramatic moments of that year (1898) occurred when Colonel Henry, who had forged one of the documents, *le petit bleu*, initially placed in Dreyfus's file, was discovered to have done so. He admitted to it, was arrested, and apparently committed suicide the same night in prison. On June 3, 1899, the Court of Appeals declared that a retrial was to take place, sending the Dreyfus case back to the military tribunal for judgment.

On August 7, 1899, the retrial of Dreyfus, who had been brought back from Devil's Island for this purpose, began. On September 10, 1899, the military tribunal found him guilty of treason all over again. This time his penalty was commuted from life imprisonment to ten years' penal servitude. Dreyfus's family and friends, fearful that he would not survive the ordeal of Devil's Island any further (he had come back physically very weak) urged him to seek a pardon from the president of the Republic. He did so, and it was granted on September 19, 1899.

The move to seek a pardon split the Dreyfusard camp. Many felt that taking this route gave the appearance of an acknowledgment of guilt. Not only would this blur the issue of Dreyfus's innocence, but it would allow those guilty of conspiracy against him to go unpunished, thus leaving unexonerated many people whose lives had been ruined in defense of Dreyfus. Picquart, for instance, who spent a year in prison as a result of making public the Army's cover-up of Esterhazy's treason and its conspiracy against Dreyfus, never forgave Dreyfus for having accepted the pardon. Dreyfus himself agreed to do so only as a provisional step on the path to his complete vindication. This finally occurred on July 2, 1906, when the Court of Appeals annulled the verdict of the military tribunal and declared him innocent.

Another controversy arose within the Dreyfusard camp at this point, however. Some argued that the Court of Appeals did not have the authority to pronounce a verdict. It had therefore abused its power, not unlike the Army had done earlier. According to this faction, the Court of Appeals should have sent the case back to the military tribunal for another retrial, and continued to do so as often as proved necessary, since that was the limit of its legal authority. Other Dreyfusards argued that France had been divided long enough over the affair and needed to heal, and that the compromise served the cause of justice. The hostilities that erupted in the course of these twelve years thus continued beyond the legal resolution of Dreyfus's innocence itself.

Péguy's "Notre jeunesse" was written approximately four years after that legal resolution. It is clear from the portrait and also from Appendix C that Péguy disapproved of Dreyfus's acceptance of the presidential pardon and that he opposed the Court of Appeals's annulment of the military court's verdict. Especially the latter struck him as a prime example of the degeneration of a mystique into a politique. But his prime grievance against the Dreyfusards' betrayal of their mystique lay with the anti-Catholic legislation passed by the Waldeck-Rousseau and Combes government in 1901 and 1902 respectively. These governments had come to power because of the public disgust with the Army's and Church's roles in the Dreyfus Affair. They proceeded to pass legislation that culminated in 1904 in a law forbidding parochial school instruction in France. From 1902 to 1904, approximately 3,000 Catholic schools were forcibly closed, based on the claim that they were in violation of a law passed in July 1901 forbidding the establishment of new congregations (and their teaching wings) without prior authorization from the government. For Péguy, to have supporters of Dreyfus, especially Jean Jaurès, now president of the Chamber of Deputies, reduce the earlier fight to exonerate Dreyfus to a struggle for state control between the Radical-Socialist coalition and the coalition of the Church and the Army was forever to obscure the fact that no political party had been connected with the original impulse to defend Dreyfus. The net result of the Waldeck-Rousseau and Combes decrees, Péguy believed, was an injustice to the Church that mirrored the injustice perpetrated against Dreyfus as a Jew.

CHAPTER THREE

One Truth, Many Truths

In Chapter 1, I suggested some of the issues that Péguy's portrait of Bernard-Lazare raises, chief among them the dynamic between "us" and "them." I concluded there that this dynamic led us to certain Christian theological underpinnings—the notions of hope and incarnation. In other words, the way Péguy enacts the relationship to the other, in this case the Jews, is inseparable from a certain religious vision. The movement between "us" and "them" cannot be understood on the level of politics or rhetoric alone, although it has obvious urgency in both those realms. To clarify Péguy's thought, I would like in this section to compare him to two philosophers much preoccupied with the same issue: the religious dimension inherent in the relation to the other. The first is Emmanuel Levinas, widely known for his continual meditations on "l'Autre" and "Autrui," the other person. These meditations present themselves quite self-consciously as a translation of the Jewish vision into a philosophical vocabulary. The second is Franz Rosenzweig, whose work is also such a translation. The relation with the other is central for him as well, given additional concreteness by his famous exposition of the relationship between Jews and Christians in the third part of his magnum opus, *The Star of Redemption*.

Before proceeding with this comparison, however, I would like to draw attention to certain necessary precautions. Péguy did not talk, in "Notre jeunesse" or elsewhere, *about* the proper relation to the other. He embodied a relation to the other and the principles inherent therein in his act of writing about Bernard-Lazare. In interpreting his text, I had concluded that hope and incarnation made it possible for Péguy to recognize the humanity of the other while emphasizing his difference. But it cannot be said often enough that hope and incarnation are not *theories* that Péguy applies in order to perceive Bernard-Lazare in a certain way. In fact, they precede any and all theory. That is, they are already at work when Péguy's theories about the Jews, also present in the text, come into play. After all, Péguy's whole point about incarnation is that it reveals a reality more deeply embedded than theory. His whole point about hope is that it too is incarnated: the acceptance of defeat and yet the refusal of it for the sake of the other occur on a level prior to deliberation.

It is important to underline the embedded nature of hope and incarnation in Péguy's relation to Bernard-Lazare because, in interpreting his text, we inevitably place ourselves in a strange bind. We bring up to the level of theory something that does not function this way in his work. It does not help that what we bring up to that level is the notion of embodiment. For the theory of embodiment is not the same thing as embodiment. The most correct formulation of how the universal hides within a particular is still no guarantee that, when faced with the particularity of a person standing before oneself, one will respond to that universal. That recognition of universality in the midst of difference, without erasing difference, will depend, not on a theory, but on a commitment so deep that there will be no need at the moment of confrontation to resort to any theory at all. The problem with speaking about hope and incarnation, then, is that it may give the impression that it is all a matter of understanding the theory.

But if it is not, then cannot the intellect guide us at all in our quest for justice? Are commentaries such as this useless because they cannot convey the immediacy of response to the other that is the only thing that will suffice in an actual encounter? While there may be many moments when one is inclined to think so, the alternative is to assume that that immediacy is a natural, spontaneous, unschooled phenomenon, integrally part of the human psyche. It does not take much looking around to notice that this is not so. People do not seem, on a regular basis, to notice each other's humanity in the midst of difference. It might just be, even though it sounds paradoxical, that that immediacy is learned, that it needs to be formed, guided. Part of that guidance surely involves the intellect. After all, Péguy reflected on hope and incarnation a good deal both before and after he wrote "Notre jeunesse." Perhaps it is only a long time spent mulling over what initially is mere abstraction that allows it to penetrate deeper reaches or to maintain itself in deeper reaches. In any case, we have no choice. Even if the intellect cannot serve us at the crucial moment, we have only the intellect to warn us about this very shortcoming.

All of this has to be kept in mind as we situate Péguy's portrait of Bernard-Lazare in the context of twentieth-century religious reflections. To compare his way of entering into relation with Jews to somebody else's theory about the Jews, for instance, would miss the difference of level. It would be comparing theory to what is not theory. This is not to say that there are not plenty of theoretical statements about the Jews in "Notre jeunesse." One need only recall Péguy's frequent assertions that the Jews are a prophetic people. But his relation to the Jews is not completely contained in those statements. It is revealed in those turns of phrase and forms of address that continually maintain a tension between the universal and the particular. These turns of phrase, these forms of address, rarely appear as part of the overt argumentation. They are in the fabric of that argumentation but are not the argument itself.

This being "in the fabric," so central for understanding the deepest level of Péguy's thought, is also central to the thought of Levinas and Rosenzweig. These Jewish philosophers, just like Péguy, insist on embodiment, on situating the intellect vis-à-vis something that precedes it and exceeds it. In that embodiment lies the religious dimension and also the possibility of justice to the other.

Emmanuel Levinas

Emmanuel Levinas, who was born in Lithuania in 1906 but lived in France from 1923 to the time of his death in 1995, is a philosopher whose work has influenced both the Jewish and the non-Jewish world. Originally a student of Husserl and Heidegger, he devoted his life to rethinking the premises upon which philosophy is built, not only that of his immediate teachers, but also that of all philosophers, going back to the ancient Greeks. There is a violence in the systematizing impulse of philosophy that Levinas wants to expose. His inspiration for discovering another way comes, at least in part, but it is a central part, from Jewish sources.

I cannot here give a comprehensive view of his philosophy, for my intent is merely to point to one of his central themes and show its affinity with Péguy's approach. In any case, I am not sure it is possible, even under different circumstances, to give a comprehensive view of Levinas's philosophy. It refuses quite consciously to become a system, and those who make it into a neat series of propositions do it a disservice. I therefore focus on one of his short essays, which should nonetheless suggest one aspect of his central insight.

This essay is not from his philosophical work properly so called. It is from his Talmudic commentaries, which he himself always considered as something of an avocation, to the side of his philosophical writings.[1] But the Talmudic commentaries were composed simultaneously with his major philosophical works and reflect all the same concerns. Because they are written for a more general audience, they often provide easier access to his thought, as the vocabulary is less technical. Nonetheless, the Talmudic essay "The Temptation of Temptation" presents many challenges of its own, not least philosophical challenges.[2] Since it is a commentary and not an expository essay, it does not develop along the lines of an argument. Rather, Levinas makes his points in response to particular passages in the rabbinic text he has chosen, letting the zigzag of the discussions in the text set the pace for his own reflections. We shall follow him in this, but not at every point. That is, I make available the specific Talmudic passages upon which he is commenting, but I skip a few in order to focus on the central thought. The reader unfamiliar with the style of Talmudic discussion should be forewarned that, on the surface, the different exchanges seem to come from thin air and to be unrelated to each other. A practiced eye can detect connections, however, and that is in large part what Levinas's Talmudic commentary involves.

The rabbinic text Levinas has chosen for this particular reading is about the giving of the Torah to the Israelites, revelation. It begins with the following, rather peculiar statement: "Rav Abdimi bar Hama bar Hasa has said: This teaches us that the Holy One, Blessed be He, inclined the mountain over them like a tilted tub, and that He said: If you accept the Torah, all is well; if not, here will be your grave."[3]

The people referred to in this passage are the Israelites standing at the foot of Mount Sinai. How did Rav Abdimi come up with the idea that God had turned Mount Sinai upside down and was threatening to drop it on the Israelites unless they accepted the Torah? Levinas explains that it has to do with the Hebrew preposition *btachtit*, normally translated as "at the foot of," but literally meaning "underneath." In order to get his image of the upside-down mountain, Rav Abdimi has decided to translate the preposition literally. They were beneath because God was holding the mountain up over them.

Levinas is quick to point out that this whimsical interpretation actually contains a question about the nature of revelation. Is revelation like any other truth, which we acquiesce to by weighing sides, deliberating, in short, reasoning? It seems, from Rav Abdimi's imagery, that it is not. Revelation imposes itself, *forces* itself on us. We have no time to deliberate, because of the urgency of what presents itself.

The way revelation reveals itself and the way it is accepted is also the topic of the next rabbinic passage: "Rav Simai has taught: When the Israelites committed themselves to doing before hearing, 600,000 angels came down and attached two crowns to each Israelite, one for the doing, the other for the hearing."

Rav Simai is referring to a striking feature in the Book of Exodus. We are told there that when Moses asked the Israelites whether they would accept the Torah, they replied, "Naaseh v nishmah," "We will do and we will hear" (Exod. 24:7). Surely, this is a strange order. Normally, when asked to do something, we first examine what it is we shall have to do. But here, the Israelites commit themselves to the Torah without first having heard its contents. It is a commitment prior to any deliberation or weighing of sides.

This way of committing oneself, rather than being censured, received praise from the rabbis, as is evident in the passage quoted above. Each Israelite gets two crowns, one for the doing, one for the hearing. Levinas tells us that there is another tradition in which each Israelite gets three crowns, one for the doing, one for the hearing, and one for the reversal of the order. Slightly later in the rabbinic discussion, the doing before the hearing will be referred to as the secret of angels.

But is it not sheer foolishness to behave this way? A Sadducee, someone who does not accept rabbinic authority, makes a reproach that no doubt echoes that in the reader's mind: "People in a hurry, for whom the mouth passes before the ears, you always find yourself in a state of headlong haste. You should have listened in order to know whether you were able to accept, and if you were not able to accept, you should not have accepted."

Levinas expands on this objection. Is this haste in committing oneself to do the Torah before having examined its contents not either naïve or dangerous? That is, is it not likely that once the contents are examined, people will back out of a commitment made in a moment of enthusiasm? Does not naïveté, for this very reason, always indicate a temporary commitment, soon to be broken? Besides, is it not dangerous, both to oneself and to others, to rush into action without properly evaluating the implications and consequences?

These criticisms would be justified, Levinas responds, if the giving of the Torah revealed a content, specific injunctions and tenets. But, Levinas argues, the Torah as described here, prior to being a specific content, is the revelation of the Good. The Good, he continues, is not a set of propositions but the imposition of an obligation to the other person. After all, Levinas points out, quoting from the daily Jewish prayers, the Torah is given in the light of a face.[4] That is, what the Israelites accepted was not an idea but a relation of obligation that occurs *as soon* as the face of the other appears. This obligation is not the result of deliberation about obligation. It *immediately* binds one. One can notice that one has been bound and accept it, but that is not tantamount to reasoning about whether one should be obligated to another and *then* becoming obligated. What revelation reveals, therefore, is an obligation we have incurred prior to our reasoned consent.

Thus, when the Israelites accepted the Torah prior to knowing its contents, they were not acting on blind faith. For blind faith implies acquies-
cence to propositions one refuses to question. But, here, in revelation,
there are no propositions to examine. There is only a human face to respond to. The Good is precisely that violent imposition of obligation, violent because it doesn't give us the leisure to decide whether we are obligated or not. The Good seizes the self before the self has had a chance to
turn back on itself and reflect. In Levinas's words:

> The subjectivity completely made for the true would be the one which would enter
> into an alliance with it prior to any manifestation of this truth in an idea. But here
> is where the logical integrity of subjectivity leads: the direct relation with the true,
> excluding the prior examination of its terms, its idea—that is, the reception of Rev-
> elation—can only be the relation with a person, with another. The Torah is given
> in the Light of a face. The epiphany of the other person is *ipso facto* my responsi-
> bility toward him: seeing the Other is already an obligation toward him. A direct
> optics—without the mediation of any idea—can only be accomplished as ethics.
> Integral knowledge or Revelation [the receiving of the Torah] is ethical behavior.[5]

This relation to the Good does not mean, Levinas makes clear, that reason has no role to play. He points out that when the Sadducee makes his
objection about the Jews' headlong haste, he makes it to Raba, who, according to the rabbinic text, "was buried in study, rubbing his foot so
hard that blood spurted from it." Raba, a man who accepts doing before
hearing, spends his life thinking so intently over the meaning of the par-
ticulars of the Torah that he draws blood from his foot, indicating the
strain of his effort. The commitment to the Good precedes reason, but reason is still needed to affirm this reversal and thus to guarantee its proper
functioning in the myriad details of daily life. After all, the crowns the
Israelites received were not only for the doing. They were for the doing,
followed by the hearing. As Levinas puts it: "The yes [to the Torah] is a
lucidity as forewarned as skepticism but engaged as *doing* is engaged."[6]
In other words, accepting the responsibility for the other must involve
weighing what that responsibility may involve in specific moments. But
this weighing does not decide the initial commitment, which is independently there, evoked by the presence of a human face.

Levinas also does not imply that once the commitment to the Good is
made, there will never be failure to enact it. We find out, in fact, in the very
same passage previously cited that praised the Israelites for the "We will do
and we will hear," that they sinned soon thereafter and were bereft of their
crowns: "As soon as Israel sinned, 1,200,000 destroying angels came down
and took away the crowns, for it is said (Exodus 33:6): 'The children of Israel gave up their ornaments from the time of Mount Horeb.'"

Levinas, in commenting on this passage, makes a distinction that accounts for the title of the essay, "The Temptation of Temptation." He differentiates between temptation and temptation of temptation. The children of Israel were indeed tempted at Mount Horeb. They were presented with a choice between good and evil and were lured into evil. In order to be tempted, then, what is good and what is evil must already be agreed to, in order for temptation to be viewed as temptation in the first place. The temptation of temptation, on the other hand, occurs when one claims that the standard for good and evil is yet to be determined and that one's own experience provides the basis from which to reason about what good and evil are. In such a case, one is always on the threshold of committing oneself to the Good but never quite doing it, since more experience will obviously provide more knowledge, which requires more experience, ad infinitum. Thus, one is never tempted, since temptation implies a predetermined good and evil. One is always one step before temptation in the temptation of temptation.[7]

Levinas argues that in the rabbinic passage just quoted, the Israelites do acknowledge that they violated the Good, since they willingly gave up their ornaments. They do not claim to justify their action on the basis that it provides them with more knowledge, through which alone the Good can be determined. This latter attitude skews not only ethics, but reason, according to Levinas. For a reason that does not recognize the obligation to the other as prior to all knowledge is a reason that can be bent in any direction. It walks in tortuous paths rather than in integrity, as in the last rabbinic quotation in the passage, Raba's answer to the Sadducee. "It is written about us who walk in integrity: 'The integrity of the upright guides them'; about those who walk upon tortuous paths, it is written: 'The crookedness of the treacherous destroys them'" (Prov. 11:3). For Levinas, these words are not just pious moralizing. Integrity is integrity precisely because reason follows an unreasoned commitment to the Good. Crookedness is crookedness because that prior relation to the Good is missing.

"The Temptation of Temptation," like the rest of Levinas's Talmudic commentaries, does more than merely speak about responsibility to the other person. It also already embodies it. Traces of this embodiment can be glimpsed at different points in the essay.

Before he begins his textual analysis, Levinas informs his readers that he will seek "for the unity and progression of thought in the text which, as you can already see, is made up of apparently unconnected observations."[8] The indicator of embodiment is that he assumes that there is unity in the text *before* he has actually found it. Reason follows, explicating the text. But the coherence reason brings to light is accompanied throughout by the prior conviction that such coherence exists. Is this not reminiscent of the "We will do and we will hear," committing oneself before having examined the contents of what one has committed oneself to?

A concrete example of this reversal occurs in Levinas's discussion of Rav Abdimi bar Hama bar Hasa's translation of the preposition *btachtit* to mean "beneath." "The commentator is quibbling over a Hebrew expression. Is he sticking to the letter? Does he not know Hebrew? Is he so uncultivated as to lend an absolute meaning to prepositions without taking account of the meaning that derives from context? Or is Rav Abdimi pretending to be doing all this in order to convey a teaching?"[9] Levinas chooses the last, of course. But he chose it before he knew what the teaching was.

It remains for us to see how this reversal of the normal order—trusting that there is a teaching before knowing what the teaching is—is connected to that responsibility to the other person, awakened at the moment of his presence. Later in his commentary, Levinas remarks upon the image of Raba, immersed in study, rubbing his foot so hard that he draws blood from it. He takes it to be an image for interpreting itself. "Has anyone ever seen a reading that was something besides this effort carried out on a text? To the degree that it rests on the trust granted the author, it can only consist in this violence done to words to tear from them the secret that time and conventions have covered over with their sedimentations, a process begun as soon as the words appear in the open air of history. One must, by rubbing, remove this layer which corrodes them."[10]

The reader's responsibility here is to wrest the author's words from time, to make them mean something in the present. It is, on another level, the same responsibility one shows to a living human being, whom one is obligated to shelter and feed, the way Abraham in Genesis 18 shelters and feeds the three strangers who pass by his tent.[11] In both instances, the responsibility, awakened by the presence of the other, is to keep alive, protect the vulnerable. And just as, in the case of the encounter with a living human being, that obligation is already in place by the time we try to figure out how best to fulfill it, so in the case of reading a text, our obligation to find a teaching, truth, in the text, is there prior to the specific truth we find. Otherwise, we may never find it.

This does not mean that a reader can never disagree with the position of a given author. The rabbis Levinas quotes disagreed often enough with their predecessors, but, as Levinas puts it in another Talmudic reading, "the authority of the text is always disputed but remains indisputable."[12] One can disagree with the contents but only within a prior openness to the possibility of receiving a teaching.

Péguy and Levinas

In most respects, Levinas's Talmudic lesson and Péguy's portrait of Bernard-Lazare are not comparable. And yet the common emphasis on embodiment is unmistakable. For Levinas, revelation is not a content, a set of ideas one adheres to. It is the imposition of an obligation. The acceptance of this obligation manifests itself in its enactment. That is, it is responsibility toward the other, on the move, in the act, that reveals revelation. Similarly, for Péguy, hope is not an idea. It is the father's visceral working for his son's happiness, so profoundly rooted he even remains unaware of it as a separate thought. Hope is a movement on behalf of the other, preceding any deliberation about whether it ought or ought not to occur. Similarly, when Péguy notices Bernard-Lazare's invincibility in the midst of defeat, he does so through a hope that is already in place, before he starts thinking.

It is, in fact, striking, once one reads Levinas, to find how many passages in Péguy's portrait of Bernard-Lazare echo those in "The Temptation of Temptation," as though Péguy had read Levinas. Levinas did read Péguy, as most of his educated French countrymen have read him.[13] But Levinas's main sources of inspiration clearly do not come from him. Levinas's reference points, as he himself indicates in his brief intellectual biography,[14] are Bergson, Husserl, Heidegger, and Jewish texts.[15] It is thus extremely unlikely that, in hearing echoes between the two authors, we are in the presence of any direct influence. Yet these echoes are so strong that they demand some sort of explanation. I shall attempt to suggest one a bit later, after turning to the echoes themselves.

Most of these echoes occur in Péguy's description of Bernard-Lazare himself: "He had a gentleness, a goodness, a mystical tenderness, an even-temperedness, an experience of disappointment and ingratitude, a kind of goodness that could not be outdone, perfectly informed and perfectly learned, of unbelievable depth. As if he had goodness to spare."

The emphasis in these lines is obviously on the special quality of Bernard-Lazare's goodness. It is not a naïve goodness, Péguy stresses, but experienced, well-informed. Is Péguy not striving to describe a commitment to the Good that, while accompanied by knowledge, is not established or disestablished by it? The second passage repeats this theme, with variations. "I still see upon me his nearsighted gaze, so intelligent and so good all at once, with so invincible, so intelligent, so enlightened, so enlightening, so luminous a kindness, with so untiring, so experienced, so enlightened, so disabused, so incurable a goodness."

Again we meet with that goodness commingled even more than in the previous passage, with intelligence. The gentleness is intelligent, illuminating, giving of light. It is as though, at least in the first part of the sentence, the kindness in itself causes intelligibility. It enlightens, is luminous. Again, this cannot help but bring to mind Levinas's previously cited assertion that "a direct optics . . . can only be accomplished as ethics."

Shortly thereafter Péguy switches the emphasis suddenly; his focus is no longer on Bernard-Lazare's gentleness but on his passion.

. . . a heart that beat to all the echoes of the world, a man who would leap on a newspaper and who in its four, six, eight, in its twelve pages with a single look like lightning would seize upon a sentence, and in that sentence there was the word *Jew*, a man who flushed, paled, an old-timer of a journalist, a regular, . . . who would pale . . . a heart that bled in all the ghettoes of the world . . . a heart that bled in Romania, in Turkey, in Russia . . . everywhere the Jew is persecuted, which is to say, in a certain sense, everywhere. . . . A perpetual tremor, a perpetual vibration. All that is needed to die at 40. Not a muscle, not a nerve that wasn't tensed for a secret mission, that wasn't perpetually vibrating for the mission. . . . A being perpetually tensed. . . . Not a feeling, not a thought, not a shadow of a passion that was not tensed, that was not commanded by the commandment 50 centuries old.

This passage conveys the immediacy of Bernard-Lazare's reaction to the suffering of others. That is, his commitment to the Good manifests itself not in theoretical pronouncements but in his visceral reaction to the vulnerability of particular people. It is as if, in this passage, Bernard-Lazare acts like a man possessed. Would this not be the very image of what Levinas meant when he spoke of the Good as that which violently seizes a person?

Péguy emphasizes in this passage that it is to the Jews that Bernard-Lazare reacts in this manner. But we also know, from the same essay, that he reacted to the plight of the Armenians in Turkey and to that of the French Catholics. His responsibility was primarily, although far from exclusively, to the Jews. It was a responsibility, Péguy tells us, that resulted from a commandment issued fifty centuries before. In other words, it was not an attitude he had tried on for size. He lived it, as though it were imposed upon him, as though that mountain were still hanging upside down, ready to crush him, unless he accepted responsibility.

The sense of a responsibility not freely chosen emerges from the next passage as well.

I still have upon me, in my eyes, the eternal goodness of that infinitely gentle gaze, that goodness that did not hurl itself out but was poised, informed. Infinitely disabused; infinitely informed, itself undefeatable. I still see him in his bed, that atheist dripping with the word of God. Even in death, the whole weight of his people bore down on his shoulders. He could not be told that he was not responsible for them. I have never seen a man burdened in such a way, so burdened with a task, with an eternal responsibility. As we are, as we feel responsible for our children, for our own children in our own family, just as much, exactly as much, exactly thus did he feel responsible for his people.

Lazare is responsible for his people the way parents are responsible for their children.[16] Parents don't decide to create a bond of obligation to their children. They are obligated whether they want to be or not. They can fail to acknowledge their obligation or fail to carry it out in specific instances. But neither failure erases the fact of obligation, which is simply there, before we choose it, unshakable, even if we act as though we could shake it off. It seems that it is precisely through this visceral, unshakable obligation that the word of God speaks.[17] And here again, one hears the conclusion of "Temptation of Temptation," in which Levinas refers to that responsibility as the impossibility of escaping from God.[18]

I cannot resist pointing to yet another passage, which echoes Levinas's themes so strongly as to outdo him. It is not from "Notre jeunesse" but from "Clio—Dialogue de l'histoire et de l'âme païenne" ("Clio 2"), one of Péguy's essays on history, and it speaks about the peculiar contractual relation between author and reader:

> Here you have it, my friends, the implied contract and all the responsibilities it bears with it. The contract made without us, in which we are bound without having been asked our opinion. Among so many other, implied contracts, which hold us bond at the wrists for our entire temporal life, and maybe for a little beyond. Here is one. On the one hand, the author, from his side, puts in his work. On the other hand, from our side, we bring the entire memory of the world, we put in the common memory of common humanity. We put in this common memory, so precarious, so powerful, which incessantly makes and remakes itself. Such are the contractual assets. And the mutual connections, the relations, the ties. Such are, on both sides, the contractual obligations. It is a broken contract, like all contracts, and, like all contracts, is unbreakable. A contract about which we have never been and never shall be consulted, neither the author nor we the public. Those works are in our hands like hostages, like slave women prisoners, the wives of Darius. In the hands, alas, of what posterity. . . . Their honor, their esteem, and their life depend on us. It does not escape you, my friend, that is the greatest honor that could be bestowed upon us in time, and that we did not ask for it.[19]

The focus of Péguy and Levinas is remarkably similar. In the relation of the reader to the author, in both cases, we have the appearance of *a responsibility that the reader has never chosen*. It is up to him to place the work within the common memory of common humanity, to save it from time. The works are the most vulnerable of the vulnerable—women slave prisoners. And through the works it is always to the authors that we are responsible, the passage makes clear. It is an enormous responsibility. We can fail at it but we cannot escape it.

I am submitting that these echoes, one would almost have to find a stronger word, are not coincidental. These themes occur in the works of both authors because each faced a world in which the *priority, the immediacy* of that responsibility to the other had been obscured. Levinas, of course, faced it in the most visible of all failures of the contract—the fascist state of the 1930's and 1940's, in which that visceral response to the vulnerability of the other was considered weakness. But Péguy already faced it at the turn of the century. He faced it in the anti-Dreyfusard position, which maintained that no loyalty was higher than that to a strong state. He faced it in the Dreyfusard-socialist position once it became a party vying for power, wanting control of the state above everything else. He faced it in the positivist ideology pervading the university, insisting that in the study of man there are no presuppositions, dehumanizing the humanities and social sciences.[20] I would submit further that in Levinas's and Péguy's reactions to the temper of the times, we may be encountering the religious emphasis particular to our century. This does not mean that the notion of incarnation in Péguy's text perfectly covers the senses of the notion of revelation in Levinas. Or that words like *responsibility* in Levinas's text perfectly cover the senses of the word *hope* in Péguy's. I have spoken primarily of echoes. But, perhaps to echo Péguy, the emphasis on embodiment is the point of intersection of two mystiques—the Jewish and the Christian—face-to-face with the times. Both relocate the sacred in ethical encounter.

Franz Rosenzweig

Franz Rosenzweig (1886–1929), one of the great thinkers of the twentieth century, also gives voice to this theme of embodiment in all his work. Although he lived closer in time to Péguy, the influence of his written works has been felt more in the latter half of our century. Levinas, in fact, did much to awaken interest in Rosenzweig among his contemporaries, both through the essays he wrote about him and through an oft-quoted sentence in his book *Totality and Infinity*, in which he claims that Rosenzweig is too present in this work to be cited.[21] Levinas's thought and Rosenzweig's converge in many respects, not least on the subject of embodiment. Nonetheless, Rosenzweig's expressions of embodiment illuminate Péguy's thought from an angle different from that of Levinas.

Rosenzweig wrote his major work, *The Star of Redemption*, while a German soldier in World War I.[22] In it, he translates into a modern philosophical vocabulary his understanding of three terms key to the Jewish tradition: *creation*, *revelation*, and *redemption*. The fact that he wrote it when he did is no coincidence. As he stated to a friend several years later, he felt that European culture was on the verge of collapse and needed an infusion from spiritual sources outside it, Judaism being one of those sources.[23] He thus proposes to the educated European reader of his time a vision of the human being that had hitherto not received attention.

As *The Star* makes clear, Rosenzweig did not think that the Jewish contribution to the world lay merely in its proclamation of certain ideas about man, God, and the world. Rather, the contribution of the Jews was to remain throughout history a community apart, preserving these teachings from the encroachments of time, until, at the end of time, they will be realized in the formation of one human community, in which there no longer will be a difference between Jew and non-Jew.[24]

True to his own understanding of the human being and the role of the Jew as he outlined it in this book, Rosenzweig planned to stop writing books and focus instead on the reestablishing of Jewish communal life, centered around the traditional teachings and practices. This would require quite a bit of effort and imagination, as contemporary Jews like himself had become thoroughly immersed in German culture in particular and European culture in general. They no longer knew even some of the very rudimentary facts about their tradition at all.[25]

In keeping with this goal, Rosenzweig became the director of a new institution for Jewish learning, the Freies Jüdisches Lehrhaus, which he had been very instrumental in founding. But barely three years later, by the end of 1923, he was left motionless and speechless, as a result of what is now often called Lou Gehrig's disease.[26] Thanks to the efforts of his wife and the system they devised,[27] he managed to work on for six more years—writing essays, letters, doing translations and commentaries of Jewish texts. In the midst of his complete physical debilitation, he exhibited an altogether amazing vitality, mostly directed to the reinvigoration of Jewish life.

It is to some of the essays centered around the Lehrhaus that I shall turn to give the reader a taste of his insistence on embodiment. These essays, written both before and after the onslaught of his disease, are mostly on Jewish education, although one involves a discussion of Jewish ritual as such. As in the case of Levinas, these shorter writings make a glimpse into his thought easier than his major philosophical work. But, as in the case of Levinas, the central insight is the same for both. I shall, in any case, refer to *The Star* at a certain point in my commentary.

In several of his essays on Jewish education, such as "Toward a Renaissance of Jewish Learning," for instance, Rosenzweig dwells on the fragmentation of Jewish life among his contemporaries in western Europe.[28] He means by this that much, if not nearly all of life, is lived outside the Jewish traditional teachings or practices, so that if a Jewish life exists at all, it has become only an aspect alongside other aspects, which it leaves unaffected. For liberal Jews, for example, it has become reduced to a few ideas. For the neo-Orthodox, it is reduced to certain duties, the rituals. For the Zionists, it is reduced to a certain task, working for the creation of a Jewish state. But in each of these cases, a large chunk of life escapes, remains unrelated to what is considered the "Jewish" side. Rosenzweig claims this is so even in the case of the neo-Orthodox, who seem so absorbed in traditional practices. Yet they too go to work in a world in which they bow to another jurisdiction. That is, the world of work remains outside the Jewish world.

To live a Jewish life, according to Rosenzweig, however, is not merely to have Jewish ideas or to perform Jewish tasks. It is to act and think in such a way that every act and every thought stems from one center, a Jewish center. The Jewishness of the Jewish human being "is no entity, no subject among other subjects, no one sphere of life among other spheres of life; . . . it is something inside the individual that makes him a Jew, something infinitesimally small yet immeasurably large, his most impenetrable secret yet evident in every gesture and every word—especially in the most spontaneous of them."[29]

A bit later, he reiterates this theme, when he lays out the requisite attitude the Jew must adopt if he wants to become a Jewish human being once again: "If he has prepared himself quite simply to have everything that happens to him, both inwardly and outwardly, happen to him in a *Jewish* way—his vocation, his nationality, his marriage, and even, if that has to be, his Juda-'ism'—then he may be certain that with the simple assumption of that infinite 'pledge,' he will become in reality 'wholly Jewish.'"[30]

In these two quotations, we can already detect the centrality of the idea of embodiment in Rosenzweig's thought. The Jewish human being is not someone who operates with Jewish ideas or does Jewish deeds. Something deeper than either commands his activity as a whole. This something deeper manifests itself most in the spontaneous gesture and act—the one that is not consciously chosen. To be a Jewish human being, then, is to see and do through an invisible framework that orders everything, even the "non-Jewish" deeds or thoughts, even the "Jewish" deeds or thoughts.

The problem Rosenzweig confronts is how to regain this wholeness, given the fragmented lives of Jews at the present moment. The reading and writing of books cannot by itself bring back this wholeness, for books provide people with knowledge, but if this knowledge is not integrated into life, it remains mere idea. And how is it to integrate into life, if there is no life such as the one it enlightens about to refer back to? In such cases, books only add to the piling up of ideas, contributing to the fragmentation of life rather than healing it.

There is, of course, no choice but to resort to the intellect anyway. In an earlier letter to his parents, Rosenzweig wrote: "If we were still keeping Kosher, I could have spared myself the effort of writing *It Is Time* [an essay on Jewish education], but now that the way to the heart is no longer through the stomach, it must be through the spirit."[31] The word *spirit*, in this context, means self-conscious understanding, the intellect. And, in fact, when the Freies Jüdisches Lehrhaus was founded in 1920, it certainly centered on book learning—Hebrew language courses, history and philosophy courses, study of Jewish texts.³² Nonetheless, in describing this path back, Rosenzweig repeatedly limits the place of the intellect by forcing it to enter into relation with something beside itself.

Rosenzweig did not want the Lehrhaus suddenly to spring up full-blown, with its curriculum presented to unsuspecting students. Rather, he proposed as a prerequisite to any setting of curricula, that those who were eager to rediscover their heritage as Jews gather in one public space and exchange ideas, doubts, wishes about what such an education might be. This space and time in common would in itself create the seeds of a communal life. However tenuously, it would create the experience of belonging to a people engaged in a common enterprise. Thus when one began to read texts describing Jewish life, the readings would fall, not into a void, but onto a soil, no matter how thin:

It is essential that the discussion place be a single room—without a waiting room. The discussion must be public. . . . The discussion should bring everybody together. For it brings people to each other on the basis of what they all have in common—the consciousness, no matter how rudimentary, no matter how obscured or concealed, of being a Jewish human being. That one can meet others on such a basis, that one can desire in common with others—this will be an experience, even if the desire remains unsatisfied.³³

For Rosenzweig, this common space was only a beginning. It should lead, in fact, to the creation of a Lehrhaus, with its variety of course offerings. But Rosenzweig considered the Lehrhaus itself but a point of passage into fuller Jewish learning and communal life, which would arise as a consequence, in ways that could not be anticipated in advance.³⁴ He was not in the least bit worried when he wrote the essay "Toward a Renaissance of Jewish Learning," that he did not yet know either what this fuller life would be like or what the curriculum of a Jewish house of learning would be. On the contrary, not knowing, at this stage, was exactly as it should be. In this essay, again and again, he states that ready-made plans cannot work, if the goal is infinite:

What is intended to be of limited scope can be carried out according to a limited, clearly outlined plan—it can be "organized." The unlimited cannot be attained by organization. That which is distant can only be reached through that which is nearest at the moment. Any "plan" is wrong to begin with—simply because it is a plan. The highest things cannot be planned; for them readiness is everything.³⁵

A bit later, he calls this readiness by another name, confidence:

Confidence is the word for a state of readiness that does not ask for recipes, and does not mouth perpetually "What shall I do then?" and "How can I do that?" Confidence is not afraid of the day after tomorrow. It lives in the present; it crosses recklessly the threshold leading from today to tomorrow. Confidence knows only that which is nearest, and therefore it possesses the whole.[36]

To regain that center, that wholeness, then, one needs most of all to discard preconceived notions of how to get there. For it is not in the notion but in the encounter with specific events, teachings, deeds, previously not encountered, that the whole is revealed. The whole is not something one arrives at at the end, when one has acquired all the items necessary. It is not a body of information. Rather the whole can become present at any moment. It is in the nature of an insight, illuminating all things. This mode of learning, gleaning the whole from the particular instead of amassing it as a quantity of information, makes possible an embodied knowledge, a knowledge that can turn into spontaneous gesture and act.

This encounter with the particular is not completely haphazard, however. For it is directed from the beginning by a pledge: "the simple resolve to say once: 'Nothing Jewish is alien to me.'"[37] Expressed differently, it is the resolve to have everything that happens to oneself happen in a Jewish way—one's vocation, nationality, marriage, Judaism. In Rosenzweig's view, then, two elements must concur if one is ever to recover that secret center. On the one hand, time must be given its due, nothing can be planned ahead of its proper moment. On the other hand, the decision to engage in being a Jewish human being cannot be made in the course of time. It must be made beforehand, before one knows the contents of the teaching one desires to regain. It is this decision that signals the readiness to begin on the path whose contours only time will tell.

In this vision of how to return to the Jewish tradition, we note the emphasis on embodiment in several ways. In the first place, community, the exchanges within a group focused on a common goal, need to precede and accompany learning, giving it a home in concrete experience, rather than in the logic of ideas alone. Secondly, learning is not a matter of amassing a vast body of knowledge systematically. It is a matter of responding to a particular, in which the whole lies hidden. Rosenzweig *did* want a broad and thorough knowledge of Jewish sources. But that knowledge could only turn into Jewish learning through that attention to particularity. Thirdly, individuals must decide that the pursuit is worthwhile before they have begun it. In all these cases, the intellect is as though cushioned against something else, which curbs its autonomy—whether it be community, the factor of time, or a trust prior to the knowledge the intellect provides. It is perforce related to factors beyond it and made to take its direction from them.

All of the above has been about the rediscovery of Jewish teachings, the reentry into Jewish texts, as the path to the Jewish center. We know, how-

ever, that unlike Martin Buber, with whom he associated closely, Rosenzweig thought that the way back also involved Jewish rituals.[38] As in the
case of the reentry into texts, he cautions against allowing the intellect to
dominate, but, surprisingly, given his emphasis on embodiment, the ritual
life is not by itself the solution to that secret center permeating all one's
activities.

In an essay addressed to Buber, "The Builders," he argues against the
latter's view of Jewish Law, of ritual, as something worthy of reverence
but no longer to be practiced. Instead, he claims that just as one must go
through all the Jewish teachings available to rediscover the Jewish human
being, so one must go through all the ritual, the Law. For it is not enough
to study ritual. In order for ritual to be ritual, it must be done; "what is
doable and even what is not doable yet must be done nonetheless, cannot
be known like knowledge, but can only be done."[39]

But why is it not enough to study it, as part of an honorable heritage?
In the face of all kinds of psychological and sociological explanations miti-
gating against its practice, Rosenzweig states:

Psychological analysis finds the solution to all enigmas in self-delusion, and historical sociology finds it in mass delusion. The Law is not understood as a commandment addressed by God to the people but as a soliloquy of the people. We know
it differently, not always and not in all things, but again and again. For we know it
only when—we *do*.

What do we know when we do? Certainly not that all of these historical and sociological explanations are false. But in the light of the doing, of the right doing in
which we experience the reality of the Law, the explanations are of superficial and
subsidiary importance.[40]

The reason why study is not enough and explanations of ritual are
not sufficient is, then, that something happens in the *specific enactment*, in
the doing, that is simply different from any theoretical knowledge, even
the most correct. The doing does not give knowledge. It puts in relation:
"Only in the commandment can the voice of him who commands be
heard. . . . We wholly realize that general theological connection only
when we cause it to come alive by fulfilling individual commandments and
transpose it from the objectivity of a theological truth to the 'Thou' of the
benediction."[41]

Rosenzweig does not claim that this happens every single time a ritual
act is performed, automatically, as if by magic; rather, it occurs "not always, and not in all things," he says. But he claims that this being put in
relation cannot happen through theoretical understanding. It can happen
only through doing. Thus, his argument against Buber, in a way, and
against psychological and sociological reductions of ritual is that there can

be no argument either for or against ritual, understood theoretically, because it reveals its truth only in the doing.

Given this view and given his emphasis on embodiment, in general, one might surmise that Rosenzweig advocates an embrace of the ritual life in its entirety from the start. In fact, he disadvises it:

What I have tried to give in "The Builders" is a hygiene of return. What it warns against is the somersault into the Law, which is tempting because of the biographical crisis preceding it. Despite the existence of the great crisis, the individual should nevertheless wait for smaller events to actualize, through their biographical energy, the new "I can." In this way, the person who returns maintains throughout the process of his return his accustomed—un-Jewish—mode of life, and is able to stay alive.[42]

Here he calls embracing all of the ritual, the Law, all at once a temptation. Perhaps it is the temptation of having a visible sign that one has arrived at that invisible center. Perhaps it is the temptation of finding a system, a formula, by which one can be guided. He advises, instead, much in the same way he had advised regarding Jewish teaching, that, after the decision to rediscover the Jewish human being has been made, one should proceed from what is nearest at hand, allowing particular events to lead one more gradually into a fuller embrace.

An example of this more gradual approach can be found in his own life, when he explains in a letter:

Originally I made it my principle to refrain from all business correspondence on the Sabbath, but saw no harm in writing letters to friends. Nor did I give up this liberal interpretation of keeping the Sabbath until once, when Henry Rothschild and I were discussing some matter concerning the Lehrhaus, he tried to make me jot down notes since—so he said—I did not mind writing on the Sabbath. That experience, which taught me how unfeasible it is to draw such fine distinctions unless everyone else draws them too, finally drove me to accept the orthodox practice on this point, though to come to the decision was not easy for me.[43]

The reason Rosenzweig gives for proceeding in this more gradual manner, to refer back to his own words, is that in the process a person maintains his un-Jewish mode of life, and is able to stay alive. I take this to mean that the goal of keeping the commandments is not to replace the un-Jewish with the Jewish but to discover that hidden center within all activity. For this, integration, rather than outright cutting off, is needed.[44] This is, in fact, what he says, in the speech he delivered at the inauguration of the Lehrhaus:

All of us to whom Judaism, to whom being a Jew, has again become the pivot of our lives . . . we all know that in being Jews we must not give up anything, not renounce anything, but lead everything back to Judaism. From the periphery, back to the center; from the outside, in. . . . It is not a matter of pointing out relations between what is Jewish and what is not Jewish. There has been enough of that. It is not a matter of apologetics, but rather of finding the way back into the heart of our life.[45]

Of course, when it comes to practicing the Law, certain activities, of necessity, have to be abandoned. Nonetheless, the Law is to function as an illumination for what undergirds one's activity as a whole, rather than as a dividing post between Jewish and non-Jewish. As much as Rosenzweig argued for the reentry into ritual practice—and he himself became fully observant—he did not want this ritual practice to become the circumscribed "Jewish duties" of the neo-Orthodox, but a vehicle for that secret center from which spontaneous gesture and thought emanate.[46]

This concern to prevent the reifying of the Law, turning it into a commodity for becoming Jewish, is present also in "The Builders," when he argues against Buber on behalf of its continuing practice. Buber had claimed that one must go through all the Jewish teachings in pursuit of that center, or wholeness. But even for a person who had gone through all the teachings, the goal was not the knowledge those teachings provided but something else, which at this point Rosenzweig refers to as pathlessness: "Even such a one [the one who had gone through all the teachings] could say no more than that he had gone the whole way but that even for him the goal lay a step beyond—in pathlessness."[47] Even though Rosenzweig wants to include the rituals alongside with the teachings as a way to that pathlessness, nonetheless, it is pathlessness, not the rituals which are the goal in both cases: "All this holds for the Law, for doing. . . . There [for the teachings], the way led through all that is knowable, here [for the Law] it leads through all that is doable."[48]

In conclusion, the notion of embodiment that pierces through Rosenzweig's essays on reentering Jewish life should not be understood as a value placed on action as opposed to reason. Embodiment in his thought is a recognition of something underlying both action and reason, unattainable through any formula, but which is nonetheless learned, through both action and reason.

Péguy and Rosenzweig

Once again, as in the case of Levinas and Péguy, we seem to be in two completely different universes. What do these essays on Jewish education and Jewish law have to do with the Dreyfus Affair and Bernard-Lazare? Yet these essays on education and law nonetheless shed light on one of Péguy's key terms, the term *mystique* itself.

Earlier in this commentary, I spoke of mystique as disinterested action—action not for the sake of glory or power or wealth but for the sake of truth. I also mentioned that, without opposing reason, commitment to that truth is not arrived at through logical deduction. It is this latter dimension of mystique that Rosenzweig's essays illuminate, especially his discussion of the Jewish human being.

As will be recalled, the Jewishness of the Jewish human being was not, for Rosenzweig, a set of ideas or a package of activities. It was a secret center made manifest in every single thought and action, especially the most spontaneous of them. When we look back at "Notre jeunesse," we notice that this is also the way mystiques function. They are not ideas about truth or justice, although they do receive expression at the level of ideas. They are ways of being that permeate everything a person does and thinks. This is evident from the very beginning of the essay.

Péguy's portrait of Bernard-Lazare does not initiate "Notre jeunesse." It starts some 50 pages into it, as an illustration of the dynamic between mystique and politique. The two terms get introduced earlier, appearing for the first time when Péguy is speaking about a collection of archival material, mainly private letters, that his journal will be publishing in the coming issues. They are letters from certain republican milieus of the nineteenth century. In order to make them more appealing, Paul Milliet, the person who presented the letters to Péguy, mentioned that among them are a few from Victor Hugo and Henri Béranger, famous names. Péguy refuses the famous names. He wants to publish the letters from republican families who have remained obscure, because they will reveal how the republican spirit expressed itself in ordinary people, those about whom the historians of his time did not trouble themselves.[49] The way he words his interest in these unknown families merits attention:

What we want to know is of what fabric was this people woven, this people and this party, how an *ordinary* family lived, average as it were, unknown, as it were chosen at random, chosen from ordinary fabric, chosen and cut from a wide span of fabric, from the cloth itself, what one believed there, what one thought there, what one did there, for they were men of action—what one wrote there; how one married there, how one lived there, by what means, how one raised children there; first of all, how one was born there, because in those days, one was born—how one worked there, how one spoke there; how one wrote there.[50]

What captivates Péguy is the whole range of these people's thoughts and actions, and he uses the image of cloth and fabric to indicate their interwovenness. Strangely enough, these are not just thoughts and actions regarding politics, regarding the republican form of government. They are thoughts and actions regarding work, child-rearing, and marriage—everything, in short. Thus, the republican spirit, for Péguy, was not just an ideology. It permeated the human being through and through. A while later, he refers to this permeation as a mystique: "It was these families, almost always the same families, who wove the history of what historians will call the republican movement, and that we shall resolutely call, which one must call, the proclamation of the republican mystique."[51]

A few pages later, he speaks of the deterioration of that mystique. It involves the loss of that wholeness. What remains are merely ideas, arguments, but they no longer spring from a source infusing a person's entire life.

I am seized with fright when I see, when I simply observe what our elders do not want to see, which is as clear as daylight, which it takes only the willingness to see: how much our young people have become strangers to everything that once was republican thought itself and the republican mystique. One can see this above all, and naturally, as one always sees such things, from the fact that what for us were thoughts had become for them ideas, what for us, for our fathers, was an instinct, a race,[52] thoughts had become for them *propositions*, what for us was organic became for them logical.

Thoughts, instincts, race, habits that for us were nature itself, which went without saying, from which one lived, which were the pattern of life, about which, consequently, one did not even think, which were more than legitimate, more than beyond discussion: undeduced, have become the worst thing in the world: historical theses, hypotheses, I mean the least solid, the least existing thing there is.[53]

We see here, first of all, a distinction between what in the French are *pensée* and *idée*.[54] The former, which I have translated as thought, has intellectual content but, in the above passage, it functions very differently from *idée*, idea, which is only logic. The former was so deeply rooted that one did not even think about it. It was as if it were an instinctual reaction, what Rosenzweig might have meant by that spontaneous gesture and expression. The latter, being argument and proposition, is mainly a way of fighting an opponent. Péguy's description of it is reminiscent of that book-learning, unintegrated into life, against which Rosenzweig warned.

With this as foreground, it is possible to move directly into the portrait of Bernard-Lazare and to reflect once again on that famous line: "I still see him in his bed, that atheist dripping with the word of God." This dripping (the French word, *ruisselant*, even more immediately suggests sweating) captures both its involuntary nature—one does not sweat at will—and its all-pervasiveness—one sweats from every pore. Bernard-Lazare's responsibility for his people was not just a consciously held notion, although it was also that. It was something directing his entire being, overflowing, like his goodness, of which Péguy tells us he had so much, he had some to spare. This aspect must be kept firmly in mind when we try to understand why Péguy presented Bernard-Lazare as his chief example of a man acting according to a mystique.

Given the strong echo between Rosenzweig's and Péguy's preoccupations, it is not surprising to find other instances of affinity, which make that echo even louder. It will be remembered, for example, that, for Péguy, the socialists who followed their mystique in defense of Dreyfus, exhibited more Christian charity than the Church, which exhibited many qualities in its attack on Dreyfus, including great intellectual clarity, but not charity. Péguy had also argued that the Church's decline in the modern world was due, not to the rise of science, but to its refusal to stand with the most vulnerable in society, the industrial workers, and risk economic reform. The following excerpt from a letter Rosenzweig wrote in 1927 to his cousin Hans Ehrenberg (who had converted to Christianity) contains a remarkably similar thought:

> You can get a better understanding of Zionism by considering the significance of socialism for the church. Just as the Social Democrats, even if they are not "religious socialists," even if they are "atheists," are more important for the establishment of the Kingdom of God through the church than the church-minded, even the few truly religious ones, and certainly than the vast mass of the semi—or wholly indifferent, so the Zionists are for the synagogue.[55]

The coincidence between the two authors here derives from their similar emphasis on embodiment. The reason the socialists and the Zionists are more important to their respective traditions than the Church or synagogue-minded is that they attempt to embody in the whole of life, in the complexities of communal relations, the teachings of their traditions. Church and synagogue attendees might maintain a private piety or morality but, to use Péguy's term, they cannot perpetuate the central mystique of their traditions. For Rosenzweig, this central mystique was the Kingdom of God, whose realization depended upon both Jews and Christians, although in different ways, and upon both God and man. This is not the term *charity*, the key word in Péguy's vocabulary when he talks about the socialists and the Church in "Notre jeunesse." Nor is it the term *hope* so central to him in a more hidden way throughout the essay. The parallels between the two thoughts are nonetheless clear. Péguy never meant by *charity* only a private giving. It is to stand publicly with the vulnerable. Nor did he mean by *hope* a passive waiting. It is a deed, on behalf of the other, arising despite one's own defeat. In both instances, the terms carry the public, ethical connotation of Rosenzweig's term, *redemption*. In both instances, embodiment is not just putting an idea into practice but the flickering of the eternal in time.

On this latter point, I cannot resist pointing out one last instance of how close Péguy and Rosenzweig sometimes are in their understanding. In *The Star*, Rosenzweig says that redemption is made possible because of revelation.[56] In revelation, God reveals his love to the specific human being. This love commands love in return. But this love, in returning God's love, turns toward the neighbor. It is a world thus exclusively made of neighbors turning toward one another that will be the redeemed world.[57] In the meantime, however, many of these movements toward the neighbor fail to reach their mark, and it is in the way Rosenzweig expresses this failure that we hear such a strong echo of Péguy: "Now this fulfillment of God's commandment in the world is not, after all, an isolated action but a whole sequence of actions. Love of neighbor always erupts anew. It is a matter of always starting over from the beginning. It cannot be diverted by any disillusionments—on the contrary: *it needs disillusionments in order to spring forth again ever anew.*"[58] Does this not sound like Péguy's description of the man of 40, defeated and yet rising anew on behalf of his son? Or of Bernard-Lazare, defeated but unstoppable in his ever-renewed responsibility for his people? Or, of mystiques in general, always defeated by politiques and always resurgent? These echoes, I must emphasize, are not haphazard crisscrossings. They occur because the work of both authors is permeated with an awareness of transcendence detectable in the ordinary,[59] an awareness of what I have often referred to as embodiment.

I would like, before leaving Rosenzweig, to spend a bit more time on the connection between embodiment and ethics in his thought. For, while it intersects at significant points with that of Péguy, it nonetheless reveals aspects different from his. The points in common should not obscure the fact that their writings do not coincide.

We have already caught a glimpse of the relation of embodiment to interhuman exchange in Rosenzweig's essays on Jewish education, when he stresses the importance of community. The proper embodiment, in which every thought and gesture emanates from one secret center, is made possible only as a result of the relations between human beings. One cannot produce it by oneself, simply through the reading of books. It is in the course of discussing with others, living with others, teaching and learning with others, that Jewish spirituality, what he calls the Jewishness of the Jewish human being, is passed on and enters at a level below that of ideas alone. But community is not only prerequisite to embodiment; it is also the end result of embodiment. That is, embodiment also produces community. In order to understand this dialectic better, I would like to turn, briefly, to *The Star*.

In the one community at the end of time, Rosenzweig tells us, there will no longer be either Christians or Jews. Nor will the Name of God be pronounced. Since the outstanding mark of this community is that all will recognize the one God, he need no longer be named, for names separate out from other names. But there will be no other name to which the name of God will be in opposition:

Redemption redeems God by releasing him from his revealed name. The process of redemption in the world takes place in the name and for the sake of the name.

The end, however, is nameless: it is above any name. . . . Beyond the word—and what is name but collective word—beyond the word there shines silence. There where no other names any longer confront the one name, where the one name is al[l]—one and all that is created knows and acknowledges him and him alone, there the act of sanctification has come to rest. For sanctity is meaningful only where there is still profanity. Where everything is sacrosanct, there the Sacred itself is no longer sacred, there it simply exists. This simple existence of the Highest, such unimpaired reality, omnipotent and solely potent, beyond any desire for or joy in realization, this is truth. For truth is not to be recognized through error, as the masters of the school think. Truth attests itself, is one with everything real; it does not part in it.[60]

Thus, at the end of time, when God is universally recognized, universally acknowledged, he will be most hidden, in that he will no longer be invoked by name. The truth that Rosenzweig refers to in the above passage, however, is not a matter of cognition, of a proposition agreed to. For the recognition of God, as Rosenzweig tells us elsewhere, occurs when "God dissolves in us,"[61] that is, when his act of love toward the human being propels that human being toward the neighbor. It is in that movement that God is recognized, in the act itself. He gives a wonderful description of this movement in a letter to his future sister-in-law, written after *The Star* itself:

No man can help himself. Though the world is full of people who try to make themselves believe that they can, they succeed no better than Muenchhausen did when he tried to pull himself out of the mire by the scruff of his neck. Each of us can only seize by the scruff whoever happens to be closest to him in the mire. This is the "neighbor" the Bible speaks of. And the miraculous thing is that, although each of us stands in the mire himself, we can each pull out our neighbor, or at least keep him from drowning. None of us has solid ground under his feet; each of us is only held up by the neighborly hands grasping him by the scruff, with the result that we are each held up by the next man, and often, indeed most of the time . . . hold each other up mutually. All this mutual upholding [a physical impossibility] becomes possible only because the great hand from above supports all these holding human hands by the wrists. It is this, and not some nonexistent "solid ground under one's feet" that enables all the human hands to hold and to help. There is no such thing as standing, there is only being held up.[62]

In this passage, God reveals himself through the wrist of the person holding his neighbor's head above the mire, although he too is in the mire. It is, of course, possible to see only the person's wrist, and not the lack of ground underneath, requiring that the wrist itself be supported. Thus, here as well, God's manifestation is tantamount to his hiddenness. His presence is inseparable from the human act of help toward the other.

In *The Star*, such mutual upholding—on the scale of the entire world, where everyone turns toward his neighbor—is redemption. As has already been mentioned, both Judaism and Christianity are required for its realization. Judaism, through its separation from the nations of the world, maintains its oneness through time, already anticipating the oneness of all mankind. Through its very perpetuity, it provides the world with a representation of that one community at the end of time. Christianity, on the other hand, does not keep itself separate. Its mission, on the contrary, is to mingle with the nations, adopting their customs, sharing their history. Only working from within can it break down barriers between people, making them all brothers in Christ. But Christianity soon becomes embroiled in the very differences it is trying to erase, confusing the reign of a particular group with the Kingdom of God. Only the Jews, stubborn outsiders refusing to enter the times, remind the Church that the world still awaits redemption.

Although the Jews await redemption like everyone else, at particular moments, according to Rosenzweig, they already live it. He speaks of one such moment and the steps preparatory to it in his section "The Fire or the Eternal Life." These preparatory steps, like the moment to which they lead, all involve the creation of a certain kind of silence. The first step toward this silence occurs during the delivery of the traditional sermon, always based on the recitation of Torah and rabbinic commentary.[63]

He claims that a sermon functions in a very different way from other types of public speaking, for most sorts depend, in order to be successful, on engaging the audience, making it approve or disapprove. When the audience does so, it is itself speaking, either through its cheers and jeers or through various physical signs. A sermon, however, is not meant to engage the audience in a dialogue. It is to silence it before the recitation of sacred text. A real sermon, then, causes the audience to listen silently. The speaker, as a result, does not derive his cues from it. He too is as if silent before the text, allowing it to be heard through his commentary. The silence gives expression to a community, bound not only through personal relations but through a common center.[64]

In the second preparatory step to the experience of the end of time in the present, silence also occurs. It happens as a result of sharing a meal in common, after the sermon, the Shabbat meal. Eating together establishes a common bond not so much through the table talk as through the renewing of life together, the sharing of food. After a meal taken together, if participants see each other again, they greet each other: "And so, when the guests leave, they are no longer strangers to one another. They greet one another when they meet again. Such greeting is the loftiest symbol of silence. They are silent because they know one another. If all men, all contemporaries, all the dead and all the still unborn, were to greet one another, they would have to eat a pound of salt with one another—as the saying goes."[65]

Silence here is not the absence of speech. People greet one another. But the greeting, the recognition of the person in his specificity, rests on the experience of renewing life together, which need not be mentioned. Undergirding the greeting is a common bond, which conditions the greeting without ever being named.

These two preparatory steps culminate in a moment of community in which the whole world is experienced in its oneness, in that very moment. It is the breakthrough of the end of time, eternity, into the present. For Rosenzweig, this moment is the Day of Atonement, Yom Kippur. Throughout its span, the Jew is not just a member of a particular people. He is man, weak, sinful man, praying with all the sinners—that is, with all of mankind.[66] In the course of the liturgy, it is recounted how, when the Temple still stood, the High Priest, at a certain point in the service, would pronounce the name of God, unutterable at any other time of the year.[67] The Jew, in immediate response, kneels, not in fear, but because of God's sudden proximity: "Kneeling in common before the Lord of all in the world, and 'of the spirits in all flesh,' opens the way for the community and only for this community and the individual within it, the way to the all-embracing common unity where everyone knows everyone else and greets him wordlessly—face-to-face."[68]

It is Yom Kippur, then, that brings redemption into time and yet makes the Jew thirsty for its realization, for this community is only symbolically the whole world. Its description, above, rejoins descriptions we have encountered in earlier passages. People will greet one another, recognize one another in their specificity, on the basis of commonality they need not mention. Here, too, there is silence, something unspoken, recognized by all in their very act of greeting one another. Is this silence not another word for embodiment?

This brief excursion into *The Star* should bring out in greater relief than before that Rosenzweig's notion of embodiment is through and through related to ethics, to the relations between human beings. It should also support my earlier contention that in finding echoes between Rosenzweig's and Péguy's thought, I made no claim to an identity between them. Rosenzweig's writings—at least my selection of them—push one in the direction of questions about education and community. Péguy's "Notre jeunesse" takes us elsewhere, to other questions, about the relation of religion and politics, for instance. Still, the echoes remain and it is in these echoes, I contend, that we can hear one of the significant religious currents of our century.

If one wants to give this current a name other than the one I have already given it—embodiment—one could call it the current against ideology, both in the sense that the thinkers in this current were careful to distinguish between *pensée* and *idée*, and, even more significant, that they were for defining a realm in which the intellect must subordinate itself to something more fundamental—the realm of ethics, the movement toward the other.[69] Both Levinas and Rosenzweig, as unsystematic as they are, are nevertheless more systematic than Péguy in carving out this realm. Péguy's work, however, in its very concreteness, may come closer to showing the movement toward the other in action. His portrait of Bernard-Lazare is a living example of such a movement. This is not to say that he was unaware of what he was doing. The very opposition between mystique and politique indicates a concerted effort to point to a domain of human activity outside ideology. His many reflections on both hope and incarnation in works other than "Notre jeunesse" testify to a similar self-conscious combating of ideology.[70] Nonetheless, the value of Péguy's portrait of Bernard-Lazare lies not in his explicit statements against ideology but in the fact that it is itself an embodiment of something beyond ideology.

Conclusion: Of Jews and Christians and the Nature of Comparison

Before closing this chapter, I would like to reflect more on what comparing Péguy to Levinas and Rosenzweig might mean. I have just suggested that the echoes in their thought came about because all three faced, if not identical histories, at least similar mental universes, what Péguy, in one of his writings, refers to as the chief feature of the modern world: "the glorification of the intellect at the expense of charity."[71] All three thinkers rose up against the subordination of the ethical relation to something else, be it called intellectualism, positivism, or statism. It is this fight, conducted independently, but against the same enemy, that, I claim, led to the similar emphases in their thought.

But without in the least contradicting this view, one might also account for the echoes in other ways. In the first place, I want to come back to a thesis that I summarily rejected earlier. Several people had suggested that there is a Jewish resonance in Péguy's thought, or that his thought is in fact Jewish.[72] I thought phrasing things in this manner, especially the latter way, obscured both the difference Péguy always insisted upon maintaining between traditions and the Christian underpinnings of his thought. But now that I hope to have shown his insistence on difference as well as his Christian underpinnings, I feel I may have been too hasty in dismissing those commentators who saw something Jewish in his thought. After all, could not Péguy, while remaining perfectly Catholic, still have assimilated or integrated a Jewish emphasis?

It seems highly unlikely that this integration would have come about through Péguy's reading of classical, that is, rabbinic, Jewish sources. They were not widely available and, with the exception of a few, his Jewish friends themselves were not learned in them. As has already been mentioned, those friends were for the most part, secularized, at some remove from Jewish teaching and practice. Bernard-Lazare himself knew a good deal of Jewish history, including some of its classical textual sources, but the progressivistic, positivistic attitudes of his time, as reflected in his *Antisemitism: Its History and Its Causes*, did not always lead him to interpret them sympathetically.

Péguy, we know, did read contemporary works about Jews, by both non-Jews and Jews. No doubt, many of his statements in "Notre jeunesse" can be traced back to Renan or Darmesteter or Bernard-Lazare himself. Yet the emphasis I have labeled embodiment—the multidimensional interpenetration of temporal and eternal, with its peculiarly ethical focus—does not find its equivalent in those works. Pie Duployé suggests that it was Péguy's observation of contemporary Jewish life, of the political events swirling about his many Jewish friends, that led him to understand the Jewish role in history.[73] I would like to extend this line of reasoning, in agreement with several other commentators, to suggest that this same observation might have led to an incorporation of a Jewish element into his thought.[74] The Jews' struggle for justice, their way of encountering both defeat and victory may have helped to shape his Christian vision, giving the terms *hope* and *incarnation* accents they might otherwise not have had. This ability to think in a certain direction is perhaps what he had in mind when he once said: "I side with the Jews, because with the Jews, I can be a Catholic in the way that I want; with Catholics, I couldn't."[75]

Whether such an integration actually occurred remains, of course, difficult to substantiate. But whether it occurred or not, the presence of echoes between the thought of Péguy, a Catholic, and that of Rosenzweig and Levinas, Jews, raises the issue of the relation between truths. How does the truth of one's own tradition relate to the truth of others? Is it a question of denying the truth of others? Or do truths interpenetrate? But, if so, how? All three of our authors devoted a good deal of their writings to these very questions. In fact, from a certain angle, this is the center of all their thoughts. One might object, of course, that for all three the discussion limited itself to the pagan (classical Greek, and in the case of Péguy, also the Roman), Christian and Jewish traditions.[76] In this respect, they fell prey to the provincialism of their times, which we can hardly boast of having overcome. However, despite this, since the problem of the One and the many already presents itself when there are only three traditions, each one contending it has the truth, what our authors have to say on this topic is bound to address our discussion about the relation between truths.[77]

To start with Péguy's reflections on this topic, it is clear that the truths of different religious traditions can coincide or converge. One need only remember that his portrait of Bernard-Lazare describes the Dreyfus Affair as the point of intersection between three mystiques, the Jewish, the Christian, and the French. (He sometimes includes the socialist as a fourth.) That is, all three (or four) responded to the fact of Dreyfus's unjust sentence in the same way. Neither here nor elsewhere in "Notre jeunesse," however, does Péguy specify *how* these traditions interpenetrate, how their truths relate to one another. He simply states that they do interpenetrate.

In other texts, though, we get farther. The first I would like to adduce is found in Clio 2, in that same discussion of the classical Greeks I have already mentioned.[78] The reader will recall that this is where Péguy claims that the classical Greeks had a secret contempt for their gods, envying them their power, immortality, and endless amusements, but reserving their true admiration only for human beings. The latter, facing the three miseries, which Péguy also refers to as the three greatnesses—destitution, risk, and death—rise to a height the gods, in their very lack of limitations, can never know. In the course of his analysis, Péguy briefly, even parenthetically, compares this Greek spirituality to the Christian one: "(The particular import of Christianity is not that it invented *de nihilo* the three miseries [the three greatnesses], death, destitution, risk, but that it found their true intent, having added sickness, that half of modern man.) And to have assigned their true, full greatness to these four, to have given them their true, full weight."[79]

In these lines, Christianity is not a separate truth but a manner of recognizing, accenting, emphasizing what is already present in the Greek tradition and, perhaps by extension, in every other tradition. Péguy sees what he sees in the Greek texts, then, because, as a Christian, the paradoxical reversal of lowliness and height is intimately known to him. This does not mean, however, that the themes he detects in the Greek tradition are not present within it. Rather, one can extrapolate from his sentences above that Christianity provides an interpretative key to the tradition of the Greeks. One's own truth makes it possible to detect truth elsewhere. This does not mean distortion. On the contrary, it makes discovery of the truth possible in the first place.

One way of using this insight is simply to state that Rosenzweig's and Levinas's emphases give articulation to what is already in Péguy's work but in a less sharply focused way. The theme of embodiment, in its ethical thrust, permeates all of Péguy's writings. Yet, it takes a Jewish reading to show its importance. In this formulation, I am, of course, claiming for the

Jewish tradition what Péguy claimed for Christianity, mutatis mutandis. Judaism did not invent embodiment in its ethical modality. It has merely assigned it its true weight. Every tradition, then, would have the capacity to illuminate every other from one particular angle.

This view of the relation between the truths of traditions is reinforced by another of Péguy's texts, "Bar Cochebas," written somewhat earlier than the previous two. In it, he opposes the evolutionistic or progressive view of history, in which earlier metaphysics, philosophies, and religions are not only replaced but improved by those coming later. He claims instead that not only is each metaphysic unique, and therefore irreplaceable, but also that, in this realm, as opposed to the realm of technology, one cannot talk of improvement. Each metaphysic, he says, is a human response to God, who speaks to his creatures through the signs of his creation.[80] In its response, each metaphysic captures one object of this creation and is complete unto itself when it comes to that object.

As a result, if one wants to speak about certain objects, or certain aspects of reality, one has to refer to that tradition whose language is best honed to deal with that object. In short, because traditions are not interchangeable, each tradition needs the other in order to enter into a certain realm:

> Which means that there is always only one language, only one, for each object, only one word to say when one wants to say this or that. Whoever would want to speak of the intelligible and physical world, of ideal reality and transitory appearance, of dialectical ascension and of mythical symbolization, and of the insertion of spirits or souls in bodies will have to speak the language of ancient Hellenic Greece, one of these languages called Platonic philosophy and Plotinian philosophy. Whoever would want to speak of the just and jealous God, of a single God, and of temporal justice, pursued almost frenetically, and of the chosenness of people, and of the destiny of man and of a people, he will eternally have to speak the language of Israel. . . . Whoever would like to speak of fall and redemption, of eternal judgment and salvation, of God become man and of man made in the image and likeness of God, of a single God in plural persons, infinitely a Creator, infinitely all-powerful, infinitely just and infinitely good, of eternal communion, of the eternal city and of eternal charity, eternally he will have to speak the language of the Christian people.[81]

In this passage, while Christianity seems to cover a broader range than the other two traditions mentioned, it nonetheless does not have a monopoly on the real. If, for instance, it wants to speak about justice on earth or the destiny of a community of people, it too will have to resort to the language of the Jewish tradition. To return to these echoes of Levinas and Rosenzweig in Péguy's voice, their presence could be accounted for by the fact that when facing a situation requiring the mobilization of a people for the sake of correcting an injustice, the Catholic will always have to speak a Jewish language.

The passages I have just cited hardly exhaust Péguy's reflections on this question, but they do indicate one of its major directions, most fruitful for understanding what underlies our comparison. In turning to Levinas and Rosenzweig, I feel more uneasy, because I shall be presenting what may appear to be mere asides rather than addressing their elaborate formulations of the relation to the other or their understanding of truth. I have, however, attempted to intimate those already, in this whole chapter. The advantage of the passages that I do cite rests in the fact that they occur in the very thick of interpreting, allowing us to see their attitude toward the truths of other traditions, at work, as it were. While these passages have even less claim than those from Péguy to convey the problem as expressed in the entire thought of these authors comprehensively, they nonetheless illuminate our comparison from interesting angles.

Levinas's reflection comes from one of his Talmudic commentaries, "As Old as the World?" In the process of commenting on a Talmudic text on the Jewish court of justice, the Sanhedrin, he is brought to notice a similarity with the Greek conception of justice. Both the rabbis and the classical Greeks thought of the place where justice was dispensed as the navel of the universe. This similarity between the two traditions, deepening yet further upon Levinas's rereading of the *Oresteia*, elicits the following response from him:

Where then, is the difference between Delphi and Jerusalem? Let us be on our guard against facile and rhetorical antitheses: we are justice, they are charity: we love God, they love the world. From authentic spiritualities, no spiritual adventure is withheld. And Hellenism is probably a somewhat authentic spirituality. It is in the nuances of the formulations, in the inflections of the speaking voice, as strange as this may appear, that the abysses which separate the two messages open . . . in returning to our text . . . we may perhaps have occasion to discover in the Sanhedrin an aspect slightly different from the one which emerges when one reflects upon the other navels of the world.[82]

In this passage, Levinas seems to rejoin, at least in part, and from an altogether different direction, Péguy's observation that Christianity did not bring anything new but merely brought to light the full dimensions of what was already there in other traditions. For when Levinas says that every authentic spirituality holds within it all spiritual adventures, is he not claiming that no tradition has a truth that is somehow not also available, at least potentially, in all others?

Within this view, what might be called the Jewish echoes in Péguy's thought could be read as the dimension of Christianity that resonates with Jewish themes but is not of Jewish provenance at all, just as the resonances between the Talmudic passage on the Sanhedrin and Aeschylus do not be-speak a direct influence of one upon the other. Rather, given Levinas's passage above, both, as authentic spiritualities, contain within them a theme that no authentic spirituality would leave out. According to this reading, then, the ethical bent in Péguy's emphasis on embodiment may simply reveal an aspect of the religious dimension as such, discoverable also among Buddhists, Muslims, the Bemba, and so forth.

Levinas had also maintained that, against that background, there are irreducible differences, detectable when listening to the speaking voice, in its inflections and nuances. In this commentary, I have not pursued these differences, although I have insisted on the word *echo* rather than *coincidence*. Still, I wonder if that combination of melancholy and humor so characteristic of Péguy's tone is not one such difference. This tone, present in all of Péguy's expressions, is completely absent from both Levinas and Rosenzweig. This could, of course, be a matter of individual temperament. But perhaps it also points to one of those abysses of difference between traditions, created by the fact that one involves a crucifixion and a resurrection and the other does not. In any case, if we follow Levinas's suggestion, it is precisely in such apparently extraneous details that the differences lie.

The contribution I have chosen from Rosenzweig on this topic of the relation between traditions may, at first, not seem to apply at all. It is about the relation between languages. Rosenzweig's reflections arise out of very practical endeavors, since he was himself engaged with Martin Buber in a new translation of the Hebrew Bible into German, and in his own translation of the poems of the medieval Jewish poet and philosopher Yehuda Halevy, also from the Hebrew into the German.[83]

Against some of the prevailing standards of translation in his day, he did not want the translator to level out differences between the two languages, making the original sound completely like the colloquial speech of the home language. Rather, the language of the foreign work must inflect the very structure of the home language. It must bring something new to it, a way of expressing things it did not have before. In describing this renewal of one language by another, he reveals his fundamental assumption about the relation prevailing among all languages:

All languages are virtually one. There is no trait in any one language which is not at least latent in every other, though it may appear only in dialects, in the vocabularies of trades and callings, or in the chatter of the nursery. The possibility and the function of translating, its can-be, may-be, and should-be, are based on this essential oneness of all languages and on the command springing from the oneness that there shall be communication between men.[84]

We rejoin here Levinas's thought about each spirituality containing all spiritual adventures within it, transposed to the level of language. But since the texts Rosenzweig had in mind when he discussed translation were all classical texts, in many cases religious texts, and since the texts he himself translated were all religious texts par excellence, the line between what he says about language and what he says about religious tradition cannot be drawn too tightly.

The accent that is new in Rosenzweig's formulation is his insistence on the necessity of translating. We must translate "so that the day may come when there shall exist among languages the accord that can grow up out of all individual languages but never out of the empty spaces 'between' them."[85] Translation brings about understanding, not by making all languages uniform, but by making each responsive to the other, receptive to its mode of expression, by transforming the very structure of speech through contact.

What light does this shed upon our comparison of Péguy to Levinas and Rosenzweig? It may mean that he found, through contact with Jewish people, a way of translating one of their fundamental attitudes into the language of Christianity. The terms *temporal* and *eternal* are good Christian words, but Péguy's struggle, evident throughout the portrait, to convey a temporally eternal and eternally temporal reality, his plays with those categories, may indeed indicate an attempt at just such a translation.[86] On the other hand, and I would like to stress this, it may also mean that by juxtaposing his writing to that of two Jewish authors, I have myself translated his Christian language into a Jewish one. What in Péguy figures as incarnation I have rendered, awkwardly, as the embodiment with an ethical thrust. There must be a more mellifluous way of conveying Péguy's intent, but at least the awkwardness of my terminology points to the effort of translation.

But which way is it? Is it that there are Jewish echoes in Péguy's thought or that I have translated Christian emphases into a Jewish language? Who knows? At a certain point, there is a moment of accord, and at that moment, "Jewish" or "Christian" become mere labels. I do not mean, after so many pages spent in reflecting about the relation between the two, to suggest that these terms are always mere labels. On the contrary. But is it not the great aspiration of all thought, to glimpse, if only for a second, beyond all differences, something simply human?

This last point brings us to the national debates about multiculturalism and diversity.[87] To claim today that the goal of the intellectual life in the humanities and social sciences is to discover the human, the universal, is to become subject to the charge that one is trying to suppress diversity by privileging one model of the human over others. But the human we get an occasional glimpse of, as described here, is always the result of an encounter, in which the other's humanity inflects mine and vice versa. In short, it requires diversity to manifest itself. I would also like to draw attention to the fact that a diversity that refuses a search for the universal breaks down into a struggle for power between sealed groups, in which the weaker parties are suppressed anyway. That sort of diversity tags along its own hidden universal claim: that in the end, the hunger for power is the defining trait of the human being. The three authors I have presented here spent their entire life's work pointing to something else.

CHAPTER FOUR

Religion and Politics

Jews and Communism: 'The Generation'

In this last chapter, I would like to place Péguy's portrait of Bernard-Lazare alongside the work, not of philosophers, but of historians. "Notre jeunesse," whatever else it may be, is also a historical analysis of the Dreyfus Affair. This analysis, as I have tried to show, is informed by a certain philosophy of time, in which the transcendent manifests and hides itself in the temporal. Two emphases of this interplay between eternity and time, sacred and secular, are captured by the terms *incarnation* and *hope*. Péguy's historical analysis is far from being the only one structured according to such a vision of history. Juxtaposing his work to two other histories may thus give us another occasion to understand the notions of incarnation and hope, this time as hermeneutical principles, discovering and shaping historical evidence.

The first work I would like to examine in this context, Jaff Schatz's *The Generation*,[1] is a study of a group of Polish Jews born around 1910. They all became communists in the late 1920's and early 1930's, continuing as faithful party members until their forced emigration from Poland in 1968. In telling their story, Schatz makes it clear that he is also telling part of the story of Judaism in this century. His way of doing so is very reminiscent of Péguy's view of the Dreyfus Affair as a continuation of both the Jewish and Christian traditions. Péguy, it will be recalled, saw Bernard-Lazare's actions in the affair, as well as the eventual actions of the Jews as a whole within it, as a manifestation of the prophetic spirit, despite the fact that the Jews in question, Bernard-Lazare most of all, were secularized, positivistic, atheistic, and so forth. He made a parallel claim about the socialist supporters of Dreyfus. Standing with the vulnerable and persecuted, they were demonstrating a charity that the Church hierarchy, concerned with perpetuating its alliance with the Army and the proponents of the Old Regime, seemed to have forgotten. In both cases, Péguy claimed, something central to their respective religious traditions seeped into the political activities of those who considered themselves secular. They were thus in continuity with their tradition despite themselves.

Schatz's description of the Polish Jewish communists' relation to Judaism follows similar lines. These were people who vehemently rejected all religious affiliation, making it a point of honor, in fact, never to attend a religious ceremony of any sort, including weddings or circumcisions within their own families.[2] For them, religion created barriers between people, duped them as to their real conditions, made them sectarian. Yet it was this very tradition, perceived as narrow and blind, that bequeathed to them a vision of one mankind, making them receptive to communism in the first place. The generation of 1910, most of whose members were raised in observant Jewish homes, was exposed, through prayers, historical memories, and ritual celebrations, to a messianic thirst that had animated the Jewish community for at least two thousand years.

In stating this, Schatz is not claiming that there is a perfect fit between Judaism and communism. Rather, he is saying that in the face of the corrosive influences of industrialization, the modern state, and Enlightenment ideas, combined with the marginalization of Jews in Polish society, the element of Jewish tradition that rose to the fore was messianic hope.[3] This hope, breaking through the restraining barriers often imposed on it by other elements of the tradition, envisioned a society in which all divisions between people disappear, and one humanity finds a way of living in peace.

Schatz does not argue that the messianic urge expressed itself exclusively through communism. Zionism and Bundism were also expressions of it,[4] each stressing a different aspect of the cluster of themes associated with messianic times. These two movements, to be sure, emphasized Jewish national existence in contradistinction to the communists. But whether in one form or another, messianism, in Schatz's reading, becomes one of the chief Jewish religious expressions in the twentieth century. Just like Péguy, he sees modern politics as an extension rather than an interruption of the religious urge.

Again, Schatz is not proposing that communism or Zionism or Bundism constitutes the entirety of the Jewish religious impulse. If they represent continuity, they also represent a rupture, especially in their emphasis on radical activism and antinomianism. But even in their break, they are in continuity with other breaks from the Jewish tradition, such as Sabbateanism, for instance, a messianic movement that shook the entire Jewish world in the seventeenth century. Thus, communism, as lived out by Polish Jews, was both an extension of the heart of the tradition and an extension of a common departure from it.

Throughout Schatz's analysis of the religious impulse within the secular, we bump across the notion of incarnation or embodiment, although Schatz does not use these terms. However, he makes it clear that Polish Jewish communists' actions and thoughts were informed by something they had not, as it were, chosen.[5] For while they consciously deliberated whether to become Zionists, Bundists, communists, or something else, and made the choice for communism, they did not consciously deliberate about the messianic thirst that propelled them in the first place. Transmitted to them through the many details of their childhood and adolescence, this thirst infused itself into them without asking for their consent. It was already there by the time they made their choice to join the Communist Party.

Embodiment or incarnation also figures prominently in another aspect of Schatz's account, the Polish Jewish communists' efforts to shed their ethnic identity. On fire with the idea of eliminating all differences between people based on class, religion, or nationality, the members of the generation of 1910 were very eager to shed their own Jewish particularity as a way of entering into the universal. In this, they were similar to the French Jews Péguy encountered, who wanted nothing more than to be French, associating French civilization with the universal. Shedding one's particularity, however, is not as simple as one might think. Péguy points out how that secularized assimilated community of French Jews of the late nineteenth century exhibited both the politique and the mystique characteristic of its long history. Similarly, Schatz recounts many incidents in which Jewish particularity stubbornly asserted itself at the very moment when it was most actively discarded.

While there were a good many ways of shedding one's ethnic identity, Schatz singles out two, that of the "non-Jewish Jews" and that of the "Jewish Jews."[6] In giving up their Jewish particularity, the former most often exchanged it for Polish particularity. They insisted on speaking Polish instead of Yiddish, dropped Jewish customs for Polish ones, exchanged their names for Polish-sounding ones, intermarried. The motivation for these exchanges was mixed, with a dose of opportunism present in varying measures. But opportunism is far from telling the whole story, for these exchanges were also lived as an advance, away from narrow sectarianism, into the one humanity of the future.

A not negligible proportion of these Polonizing Jews did manage to merge into Polish culture. Nonetheless, many of them, despite themselves, retained their Jewish particularity. This was not simply a result of Polish antisemitism but of certain inescapable predilections. For instance, when these Polonizing Jews would "work the non-Jewish street"—that is, attempt to convince non-Jews of the truth of the communist vision—they managed to convince mostly other people like themselves—that is, other Polonizing Jews.[7] In the 1930's, when a great number of them spent time in Polish prisons along with communists of other nationalities, and the leveling of differences among groups was at its height, they retained their particularity as well, if for no other reason than that they were all literate, while their non-Jewish comrades often were not. In the intense study of communist doctrine that went on in those prison years, they appropriated texts in a manner reminiscent of their earlier Talmudic training. Besides, their very desire to lose their ethnic identity was more intense than that of their fellow communists.[8]

In the 1950's and 1960's, with the Communist Party in power and Polish Jewish communists in prominent positions, they nonetheless continued to exhibit traits that made them stand out: their lack of affinity for the connection between Polish culture and Catholicism, their greater internationalism, as opposed to Polish nationalism, to name just two such traits. Perhaps as a result, and in combination with other factors, they tended to socialize almost exclusively with other Polonized Jews,[9] thus constituting a group apart. Their universalism expressed itself in such a particular way that it left them, despite themselves, within a Jewish community.

At the other extreme (although, again, Schatz emphasizes that most people fell somewhere between the two) were Jews who wished to retain Jewish culture. This mainly meant keeping Yiddish as the chief vehicle of expression for Jews, and producing some sort of communist culture in that language. Jewish Jews most often "worked the Jewish street," addressing specifically Jewish circumstances. They were, however, just as universalistic in their aspirations as the Polonized Jews, which meant being strongly anti-Zionist and anti-Bundist, and having an identification primarily with the Communist Party, rather than with the Jewish people as such.

Twice in the course of the book, Schatz relates a saying illustrating how in this very identification with the Communist Party, the Jews managed to retain their particularity instead of losing it.[10] The saying that circulated was that a Pole could be a Pole and a communist. A Ukrainian could be a Ukrainian and a communist. But a Jew could only be a communist. In other words, Jewish internationalism singled the Jews out. This is not to say that Poles and Ukrainians did not consider themselves internationalists. However, in their case, they did not feel the need to stop speaking their native language or to change their names, for instance. Their ethnic identity did not pose itself as an obstacle of the same sort.

Schatz tells two anecdotes further illustrating the particularism of Jewish internationalism. The first is a joke, told after the disenchantment with Polish communism had definitely set in. It asks who would stay in Poland if the doors to emigration were opened. The answer is that only the Jews would stay, because they would want to prove that they weren't Zionists.[11] The second anecdote records a reply Trotsky made when asked whether he felt himself more of a Russian or a Jew: "No, you are wrong," he replied. "I am a Social Democrat and only that." Schatz comments by saying that this is the reply that Polish Jewish communists of the generation of 1910 would have given, except some of them would have uttered it in elegant Polish and others in Yiddish.[12]

These and other stories bring home, often in a humorous way, the inescapable particularity of Polish Jewish communists. Once again, we meet that quality of unchosenness so characteristic of embodiment. Something continues to inform a group of people—affinities, skills, desires—of which it is not in command. A final anecdote illustrates this, in a comical fashion, although it is presented in a fictional account from Hanna Krall's novel *The Subtenant.*

After World War II, many people, both Jews and non-Jews, joined the Polish Communist Party for the first time. The members of the generation Schatz is studying, who were, by this time, old-timers, had developed a slang of their own, born of their experience in the underground, in Polish prisons, and in Soviet work camps. The newer members were not always able to follow this lingo. But in one case, the inability to follow stemmed from a different source. An old-timer, a Polish Jew identified as "Wilus Sz.," gave "a rousing speech to the officers" in May 1945, declaring, "We have already dealt with Hitler . . . and now we say to the internal enemy: DAWKIE NO!—I beg your pardon, Captain, whispered an officer next to Bernard— what does it mean, Dawkie?[13] Could, then, Bernard answer that Wilus Sz. with only four classes of primary school in Tarnopol had problems in discerning Yiddish and Polish and that Dawkie meant something in Yiddish? No, Bernard could not say that, and so he answered—This is a kind of party term, from before the war.—I see—nodded the officer with understanding—How interesting."[14]

Of course, the particularism Schatz notices throughout the decades of Polish Jewish communist activity cannot be boiled down to a Yiddish word slipping in unawares. What slipped in unawares was a whole series of attitudes and inclinations. Nonetheless, it is this very slipping in unawares that is significant. Polish Jewish communist universalism retained its Jewish hue, not willfully, but because there is no universalism independent of a particular of which it is the expression.

Schatz does not deny that, given more time, Polish Jews would have assimilated into Polish culture. During the rising antisemitic attacks in the 1960's, the members of the generation of 1910 were, in fact, much more like their non-Jewish peers than ever before.[15] This was even truer of their children. Only the intensity of the antisemitic attacks of the later 1960's and the forced emigration of most of this group halted this trend. But had the trend continued, it would not erase the irony Schatz wishes to point out. Polish Jews would not have become universal. They would have become Polish.

If the above description of Schatz's book points to the importance of incarnation or embodiment as a key structuring element of his history, the following should indicate how the notion of hope shapes his material as well. The very subtitle of the work already points us in this direction: *The Rise and Fall of the Jewish Communists of Poland*. The story Schatz tells is indeed one of hopes dashed, of what he himself refers to as an existential defeat.[16] The people he studies yearned to transform the world, to transform it imminently. They were forced when most of them were in their sixties to acknowledge the utter failure of the work of their hands. Poland did not become a society in which all differences based on class, religion, and nationality disappeared. Polish Jews were forced to leave precisely because of the virulence of sentiments based on those differences.

True to one tradition of university scholarship, Schatz wishes to present the events that marked the lives of the generation of 1910 from within. That is, he wants to make the readers see their choices as the members of that generation saw them, to make them think in the categories they themselves used. From this perspective, he conveys the great pathos of this history, both in terms of broken individual lives and in terms of the tragic end of the collective existence of Jews in Poland. The defeat was indeed bitter on the level of individuals. Each, by 1968, after devoting his or her entire life to reforming Polish society, was forced to make a choice to emigrate, either to Israel or to a Western capitalist country. Rendered stateless, made to pay the Polish government for their children's education, and accused of conspiracies of all sorts,[17] these Polish Jews were obliged to seek asylum in the very countries whose regimes they had violently opposed, Israel as a narrow nationalism, the others as capitalist oppressors. On the collective level, the departure of Polish Jews from Poland in 1968, represented the end of a relationship between Jews and Poles that had endured for close to a millennium. They were the last Jews left in Poland. Antisemitism finally drove them out only a little over two decades after the mass killings of World War II.[18]

Given this description, it might be more accurate to speak of despair, or at least disabuse, when referring to Schatz's framework. But there is another dimension, evoking hope. We catch a glimpse of it in the introduction when Schatz explains why he is writing this study. It turns out that he is himself the son of people who belonged to the generation of 1910.[19] This cannot help but bring to mind an aspect of Péguy's secret of the man of 40.

It will be recalled that, when the man of 40 discovers that no one in the whole history of mankind has ever been happy (*"l'on* n'est pas heureux"), he nonetheless continues to hope for the happiness of his son, viscerally, unthinkingly, with his whole being. Also, although he knows he has been defeated, he searches obsessively in his son's eyes for the judgment that his son is passing on him. It is this latter aspect whose echo we find in Schatz's book. That is, the story he tells of his parents' generation, those Polish Jews who became staunch communists early and remained so until the end, can be interpreted, in fact, as an answer to that look. He recognizes his parents' failure, but that is not all he recognizes. This something else he means to convey along with the defeat is made clear in his introduction. He remarks that the history of Polish Jewish communism is most often passed over in silence, both by Jewish historians and general historians. In this silence, he finds the same kind of avoidance that characterized Jewish historiography of the nineteenth century regarding Sabbateanism.[20] The silence was both a sign of moral condemnation and of misjudgment as to the significance of that event. The same holds true, Schatz claims, for the neglect of Polish Jewish communists.

In countering the negative moral judgment, he does not wish to glorify the choices of the generation of 1910. He points out how often they had deceived themselves, blindly obeyed in order not to have to reevaluate their initial commitment to the Communist Party: the Russo-German pact, the betrayals and violence within the party, the increasing terror of the 1950's. Nonetheless, when evaluating the generation, he insists that the moral condemnation cannot be complete: "In my view, the moral lessons of the lives under study here carry great importance even for our time. Trusting that one can and should learn from history, with this book, I want to preserve part of this experience and make it available for reflection. *As my own sons and their peers read the story of this generation, I would like them to learn to dare to dream great dreams and never to accept humiliation* and, at the same time, never to be blinded by promises of total denouement and to treasure always common human decency."[21]

Thus, in viewing his parents' lives, he wants to save something from their defeat—their hope for a better world, a world in which human beings are no longer humiliated. In this sifting out of what is worth preserving, he rejoins their own judgment on themselves, as he reports it in his conclusion. Most of the surviving Polish Jewish communists, now scattered over the world, regret many of their past deeds and wish they had realized the corruption of the Communist Party and the fundamental impossibility of implementing their vision through it sooner.[22] Yet, Schatz cautions, the varying degrees of anticommunism most of them now express should not be misunderstood. "Their lives have forced them to realize the impossibility of the Communist vision, not its moral falsity."[23] This remark echoes his introductory comments. In both cases, something of what Péguy would call the mystique of communism, its thirst for justice, cannot simply be dismissed.

He also wishes his study to point to the significance of this generation's rise and fall. It points, he says, to "the general existential conditions of the human predicament. . . . Having been both active subjects in large processes of social and political change and passive objects of winds and forces over which they had no influence, they embody the moral and existential dilemmas of human beings confronted with the ballast of existing conditions and institutions, yet seized by blazing visions of the future."[24] The significance of this generation's rise and fall is, then, that it illuminate, not just the Jewish, not just the communist, not just the Polish, but the human condition. As particular as their history is, it speaks to similar rises and falls. Would it not, to refer back to Péguy, be one more poignant illustration of the fact that everything begins in mystique and ends in politique?

Schatz has doubtless never read Péguy. At least he does not list him in his ample bibliography. Yet in his work we find echoes of that same notion of hope, with its accent on defeat and yet of a certain invincibility within and above it. Polish Jewish communists failed miserably, but something of the hope that motivated them remains unsullied by their defeat. It is that which Schatz wishes to salvage while cataloguing the ruins. The book is dedicated to his parents, in Polish, in an otherwise English text.[25]

Protestants and Nazism: *'Lest Innocent Blood Be Shed'*

The second historical account I would like to juxtapose to Péguy's portrait of Bernard-Lazare, Philip Hallie's *Lest Innocent Blood Be Shed*, tells the story of Le Chambon, a Protestant village in the mountains of southern France that became a refuge for several thousand Jews, the safest place for them in Europe, during the Nazi occupation.[26] The Chambonnais sheltered, fed, hid these Jews, and helped transport some to Switzerland, at great risk to themselves. In recounting these events, Hallie bumps into what, after reading Péguy, one can recognize as incarnation or embodiment. It is not the same aspect of embodiment we found in Schatz's history. The latter illustrates something akin to Rosenzweig's emphasis—that is, a secret center manifesting itself in action and word, especially the most spontaneous of them, as in that Yiddish expression in the communist leader's speech. The aspect of embodiment detectable in Hallie's book more closely resembles what Levinas emphasizes: a responsibility toward the other, there before any choice to become responsible has occurred, evoked simply by another person's face. This responsibility manifests itself in action, before any reflection. Such, in fact, was the nature of Bernard-Lazare's goodness, coexisting with his intelligence but not resulting from it, overflowing, spontaneously responding to suffering. It is this sort of reaction to others, a doing before hearing, that Hallie singles out in the Chambonnais.

Before he begins their story, though, he notices a similar "doing before hearing" in himself. Having stumbled upon a brief description of the villagers' activities during the war, he found himself, to his surprise, crying. He views these involuntary tears, as he calls them, as an "expression of moral praise, pressed out of my whole personality, like the juice of a grape."[27] Moral praise, of course, implies a standard of good and evil. But, as he explains, he had to write the whole book in order to discover what that standard is. The intellect follows a choice made without it. Hallie is a professor of ethics. It is not as though he had never thought about the subject of good and evil. Yet, in the confrontation with the Chambonnais' actions, he found himself praising a goodness he did not yet grasp intellectually.

In focusing on the villagers' deeds, Hallie is at great pains to point out how unmediated their response to the persecuted people who sought refuge with them was by any theory. One of his great examples is Magda Grilli Trochmé, the wife of the spiritual leader of the village, its pastor, André Trochmé. A spiritual leader in her own right, she describes what drove her to give assistance to the numerous helpless people arriving at the presbytery:

I have a kind of principle. I am not a good Christian at all, but I have things that I really believe in. . . . I try not to hunt around to find things to do. I do not hunt around to find people to help. But I never close my door, never refuse to help somebody who comes to me and asks something. This I think is my kind of religion. When things happen, not things that I plan, but things sent by God or chance, when people come to my door, I feel responsible.[28]

It would appear from her words that she did act according to some theory, since she herself begins by saying she has a kind of principle. But this principle boiled down to responding to someone who knocked at her door. "Come in, and come in" was her standard reply. The face of another person in need evoked responsibility from her, and her principle was to affirm this responsibility. Her statement makes clear that in so doing she was not enacting a religious belief in the customary sense.[29] That is, it was not because she believed in God that she felt responsible to vulnerable human beings. Their very appearance called her responsibility into play.

Hallie tried at various points to get Magda Trochmé to explain why she felt responsible for these strangers. Invariably, she was impatient with this sort of question and at a loss as to how to answer it. After hearing what he interpreted as a lame reply, intended to brush the question aside, Hallie concludes: "We had reached the bedrock in her thinking; there was no way to go deeper; the spade had turned."[30] In other words, Magda had no theory for why she was responsible. Her reaction to others' needs was so primary that there was nothing underneath to explain it.

Magda Trochmé's understanding of responsibility as something too basic to require explanation characterized the community of Le Chambon as a whole. Often Hallie mentions how reluctant the surviving Chambonnais he interviewed were to label their actions good or unusual.[31] Their reluctance did not stem from a desire to appear humble but from the sheer taken-for-grantedness, in their own eyes, of what they did. What else could they have done? they asked. Who else was there to do it? In replying with such questions, they were thinking of the people knocking at their doors. In the help they extended, they were responding not to political ideologies but to human faces.

It might be tempting for the reader to speculate that the villagers' unwillingness to explain why they responded to the fleeing Jews in their midst was really due to a lack of sophistication. After all, these were not intellectuals. They may have been incapable of theorizing about responsibility. While most of the villagers were indeed not intellectuals, some were highly educated, the Trochmés among them.[32] But for Hallie, lack of intellectual sophistication is not at all the issue. Rather, he accounts for their unwillingness to theorize about their gestures of help by resorting to a philosophical category, "life-and-death ethics."

Life-and-death ethics did not come into play immediately in Le Chambon. During the early stage of the Vichy government, before the refugees started pouring in, the Chambonnais resisted, but on the basis of ideological opposition to the regime. André Trochmé led the villagers in not saluting the Vichy flag. He refused to ring the bells of the church at the command of the Vichy authorities. Hallie points out, however, that "it is one thing to resist a government and its National Revolution; it is another to face a shivering, terrified Jew on your doorstep."[33] Life-and-death ethics always has to do with the latter situation, confronting a concrete, flesh-and-blood human being. Good in this ethics is helping this human being. Evil is harming him or her. The help and the harm are also very concrete. Most often they involve either extending or withholding food and shelter.

In the early stages of the Occupation, then, the Chambonnais were not facing actual people standing before them. They were resisting government policies. In the later stages, although their help to the Jews was a very powerful form of resistance to Vichy, it was such resistance only as a by-product. Their behavior did not originate to counter decrees but to feed the human beings before them. It is this latter motivation that constitutes life-and-death ethics. Thus, the Chambonnais' reluctance to theorize about what they did does not indicate an intellectual lack but the fact that the compulsion to protect the vulnerable did not arise from anything else but that compulsion itself. To put it in Levinas's terms, the Chambonnais understood the priority of ethics over ontology.

Hallie is quite aware that the Chambonnais' succor of the Jews occurred within a tradition. They were a Protestant community that had suffered over 400 years of persecution by the French government. This history of persecution had habituated them to look askance at the authority of the state, of officialdom. They were practiced at distinguishing spiritual authority from that which imposes itself by force. In the years of the Occupation, it made them what Burns Chalmers, a Quaker who knew them, called a sturdy people, not easily confused by the high-sounding abstractions the Vichy government attached to its policies.[34]

For this Huguenot community, true authority always derived from the Bible. Faced with the increasing stream of refugees to the village, the two pastors, André Trochmé and Edouard Théis, emphasized the story of the Good Samaritan and the Sermon on the Mount as keys to the imitation of Christ. A small group of Chambonnais, the Darbystes, did not accept the institution of pastors. They saw no need for mediation in what they perceived as literal truth. The way one Darbyste welcomed a Jewish woman into her home reveals the way the Bible functioned in their midst:

Once, early in the Occupation, a German Jewish refugee came to a Darbyste farm to buy some eggs on the unrationed "gray" market of the distant farms. She was invited into the kitchen. Quietly the woman who invited her in asked with the light of interest in her eyes, "You—you are Jewish?"

The woman, who had been tortured for her Jewishness, stepped back trembling, and she became even more frightened when the farm woman ran to the steps leading upstairs and called up, "Husband, children, come down, come down."

But her fright disappeared when the woman added, while her family was coming down the steps, "Look, look, my family! We have in our house now a *representative of the Chosen People*."[35]

This Darbyste woman viewed the persecuted stranger at her door through a prism totally different from that of the Vichy government. The help she extended to the Jews was not to counter that government but to obey another authority. This was the case with the Huguenots of Le Chambon as a whole.

It seems difficult to reconcile this reliance on the biblical text with the claim, presented above, that in sheltering the Jews, the Chambonnais were not applying any theories, were merely responding to human faces. Was there not, after all, some prior ideology, be it, as in the case of the Darbystes, about the People of God? In addition, André Trochmé, the great pastor of the village, was a pacifist committed to nonviolent resistance. Is there a contradiction, then, between Hallie's emphasis on the Chambonnais' response as unmediated by any theory and his emphasis on the Protestant framework that informed their actions?

One way to reconcile this contradiction is to understand tradition as precisely that which shapes a people to act without the mediation of any theory. The New Testament passages on the Good Samaritan, the Sermon on the Mount, and the Old Testament history of the Jews' relation to God influenced people through constant exposure, over generations. Such familiarity molds not just reason, but the entire person, making possible spontaneity of behavior. For instance, the enactment of responsibility toward the vulnerable could become something that went without saying precisely because it had been said so often and enacted so often in the turbulent history of the Huguenots in France.

Hallie points to this untheoretical nature of religious tradition when he describes André Trochmé's frequent meetings with the thirteen leaders of the village, the *responsables*, who would in turn meet in small study groups with other parishioners. During these sessions, people prayed, studied the texts, and discussed the problems of the refugees. Describing these meetings, Trochmé stressed the fluidity of the relation between the biblical text and daily life. "It was there, not elsewhere, that we received from God solutions to complex problems, problems we had to solve in order to shelter and hide the Jews. . . . Nonviolence was not a theory superimposed upon reality; it was an itinerary that we explored day after day in communal prayer and in obedience to the commands of the Spirit."[36] In other words, the Bible did not contain an ideology everyone knew beforehand. It released its meaning at particular moments and in the context of particular activities. In that way, its authority did not function as a system to be enforced but as a series of illuminations, available only in particular circumstances.

It is true that Trochmé referred to nonviolence as something he and his responsables had already decided upon, describing it as "help to the unjustly persecuted innocents around me."[37] Earlier, Hallie speaks of Trochmé's nonviolence as an attitude toward people, not a carefully argued theological position.[38] That is, it was remarkably similar to his wife's feeling of responsibility when someone in need stood at her door: a reaction to preserve the life of a specific person, vulnerable and oppressed. Was this reaction primary or was it, in fact, mediated by the texts of the Bible? Trochmé's reminiscence about the meetings with the responsables seems to suggest that such a question is impossible to answer. The Chambonnais were *already* helping the refugees when they turned to the texts. But would they have started without those texts? By the time they resorted to the tradition, they were already in it.

In recognizing the influence of the Protestant tradition on the Chambonnais, Hallie therefore wants to present it, not as a series of dogmas, but as something at once more elusive and more all encompassing. It resembles Rosenzweig's way of speaking of Judaism not as a series of ideas or activities but as a secret center informing both thought and behavior in an unplanned way. It also resembles Péguy's description of the republican tradition informing not only politics but marriage, literature, education, all of life, in fact, operating at the level of an idea behind the head rather than of an argument—a mystique, in short.

In any case, Hallie is adamant about one thing. The Chambonnais' responsibility toward the Jews did not arise out of a logical sequence of ideas of which it was a conclusion. They simply accepted that they were responsible. This did not prevent them from deliberating about a great many details involving how to carry this responsibility out. But the fact of their responsibility remained outside these deliberations. This responsibility, there of itself, is key to understanding the significance of what happened in Le Chambon during World War II. The simplicity of its presence, rather than being the idiosyncrasy of peasant folk, is one of the signs of our humanity.

From the above, it becomes possible to glimpse how the notion of embodiment structures Hallie's history of Le Chambon. Embodiment in this context is not the making concrete of a previously held abstraction. It is a responsibility already in action by the time one notices it. Hallie is thus understandably worried that, in telling the story of Le Chambon, he will be substituting ethical theory for the deeds that took place there. At the beginning of his book, he already cautions his reader about this problem. "But I was not going to make Le Chambon an 'example' of goodness or moral nobility. I was not going to use this story to explain some abstract idea of ethics. Ends are more valuable than means: understanding this story was my end, my goal, and I was going to use the words of philosophical ethics only as a means for achieving this goal."[39]

He returns to the danger of losing the concreteness of the Chambonnais' acts in his conclusion as well. By this point, he has offered many reasons for why Le Chambon became a city of refuge—its location, its current pastors, its history. But these factors, while they explain many things, do not explain the particularity of the Chambonnais in their actions—a taken-for-granted responsibility, in need of no justification. To convey this gap between theoretical explanation and something that occurs without the mediation of any theory, he uses the analogy of opening and closing a door.

In physics, the analysis of forces is useful. For instance, one may break down the various forces at work upon a door and upon the frame in which it is hung in order to hang the door well. But analysis is not all there is. There is another aspect to the full reality of the well-hung, opening door. There is the experience, so ordinary perhaps as to be unnoticed, of simply opening and closing a door.[40]

Just as no knowledge of physics, no matter how accurate and how extensive, can convey the simplicity of opening a door, no knowledge as to causes of the Chambonnais' behavior during the Occupation can convey the simplicity of their responsibility. This simplicity sets the limit for theory. The most theory can do is to notice that there are areas beyond its jurisdiction.

In order to preserve the nontheoretically derived nature of the Chambonnais' gestures of help, Hallie makes a decision as to the form of his writing. He chooses narrative over philosophical exposition. Still, he occasionally interrupts his narrative to speculate on the philosophical meaning of this or that aspect of the Chambonnais' behavior. In the process, we are confronted with the fact of embodiment yet again, but from a different angle. The philosophical language he employs, like all philosophical language, means to convey a meaning derived from reason alone. It intends to present the villagers' standards as normative for human beings in general, as universal. Yet, when we examine his text, this universal standard seems to be the expression of a particular tradition.

The philosophical category Hallie makes use of most often to highlight the meaning of the Chambonnais' activities is one we have already encountered—life-and-death ethics. In one of his concluding chapters, he compares it to the classical ethics of the Western tradition. Like the latter, life-and-death ethics requires a restraint of the passions, an inner balance. Unlike them, however, he claims that in life-and-death ethics, this restraint, if it is not directed toward the preservation of the other person's life, is irrelevant. The preciousness of human life, manifested in activity to save it, is its heart, as opposed to self-control as such.[41]

In comparing ethical systems, Hallie occasionally intersperses allusions to the Bible, particularly the Hebrew Bible. The very title of his book, *Lest Innocent Blood Be Shed*, is a quotation from Deuteronomy 19:10: "I command you to this day to [protect the refugees] lest innocent blood be shed in your land . . . and so the guilt of bloodshed be upon you." This verse refers to the command the Israelites were given to establish three cities of refuge in the land of Israel to protect those who had committed involuntary manslaughter from those who wished to avenge it. Hallie interprets Le Chambon as offering itself as just such a city of refuge. The biblical text thus provides him with a model for understanding the Chambonnais' perceptions of the necessity of their actions.

Biblical references also occur elsewhere, within the body of the book. He explains, for instance, that life-and-death ethics is guided by both negative and positive commandments. To illustrate a negative commandment, he points to Exodus 20:13: "Thou shalt not kill."[42] This the Chambonnais certainly refused to do. But more was involved in their actions than merely refraining from doing something. They also obeyed positive commandments. The illustration is once again primarily from the Hebrew Bible, where the prophet Isaiah urges people to "seek justice, correct oppression; defend the fatherless, plead for the widow."[43] The Chambonnais not only kept from killing but also prevented others from killing by hiding people in their homes.[44]

In the chapter he calls Postlude, Hallie rebukes contemporary intellectuals for being afraid to make ethical judgments. He comes close to describing what Levinas calls the temptation of temptation, postponing a decision about good and evil until the reasoning process is complete, which itself depends upon amassing endless experience. Hallie draws a parallel between the urgency facing the Chambonnais, who had no time to deliberate over whether to help or not, the very delay costing lives, and the urgency we all face in declaring such action good. While no lives are immediately at stake in our case, if we do not recognize goodness when we see people saving innocent people we shall always have time to defer such decision when we ourselves are faced with an urgent situation. Modern intellectuals are so afraid of being duped that they are not afraid to be left morally adrift.[45] In his criticism of our unwillingness to let the intellect rest when it must, he quotes the following passage: "We are living in a time, perhaps like every other time, when there are many who, in the words of the prophet Amos 'turn judgment into wormwood'" (Amos 5:7).[46] Again the paradigm for the wrong relation between intellect and morality derives from the Bible.

The last paragraph of his book is a final explanation of life-and-death ethics. Ultimately, it is based on an awareness of the preciousness of human life, all human life. At this point, he quotes a central Jewish prayer, the Shema: "Shema, Israel, Adonoi Elohenu Adonoi Echod" (Hear, O Israel, the Lord our God, the Lord is One). He explicates this prayer as follows.

"For me, the word *Israel* refers to all of our anarchic-hearted human beings and the word *God* means the object of our undivided attention to the lucid mystery of being alive for others and for ourselves. When I need commentary on the Shema in order to understand its meaning in practical terms, I recall Rabbi Hillel's summary of his belief in the preciousness of life:

> If I am not for myself, who is for me?
> If I care only for myself, what am I?
> If not now, when?"[47]

These references to the Jewish tradition, more frequent toward the end of the text, should not obscure the fact that Hallie does not present himself as a speaker from within it. Rather, he speaks as a philosopher. It is clear from various details strewn throughout the book that he is at some remove from the Jewish tradition, at least in terms of practice.[48] The quotations I have alluded to should therefore not be interpreted as Hallie's attempt to establish the authority of what he says. They are not proof texts. What, then, is their function? No doubt, in most instances, they serve as illustrations for concepts elaborated independently of them. But why turn specifically there for illustrations? Perhaps independently derived ethics may not be so independently derived after all.

In any case, Hallie's juxtaposing of his philosophical ethics with biblical language invites a reading of the Bible as expressing a certain ethical norm, of which his book indicates the broad lines. It also invites us to see his work as a Jewish interpretation of Le Chambon. Would somebody who did not know the Shema, did not know Hillel, did not read the prophets in a certain light have focused on precisely what Hallie does in his telling of the Chambonnais' story? Thus the universal norm he extracts from these events is the expression of a particular tradition. Something of a Jewish frame, no matter how tenuous, is giving shape to the universal meaning. This particularity is a fundamental aspect of embodiment

If embodiment structures Hallie's history of Le Chambon in several different ways, so does the notion of hope. Hallie says so explicitly both in his introduction and in his conclusion. In the former, he relates how he came to write *Lest Innocent Blood Be Shed*. As already described, while doing other reading, he stumbled upon a short account of the Chambonnais and, to his surprise, found himself crying. Here it is important to mention what that other reading was. For a long time, for a projected study of ethics, he had been reading descriptions of the Nazi treatment of children in the concentration camps. The Chambonnais' story no doubt came to his attention because they were involved in saving children, having set up two children's schools for that purpose. One of them was discovered, and all the children were sent to death camps.[49]

Hallie describes the state into which he had fallen as a result of reading countless accounts of unspeakable cruelty. It involved the undermining of the possibility of goodness ("Across all these studies, the pattern of the strong crushing the weak kept repeating itself and repeating itself"),[50] accompanied by a sense of being trapped inside himself, unable to experience anything but anger or indifference toward his fellow human beings. "My study of evil incarnate had become a prison, whose bars were my bitterness toward the violent, and whose walls were my horrified indifference to slow murder. Between the bars and the walls I revolved like a madman. Reading about the damned, I was damned myself, as damned as the murderers, and as damned as the victims. Somehow over the years I had dug myself into Hell, and I had forgotten redemption, had forgotten the possibility of escape."[51]

Reading about the Chambonnais and becoming acquainted with them personally over a period of several years broke through what he himself refers to as his prison. His sense of estrangement from others disappeared: "Solitude, estrangement from our fellow human beings, is part of our lives, as it is part of all aware people in our time, but it is not the most important part of our lives."[52] He could once again affirm an unqualified good, which he calls the awareness of the preciousness of human life, manifested in acts such as those of the Chambonnais. This awareness was no longer suspect of being a mere pious sentiment; rather, it became what he calls "true north, from which we can take the bearings of our actions and passions."[53]

His last pages express, in a very moving way, his sense of community with others, centered around that "true north." That very sense of community, lost in his confrontation with the horrors of the concentration camps, is a sign of his reborn hope, making it possible, as he says, to teach his children about the preciousness of human life without lying.[54] The hope here as always involves an affirmation of something invincible in the midst of defeat.

In a very compressed way, this invincibility in the midst of defeat finds expression in Hallie's reflection on the Shema.[55] He mentions that, in focusing on the Shema, he is focusing on the very words Jews pronounced on their way to the gas chambers. The Shema, besides being a very important part of the daily liturgy, is also the prayer that the dying person recites. At the very least, its words are a proclamation of a reality that death does not conquer. Hallie, in making the "Hear, O Israel, the Lord our God, the Lord is One" his own is also affirming the reality of something that survived the death camps. That something is the connection with the vulnerable that those deaths were meant to sever. *Lest Innocent Blood Be Shed* was written to attest to the invincibility of that connection in the face of the terrible defeat it suffered.

Conclusion: Of Religion and Politics and the Historian's Craft

Reading these historical accounts in light of Péguy's history of the Dreyfus Affair should make us more keenly aware of the key place of religious motivation in political events. The religious motivations detected by Péguy, Schatz, and Hallie were not expressed through explicitly religious ideologies. We remember this from Péguy's portrait of Bernard-Lazare, whose prophetic stance coexisted with a positivistic metaphysic. We also see this in Schatz's *The Generation*, whose members, imbued with messianic thirst, prided themselves on their definitive break with all religion. In *Lest Innocent Blood Be Shed*, the situation might seem more complicated, since the Chambonnais clearly acted within the Protestant tradition. Yet Hallie's whole focus illuminates how nonideological this Protestantism was. That is, the Chambonnais did not hide Jews because they wanted to foil the Nazis or even because they wanted to follow a specific religious creed. They hid the Jews because they were at their doors and they could do nothing else. It is true, of course, that by helping Jews they were foiling the Nazis and acting within a certain explicit understanding of the Bible. But no doubt Hallie focuses on Magda Trochmé, the agnostic, so much at least in part to underline how little this was the immediate motivation.

How, then, do these authors identify the religious, if it does not appear in explicit garb—in religious vocabulary, church or synagogue attendance, proclamations of belief? All three point to the presence of something that slips in unawares, something unchosen, as key to the religious dimension motivating the people they are studying. In the case of Péguy, we need only recall his famous line about Bernard-Lazare as "that atheist, dripping with the word of God." That word of God revealed itself in Bernard-Lazare's visceral sense of responsibility to his people, although he himself did not perceive his continuity with his religious heritage. For Schatz what slipped in unawares into his Polish Jewish communists was messianic thirst, inherited in childhood and adolescence from a long tradition of prayer and memory. For Hallie, what slipped into the Chambonnais' deeds without being asked was responsibility to the vulnerable, present, as in Magda Trochmé's case, as soon as a needy person knocked on the door. This responsibility, Hallie states at the end of his book, is for him revelatory of God. The unchosen quality of what slips in is what I have throughout referred to as embodiment.

Although all three authors recognize embodiment as crucial, Péguy's claims about embodiment are broader than those of Schatz or Hallie and rest upon a Christian vision of history. For him, the embodiment visible in the Dreyfus Affair is typical of historical events as such. He posits that religious motivations, detectable precisely through that something that slips in unawares, are key to understanding the historical process. In other words, politics is always interpenetrated by religion. "*Everything* [emphasis added] begins in mystique and ends in politique." The Dreyfus Affair, far from being an exception, is, he says, an eminent example of religion in history. For Péguy, in order to make sense of events, one must be able to detect this religious dimension revealing itself within the fabric of people's deeds and words. Schatz and Hallie might not disagree with this view. But they do not make this claim, perhaps because their interests do not lie primarily in philosophy of history, which, as we know, was one of Péguy's main preoccupations.

The second difference between Péguy and the other two authors is Péguy's explicitly religious—explicitly Christian, that is—frame of reference. That is not to say that he first adheres to dogma, which he then applies to his analysis of events. It is a much more flexible interchange. The unspoken, unchosen, slipping-in-unawares quality at the heart of people's activities gives him a new sense of the meaning of incarnation, which had itself predisposed him to certain kinds of evidence. The eternal is understood to inhabit the temporal in such a way as to permeate it, suffuse it, so as to be, in a sense, indistinguishable from it. One key to distinguishing this presence, however, is hope, pointing to invincibility in the midst of defeat in an infinite variety of ways. Although both Schatz and Hallie consciously ground their work in a notion of hope, they do not ground this hope in an understanding of time and eternity, although Hallie's concluding remarks on the Shema may hint in that direction.

Of the two principles I have singled out in Péguy's philosophy of history—embodiment (or incarnation) and hope—it may not be so far-fetched to claim that the latter does find itself reflected in more contemporary scholarship than the former. That is, while the discovery of hidden religious continuities remains rare, are not most scholars attempting to retrieve something that survives the onslaught of time? Although scholars may do so without being aware of it, are they not within that unchosen contract Péguy talks about, bound to the people they are studying, who, leaving feeble traces, are like the slave women in Darius's palace, waiting for us to save them from permanent oblivion? If this is so, Péguy's work suggests some of the religious ground we stand upon when we interpret. Given his view of what motivates events, we, too, in our hope, become part of the historical stream. We do not stand outside it.

Appendixes

The Secret of the Man of Forty

The speaker in this passage, as in the rest of Péguy's *Clio—Dialogue de l'histoire et de l'âme païenne*, from which it is taken, is Clio, the Greek muse of history. Péguy alternates between calling her Clio and calling her History. Under either appellation, she is the one who addresses Péguy throughout the text. It is here that we get one of Péguy's explicit descriptions of hope.

Look, she said, at this man of 40. Maybe we know him, Péguy, our man of 40. Maybe we are beginning to know him. Maybe we are beginning to hear speak of him. He is 40, so he *knows*. The knowledge that no teaching can impart, the secret that no method can prematurely entrust, the knowledge that no discipline confers nor is able to confer, the teaching that no school can disseminate, he *knows*. Being 40, he has, in the most natural way in the world, to say the least, received news of the secret that is known by the most people in the world, but that is nonetheless the most hermetically kept. In the first place, he knows who he is. It could be useful. In the course of a life. He knows what Péguy is. He has even begun to know it, he had seen the first outlines of it, he received the first signs in his 33d, 35th, 37th year. Most especially he knows that Péguy is that little boy of 10 or 12 with whom he was so long acquainted, walking on the banks of the Loire. He knows also that Péguy is that ardent and somber and stupid young man, 18 or 20, with whom he was acquainted for several years, freshly landed in Paris. He knows also that immediately afterward began the period one would almost be forced to call, despite the aversion one has for this word, the period, in a certain sense, of a mask, of a *Persona*, of a deformation of the theater. He knows, finally, that the Sorbonne, and the École normale, and the political parties could rob him of his youth, but that they did not take away his heart. And that they could consume his youth but that they did not consume his heart. He knows, finally, he knows as well, that the entire inter-polated period does not count, does not exist, that it is an interpolated period and a period of the mask, and he knows it is over and will not return. And that fortu-nately death will come sooner. For he knows that in the past few years, since he has passed, since he has reached his 33d, 35th, 37th year, and that he has biennially passed them, he knows he has found who he is once again and that he has found himself being who he is, a good Frenchman of the ordinary variety, and toward God a believer and a sinner of the common sort. But finally and above all he knows he knows. For he knows the great secret, of every creature, the secret that is most universally known but that, nonetheless, has never been leaked, the preeminent se-cret of state, the secret that is the most universally entrusted, little by little, from one person to another, in a lowered voice, in the course of intimate conversations, in the privacy of confessions, on chance roadways, and, yet, the secret that is most hermetically secret. The container of secrets that is the most hermetically sealed. The secret that has never been written down. The most widely revealed secret, and that from the people of 40 has never passed, beyond the 37th, beyond the 35th, be-yond the 33d year, has never descended to the people below. He knows; and he knows he knows. He knows that *one* is not happy. He knows that ever since there has been man, no man has ever been happy. And he even knows it so deeply, and with a knowledge so deeply ingrained in the depths of his heart, that it perhaps, that it is surely, the only belief, the only knowledge he values, in which he feels and knows his honor to be engaged, precisely the only one in which there is no under-standing, no mask, no connivance. To say it outright, no adherence, no compli-ance, no *goodwill*. No obligingness. No goodness. Now, note the inconsistency. The same man. This man naturally has a son of 14. And he has but one thought, that his son should be happy. And he does not tell himself that it would be the first time; that this has yet to be seen. He tells himself nothing at all, which is the sign of the deepest thought. This man is or is not an intellectual. He is or is not a philosopher. He is or is not blasé. (Blasé from pain, the worst corruption.) He has an animal thought. Those are the best kind. Those are the only ones. He has only one thought. And it is an animal thought. He wants his son to be happy. He thinks only of this, that his son should be happy. He has another thought. He is preoccu-pied solely with the idea that his son (already) has of him; it is an idée fixe, an ob-session, that is, a siege, a blockade, a sort of scrupulous and consuming mania. He has only one concern, the judgment that his son, in the secret of his heart, will pass on him. He wants to read the future solely in the eyes of this son. He searches the depths of his eyes. That which has never succeeded, never happened, he is con-vinced will happen this time. And not only that, but that it will happen as if natu-rally and smoothly. As a result of some sort of natural law. And, history said, I say that nothing is as moving as this perpetual, this eternal, this eternally reborn in-consistency; and that nothing can disarm God more, and that is the common mir-acle of your young Hope. But, she said, suddenly stopping, here we come back to lands you have cleared forever.

The Tractate 'Shabbath,' pp. 88a–b

This is the Talmudic text upon which Levinas bases his interpretation of revelation in his essay "Temptation of Temptation" (in *Nine Talmudic Readings*, pp. 30–31).

"And they stopped at the foot of the mountain . . ." (Exodus 19:17).

Rav Abdimi bar Hama bar Hasa has said: This teaches us that the Holy One, Blessed be He, inclined the mountain over them like a tilted tub, and that He said: If you accept the Torah, all is well; if not, here will be your grave.

Rav Aha bar Jacob said: That is a great warning concerning the Torah. Raba said: They nonetheless accepted it in the time of Ahasuerus, for it is written (Esther 9:27): "The Jews acknowledged and accepted. They acknowledged what they accepted."

Hezekiah said: It is written (Psalm 76:9): "From the heavens thou didst utter judgment: the earth feared and stood still (calm)." If it was frightened, why did it stay calm? If it remained calm, why did it get frightened? Answer: First it was frightened and toward the end it became calm.

And why did the earth become afraid? The answer is provided by the doctrine of Resh Lakish. For Resh Lakish taught: What does the verse (Genesis 1:31) mean: "Evening came, then morning, it was the sixth day"? The definite article is not necessary. Answer: God had established a covenant with the works of the Beginning: If Israel accepts the Torah, you will continue to exist; if not, I will bring you back to chaos.

Rav Simai has taught: When the Israelites committed themselves to doing before hearing, 600,000 angels came down and attached two crowns to each Israelite, one for the doing, the other for the hearing. As soon as Israel sinned, 1,200,000 destroying angels came down and took away the crowns, for it is said (Exodus 33:6): "The children of Israel gave up their ornaments from the time of Mount Horeb."

Rav Hama bar Hanina said: At Horeb they adorned themselves, as was just said (ornaments to be dated from the time of Mount Horeb) and at Horeb they gave them up, according to our verse: "They renounced from the time of Mount Horeb."

Rabbi Johanan said: Moses deserved to keep them all, for it is said just afterward (Exodus 33:7): "Now Moses would take the tent."

Resh Lakish said: The Holy One, Blessed be He, will give us back the crowns in the future, for it is written (Isaiah 35:10): "Those redeemed by the Eternal One will come back thus and will reenter Zion singing, an eternal joy upon their head." Eternal joy—the joy from of old.

Rabbi Eleazar has said: When the Israelites committed to doing before hearing, a voice from heaven cried out: Who has revealed to my children this secret the angels make use of, for it is written (Psalm 103:20): "Bless the Lord, O His angels, you mighty ones, who do His word, hearkening to the voice of His word."

Rav Hama bar Hanina has said (Song of Songs 2:3): "Like an apple tree amidst the trees of the forest is my beloved amidst young men:" Why is Israel compared to an apple tree? Answer: to teach you that just as on an apple tree fruits precede leaves, Israel committed itself to doing before hearing.

A Sadducee saw Raba buried in study, holding his fingers beneath his foot so tightly that blood spurted from it. He said to him: People in a hurry, for whom the mouth passes before the ears, you always find yourselves in a state of headlong haste. You should have listened in order to know whether you were able to accept, and if you were not able to accept, you should not have accepted. Raba answered him: It is written about us who walk in integrity: "The integrity of the upright guides them"; about those who walk upon tortuous paths, it is written: "The crookedness of the treacherous destroys them" (Proverbs 11:3).

Supplementary Texts from *"Notre jeunesse"*

In these pages, Péguy speaks of the Dreyfus Affair as an eminent example of Christian and French mystique.

There is no doubt that for us the Dreyfusist mystique was not only a particular instance of the Christian mystique, but that it was an eminent instance of it, an acceleration, a temporal crisis, a sort of example and passage that I would say is necessary. How to deny it, now that we are twelve and fifteen years away from our youth and that at last we see clearly into our heart. Our Dreyfusism was a religion, [and] I am using the word in its most literally exact sense, a religious thrust, a religious crisis, and I would even strongly advise anyone who would want to study, consider, know a religious movement in modern times—well-defined, well-delimited, well cut out—to seize upon this unique example. I should add that for us, among us, in us this religious movement was Christian in essence, Christian in origin, that it grew from Christian ground, that it flowed from the ancient source. We can today be our own witness to this. The Justice and the Truth that we so loved, to which we gave everything, our entire youth, everything, to which we gave ourselves wholly during our entire youth, were not conceptual truths and justices, they were not dead justices and truths, they were not justices and truths from books and for libraries, they were not conceptual, intellectual truths and justices, justices of the intellectual party, but they were organic, they were Christian, they were in no way modern, they were eternal and not only temporal, they were Justices and Truths, *a living* Justice and *a living* Truth. And of all the feelings that together pushed us, shaken up, into that unique crisis, today we can admit that of all the passions that pushed us into that heat and into that caldron, into that swelling up and into that tumult, one virtue was at the center and it was the virtue of charity. And I do not want to reopen an old debate today, now in the past, but in our enemies, on the side of our enemies, on the side of our then adversaries, historical like us, who have become historical, I see much intelligence, even much lucidity, much sharpness: what strikes me most is surely a certain lack of charity. I do not want to anticipate what is proper to *confessions*. But it is unquestionable that there was infinitely more Christianity in all our socialism than in all of [the Paris churches] St. Madeleine, St. Pierre de Chaillot, St. Philippe du Roule, and St. Honoré d'Eylau put together. It was essentially a religion of temporal poverty. Therefore, it is assuredly the religion that will be least celebrated in modern times. Infinitely the least observed. We have been marked by it so harshly, so ineradicably, we have been stamped by it so harshly, so indelibly that we shall remain marked by it for our whole temporal life, and for the other. Our socialism was never either a parliamentary socialism or the socialism of a rich parish. Our Christianity will never be a parliamentary Christianity or the Christianity of a rich parish. From then onward, we received such a vocation for poverty, even for misery, so deep, so internal, and simultaneously so historical, so factual, so eventful that we have never been able to pull ourselves out of it since, and I am beginning to think that we shall never be able to pull ourselves out of it.

It is a kind of vocation.

A destiny.

What could have deceived people is that all the *political* forces of the Church were against Dreyfusism. But the political forces of the Church have always been against mystiques. Especially against the Christian mystique. It is the most conspicuous application there has ever been of that general rule we established above.

It could even be said that the Dreyfus Affair was a *beautiful example* of religion, of a religious movement, of the beginning, of the origin of religion, a rare example, perhaps a unique example.

Lastly, the Dreyfusist mystique was for us essentially a crisis of the French mystique. This affair was for us and through us very specifically within the French line. As it had been very specifically for us and through us within the Christian line. We ourselves were very specifically within the French line as we were very specifically within the Christian line. We were of French quality as we were of Christian quality.

We exhibited properly French virtues, qualities, the virtues of the race: a straightforward valor, speed, good humor, constancy, firmness, a stubborn courage, but within measure, within good form, at once fanatical and balanced, at once driven and completely reasonable; a gay sadness, which is particular to the French; a set purpose; a resolve both warm and cold; a being-at-ease and a being aware; at once a docility and a constant revolt against events; an organic impossibility to consent to injustice, to resign oneself to anything. A knife-sharp quickness; the keenness of a sword thrust. It must simply be said that we were heroes. And more specifically heroes in the French style. (The proof of it is that we never recovered from it, that we never left it behind.) (Perhaps we'll be reservists all our lives.) One must, in fact, see clearly how the question presented itself. The question was never, for us, to know whether Dreyfus was innocent or guilty. But to know whether we would or would not have the courage to have him declared, to have him be known as, innocent.

In the following pages, Péguy posits that economic conditions in the modern world are such that they dim the difference between Jews and Christians by comparison with class differences. These pages again evince his fight against antisemitism.

Antisemites speak of Jews. I am warning you that I am about to utter something shocking: ANTISEMITES DO NOT KNOW THE JEWS. They speak about them but they don't know them. They [the Jews] seem to make them suffer, very much, *but they don't know them*. Rich antisemites may know rich Jews. Capitalist antisemites may know capitalist Jews. Antisemite businessmen may know Jewish businessmen. For the same reason I only know poor Jews and destitute Jews. There are many of them. There are so many that we don't know the number. I see them everywhere.

It shall not be said that a Christian has not borne witness for them. It shall not be said that I have not borne witness for them. Just as it shall not be said that a Christian has not borne witness for Bernard-Lazare.

For 20 years, I have put them to the test, we have put each other to the test mutually. I have always found them loyal as much as anyone, affectionate, reliable, with a tenderness all their own, matching anyone's, with an attachment, a devotion, an unshakable respect, a fidelity that passes all tests, a really mystical friendship, an unshakable attachment, an unshakable fidelity to the mystique of friendship.

Money is everything, dominates everything in the modern world, to such a degree, so entirely, so totally that the social separation between rich and poor has become infinitely more important, more dividing, more absolute, in a manner of speaking, than the vertical separation of race between Jews and Christians. The harshness of the modern world to the poor, against the poor, has become so complete, so frightening, so blasphemous to both the ones and the others, against the ones and the others.

In the modern world, acquaintanceships are made, are propagated only horizontally, the rich among themselves, or the poor among themselves. Across horizontal layers.

Poor, I shall bear witness for poor Jews. In our common poverty, in our common misery, for 20 years, I have found them of unshakable reliability, loyalty, devotion, solidity, with a mystical attachment, a respect for friendship. They are all the more virtuous in that at the same time, in addition to what the rest of us face, they have to struggle endlessly against the accusation, against the charges, against the calumnies of antisemitism, which are precisely all the accusations to the contrary.

What do we see. For in the end one must speak only of what one sees, one must tell only of what one sees; what do we see. In that forced labor of the modern world, I see them rowing at their bench, as much or more than others, as much and more than us. As much and more than us experiencing the common fate. In that temporal hell of the modern world, I see them like us, as much and more than us, wearing themselves out! Sorely tried like us! Exhausted like us. Overworked like us. In sickness, in tiredness, in depression, in all the overwork, in that temporal hell, I know hundreds, I see thousands who with as much difficulty, with more difficulty, make their miserable living in more misery than us.

In that common hell.

About the rich there would be much to say. I know them much less well. What I can say is that in 20 years, I've passed through many hands. The only one of my creditors who behaved with me, not only like a usurer, but in a manner a little beyond this, like a creditor, like a usurer from Balzac, the only one of my creditors who has treated me with Balzac-like harshness, with the harshness, the cruelty of a usurer from Balzac, was not a Jew. He was a Frenchman. I'm embarrassed to say it, one is embarrassed to say it, he was, alas, a "Christian," a millionaire 30 times over! *What would they not have said if he were Jewish.*

To what degree do their rich help them? I suspect that they help them a bit more than our rich help us. But perhaps they should not be reproached with this. This is what I said to a cheerful young antisemite—but who listens to me—in a form that I allow myself to think of as striking. I said to him: *But think of it in the end.* IT IS NOT EASY TO BE JEWISH. *You are always making them contradictory reproaches. When their rich do not support them, when their rich are harsh, you say:* IT'S NOT SURPRISING, THEY ARE JEWS. *When their rich do support them, you say:* IT'S NOT SURPRISING, THEY ARE JEWS. THEY MUTUALLY SUPPORT EACH OTHER. But, my friend, rich Christians have only to do the same. We do not prevent rich Christians from supporting us.

The following passages bring to light Péguy's references to Bernard-Lazare in "Notre jeunesse" that are not part of the central portrait. They occur later in the text.

In the first passage, Péguy reads the daily papers and combs them in the way that he has described Bernard-Lazare as combing them, alighting on references to persecutions of Jews in the midst of other news. The second passage makes available Péguy's reflections on Alfred Dreyfus. Péguy considered that Dreyfus did not live up to the great role that history had thrust upon him. By joining with some of the politicking maneuvers of the radicals and socialists, he had betrayed the Dreyfusard cause in Péguy's estimation.

Passage 1

Here is exactly what I want to say about Bernard-Lazare. In *Le Temps* of Friday, May 27, 1910, I read this simple headline, in the small print of the latest news: *Latest news—The expulsion of the Jews from Kiev—Saint Petersburg, May 26—The Kiev authorities have proceeded to expel 1,300 Jewish families, condemned by a recent circular of the Ministry of the Interior to leave the city—The misery of the expelled is very great.* (Havas) —What is poignant in this dispatch is not only its dryness and brevity. It is to what degree such dispatches go unnoticed today. What I want to say is that under Bernard-Lazare they did not go unnoticed.

Passage 2

This tragic situation [Dreyfus's weakness] reminds me of something Bernard-Lazare said. One must go back, one always comes back to something Bernard-Lazare said. These words will be the decisive words of the affair. Since they come from its greatest prophet and have bearing on its very victim. They are thus the high points both through their origin and through their destination. *Bernard-Lazare, born in Nîmes, June 14, 1865; died in Paris, September 1, 1903.* He was thus 38 years old. Because a man wears eyeglasses, because he wears a transverse pince-nez cutting off a fold of nose before two round eyes, the modern thinks he is a modern, the modern does not know how to see, does not see, does not know how to recognize the antiquity of that prophetic look. This was the time when, meeting Maurice Montégut, he would say. Montégut's stomach hurt, like everyone else's, like that of every other poor intellectual mercenary. And he too thought that his stomach hurt like everyone else's. He would say to Montégut: *Hey, Montégut,* laughing, for he was deeply light-hearted, internally light-hearted: *So, Montégut, everything's all right before eating a meal, when there is nothing in the stomach. One feels light. One works. But afterward. One should never eat.* Dreyfus had just come back. Dreyfus had just returned and almost instantly during the first procedures, during the first negotiations, during the first contact, everyone suddenly had the impression that there was something wrong, that this wasn't it, that he was the way he was, and not the way we had dreamt him. Some were already complaining. Some, in an undertone, soon publicly accused him. In an undertone, publicly, Bernard-Lazare defended him. Harshly, obstinately, tenaciously. With that admirable voluntary blindness of those who truly love, with that stubborn invincible tenacity with which love defends a being who is wrong, obviously wrong, publicly wrong.—*I don't know what they want,* he would say, laughing but not laughing, laughing on the outside but not laughing on the inside. *I don't know what they're asking for. I don't know what they want from him. Because he has been unjustly condemned, they want everything of him, he must have all the virtues.* HE IS INNOCENT, THAT IS ALREADY A LOT.

Reference Matter

Notes

Preface

1. The word *jeunesse* as Péguy uses it in this essay means, not young people as a group, but youth, as opposed to old age. In his translation of part of this essay (in Péguy, *Temporal and Eternal*, pp. 19–87), Alexander Dru renders "Notre jeunesse" as "Memories of Youth," but I have chosen to retain the French title. Since "Notre jeunesse" has never been translated into English in its entirety, the interested reader can only find it under its French name.

2. See, e.g., Péguy's essay "Zangwill," in *Oeuvres en prose complètes*, 1:1396–1451, or his essays *Clio—Dialogue de l'histoire et de l'âme charnelle* (hereafter cited as Clio 1) and *Clio—Dialogue de l'histoire et de l'âme païenne* (hereafter cited as Clio 2), in *Oeuvres en prose complètes*, 3:594–783 and 997–1214.

Chapter 1

1. One of the more common misunderstandings of Péguy's work rests on the appropriation of his thought by the Vichy government during World War II. Although the Resistance also claimed him as a source of inspiration, the image of him that seems to have stuck the most is that of a nationalist and of a Christian of simple faith. This has been reinforced by the selections of his work chosen for the *lycée* curriculum. This commentary places itself among the many works that have attempted to correct that image. I would like to cite two in particular with which it is most in sympathy, Pie Duployé's *La Religion de Péguy* and Alain Finkielkraut's

Le Mécontemporain. Both these authors present Péguy's thinking in its coherence and relevance to current concerns.

2. There is hardly a study of Péguy that does not pause, at least briefly, to reflect on these idiosyncrasies: repetition, huge quotations, punctuation peculiarities of many sorts, including the frequent absence of paragraph breaks. François Mauriac reflected the views of many Frenchmen when he remarked, upon hearing that Péguy was about to be translated into English, that he should first be translated into French (Péguy, *Temporal and Eternal*, trans. Dru, p. 7). More recently, Péguy has begun to draw a literary criticism much more appreciative of his style. For reflections on the significance of repetition in his writings, see Deleuze, *Différence et répétition*, although Deleuze rarely closely analyzes any specific text. For appreciative analyses of other dimensions of his style, see Dadoun, *Éros de Péguy*. See also the five volumes of essays edited by Simone Fraisse in the *Revue des Lettres Modernes*, most particularly, *Charles Péguy 3: Un Romantique malgré lui* and *Charles Péguy 5: L'Écrivain*.

3. The size of Péguy's oeuvre is truly impressive, running to nearly 4,500 pages of very small print in the new Pléiade edition of his prose alone. George Steiner, in his review of the third volume of this collection, remarked that "the material productivity of the man has few parallels in the history of literature; thousands of pages of verse and prose pouring from that famous steel-nibbed pen, often day and night" (Steiner, "Drumming on the Doors," p. 3).

4. Two essays argue this point in very different ways. See David A. Hollinger, "Post-Ethnic America," *Contention* 2, no. 1 (Fall 1992): 84–86, and Arthur Hertzberg, "Is Anti-Semitism Dying Out?" *New York Review of Books* 40, no. 12 (June 24, 1993): 51, 54, 55, 57.

5. I can think of no more profound thinker on this subject than the contemporary French Jewish philosopher Emmanuel Levinas (1906–95), whose work has inspired this commentary in ways too numerous to note here. See Chapter 3 for a glimpse into his thought.

6. See, e.g., the early "Pierre, commencement d'une vie bourgeoise," written in 1899 and published posthumously, as well as the much later "Victor-Marie Comte Hugo," originally published in Péguy's fortnightly *Les Cahiers de la Quinzaine* (hereafter cited as *Cahiers*) in 1910. Both can now be found in the new Pléiade edition, the first in *Oeuvres en prose complètes*, 1:145–87, and the second in, ibid., 3: 168–203.

7. The French philosopher and novelist Julien Benda (1867–1956), known as a defender of reason and intellect against intuitionism, was a philosophical opponent of Henri Bergson, whom Péguy considered one of his masters. Péguy once expressed his understanding of the opposition between them as being the opposition between the Alexandrian and Talmudic strains in Jewish thought. It was over one of Benda's novels, *L'Ordination* (1912), published in *Cahiers*, that Péguy broke with Georges Sorel (see Chapter 2, n. 17). Today, Benda is best known for his book *The Treason of the Intellectuals* (1927), in which he attacked many contemporary intellectuals for betraying their calling by politicizing thought. To the dismay of many people at the time, he included Péguy among the betrayers. See Finkielkraut, *Le Mécontemporain*, p. 16.

8. By *pulta* Péguy means the *puzta*, grazing land in Hungary.

9. *Tchernosium* refers to the very fertile soil of the steppes of southern Russia.

10. Péguy, "Note conjointe sur M. Descartes et la philosophie cartésienne," in *Oeuvres en prose complètes*, 3:1296–97.

11. Bergson and Péguy knew each other personally. Bergson once said of Péguy that the latter understood him better than he had understood himself. Péguy, in later years, reproached Bergson for no longer reading him. In a letter written in February 1914, he says, "You never suspected the pain you caused me the day you told me that you no longer had time to read me. I agreed to everything, to 20 years of growing misery and solitude, as long as I was read by three or four, among whom you were the first. Today, I work inside a grave and you do not even accompany in thought what passed from you to me" (quoted in Robinet, *Péguy entre Jaurès, Bergson et l'église*, p. 220; my translation). At the outset of the war, Bergson promised Péguy that he would take care of his family if he died in battle, and he fulfilled his promise.

12. Various questions regarding both the founding and the nature of the journal are discussed in *Charles Péguy 2: Les Cahiers de la Quinzaine*, ed. Fraisse. See also Robert Burac, "Avertissement," in *Oeuvres en prose complètes*, vol. 1, esp. pp. xv–xxxvi.

13. There are many references to Péguy's socialism in the secondary literature about him. See, e.g., Itterboek, *Socialisme et poésie chez Péguy*. The best sources, however, remain his own early writings, "De la cité socialiste" and "Marcel: Premier dialogue de la cité harmonieuse," in *Oeuvres en prose complètes*, 1:34–40, 55–117. In fact, many of the essays collected in this first volume of Péguy's prose writings reflect his socialist vision. See also Péguy's play *Jeanne d'Arc*, written at the height of his socialist involvements. In "Notre jeunesse," there are intermittent passages describing his socialism (see pp. 96–101).

14. "A nos amis, à nos abonnés," in *Oeuvres en prose complètes*, 2:1276.

15. On the novelist, essayist, and dramatist Romain Rolland (1866–1944), see Chapter 2, n. 37.

16. Some of Péguy's most famous writings on the economic plight of the common man occur in "De Jean Coste," in *Oeuvres en prose complètes*, 1:1011–58, where he makes the distinction between misery and poverty. See also his outcry on the impossible financial conditions of the *Cahiers* in "A nos amis, à nos abonnés," in ibid., 2:1268–1315, and his comments in "L'Argent," in ibid., 3:745–847.

17. Péguy had been trained as a typesetter in 1895 during a leave from his studies at the École normale supérieure. Steiner ("Drumming on the Doors," p. 3) draws attention to the care he took with the physical appearance of the *Cahiers*, observing, "No minutiae of typography, of binding, of the choice of paper, left him indifferent."

18. Péguy actually began work on a doctoral thesis that, if accepted, would have entitled him to a teaching position in higher education. An uncompleted essay, "De la situation faite à l'histoire dans la philosophie générale du monde moderne" (in *Oeuvres en prose complètes*, 2:1053–1267) resulted from this endeavor. Other essays with very similar preoccupations, such as "De la situation faite à l'histoire et à la sociologie dans les temps modernes" and "De la situation faite au parti intel-

lectuel dans le monde moderne devant les accidents de la gloire temporelle" (both in ibid.), testify to Péguy's long-term reflection on the projected topic of his thesis, the place of history in modern intellectual life. The shorter, complementary thesis required for the doctorate was to have been on typography.

19. Péguy had previously invested his wife's dowry and some of his mother-in-law's money in his initial enterprise, a socialist bookstore and publishing house. The money was eventually reinvested in the *Cahiers*, his life's work.

20. The hierarchy of the Catholic Church wanted to restore the monarchy, allying itself with the Right, which had attempted several times to overthrow the government of the Third Republic by force. During the Dreyfus Affair, as is well known, the Church's overwhelming support went to the anti-Dreyfusards. The Third Republic's reprisals against the Church under the Waldeck-Rousseau and Combes governments (see Chapter 1, n. 89, and Chapter 2, nn. 22–25, below) are part of the context in which Péguy's terms *mystique* and *politique* take on their meaning.

21. The whole family was baptized after Péguy's death. See Villiers, *Charles Péguy: A Study in Integrity*, p. 370.

22. It is often reported that Péguy did attend mass shortly before his death at the front, for the first time since his childhood; see Rondeau, "Péguy, la colère," p. 66. Péguy's devotional poems can be found in his *Oeuvres poétiques complètes*. On Péguy's relationship to the Church, both before and after his return to Christianity, see also Bastaire, *Péguy l'inchrétien*.

23. For a commentary on these poems and some quatrains missing from the original Pléiade edition, see Sabiani, *La ballade du coeur*.

24. Clio 1 and Clio 2 are cited in the Preface, n. 2, above.

25. I am giving English titles for works that have been translated, retaining the French titles for those that have not. *Le Porche du mystère de la deuxième vertu*, first translated as *The Portico of the Mystery of the Second Virtue* (1970) has been translated again as *The Portal of the Mystery of Hope* (1996).

26. The two most recent biographies of Bernard-Lazare are Nelly Wilson's *Bernard Lazare* and Jean-Denis Bredin's *Bernard Lazare*. Two doctoral dissertations have also been devoted to him: Léon Chouraqui, "Contribution à la connaissance de la pensée littéraire, morale et politique de Bernard Lazare," and Jean Guillon, "Bernard Lazare." The earliest biography is that by Baruch Hagani, *Bernard Lazare*.

27. Bredin, *Bernard Lazare*, p. 29. On the École pratique des hautes études, see also Chapter 2, n. 8. Baruch Hagani, Bernard-Lazare's earliest biographer, explains his interest in these subjects as a result of his involvement in the symbolist movement. Religious texts are, after all, replete with myths, allegories, and images. See Hagani, *Bernard Lazare*, p. 8.

28. Bernard-Lazare, *Antisemitism*, p. 9.

29. Ibid., p. 14.

30. Ibid., pp. 141–48.

31. Bernard-Lazare, *Le Fumier de Job . . . suivi de Hannah Arendt, Herzl et Lazare* (1990), p. 59. This book appears to be the first publication of all the notes Bernard-Lazare had collected in view of writing a history of the Jews. Before his death, he had asked two of his friends to publish them. This was not done. Several

decades later, one of Bernard-Lazare's brothers, Edmond Bernard, selected some of them, which appeared in 1928 as *Le Fumier de Job*, edited by Edmond Fleg. Hannah Arendt subsequently chose an even smaller number of excerpts from the earlier book and published them in 1948 as *Job's Dungheap*. The current French edition differs from both the earlier French version and from the English translation. It is a much more complete collection of Bernard-Lazare's unpublished thoughts than either, and the selection of published essays appended at the end of the book is not the same as in the book published by Arendt. Arendt had written on Bernard-Lazare a few years prior to her introduction in *Job's Dungheap*. For her, he was one of four figures in modern times who "really did most for the spiritual dignity of their people, who were great enough to transcend the bounds of nationality and to weave the strands of their Jewish genius into the general texture of European life" ("Jew as Pariah," p. 99).

32. Bernard-Lazare, *Fumier* (1990 ed.), p. 95. (All subsequent references to *Fumier* are to the 1990 edition.)

33. Theodor Herzl and Bernard-Lazare knew each other. The latter, in fact, attended the Second World Zionist Congress in 1898, only to break with Herzl in 1899. Some of the differences between them are captured in a letter Bernard-Lazare addressed to Herzl in February 1899 (quoted in Bredin, *Bernard Lazare*, p. 315), which I translate in part as follows:

> I have for a long time held opinions, ideas, thoughts, tendencies radically opposed to those that guide you, my dear friend, and that guide the action committee. You are bourgeois in thought, bourgeois in feeling, bourgeois in ideas, bourgeois in social conception. Being such, you want to guide a people, our people, which is a people of the poor, of the unfortunate, of proletarians. You can only do so in an authoritarian way, by wishing to lead them toward what you consider to be good for them. You thus act without them, above them: you want to lead a herd. Before creating a people, you create a government, acting financially and diplomatically, and thus, like all governments, you are at the mercy of your financial or diplomatic failures. . . . Your error is to have wanted to make a bank the motor of your enterprise; a bank can never be, will never be a means for national rehabilitation.

Bernard-Lazare wanted a cultural and educational renewal before the creation of political structures as such. See also Nelly Wilson, *Bernard Lazare*, p. 230.

34. This is one of the reasons given by Nelly Wilson, *Bernard Lazare*, pp. 93, 96, 97. In his *Politics of Assimilation*, p. 169, Marrus also gives this explanation, along with several others, including the Romantic influence of Maurice Barrès, making the younger generation interested in its national patrimony, and Bernard-Lazare's anarchist views (pp. 173, 174).

35. Several commentators, even those most sympathetic to Bernard-Lazare, do not hesitate to call his earliest stance on the Jews antisemitic. See Prajs, *Péguy et Israel*, p. 72; Nelly Wilson, *Bernard Lazare*, p. 10. Bernard-Lazare's early writings are especially hostile to non-French Jews. He characterizes those of Algeria, for instance, as sordid usurers, worthy only of contempt (Wilson, *Bernard Lazare*, p. 76).

His thought continues to stir controversy among Jews themselves, as evidenced by the heated discussion around the reissuing of his work. See Alain Finkielkraut, "Le Détournement d'un prophète," *Le Monde*, Feb. 19, 1982: 16; Arnold Mandel, "Bernard Lazare extérieur à lui-même," *Information juive* 34, no. 11 (Jan. 1982): 12; and Pierre Vidal-Naquet, "Relire Bernard Lazare," *Esprit* 66 (June 1982): 174–75. And see also the French translation of Nelly Wilson's *Bernard Lazare*, an expanded version of the English original, in which she reacts to this discussion (on pp. 154–58).

36. "To say that Péguy knew the Jews is to say little: he knew them as Jews. He even often rediscovered in them the Judaism they seemed no longer to remember" (Prajs, *Péguy et Israël*, p. 36; my translation). For an overview of some of Péguy's friendships with Jews, see Viard, "Prophètes d'Israël et annonciateur chrétien," pp. 334–44. See also Rabi, "Israël," pp. 332–42, and Lévy, "Mes souvenirs de Charles Péguy," pp. 1–7. Marrus claims that in the 1890's, there were only 500 Orthodox Jews left in all France, most of them eastern European immigrants (*Politics*, p. 39). This may go some way toward explaining the paucity of observant Jews in Péguy's entourage.

On a related but different issue, there is controversy among scholars about the extent of Péguy's knowledge of the Jewish tradition itself. Prajs, *Péguy et Israël*, p. 113, suggests that he was familiar with an array of Jewish texts made available to him by his observant Jewish friend Edmond-Maurice Lévy, but claims, on the other hand, that Péguy did not really know the Old Testament, including the prophetic texts, firsthand (ibid., p. 181). Duployé makes the same claim in *Religion de Péguy*, p. 427. Both Lévy, "Souvenirs," p. 2, and Rabi, "Israël," p. 338, claim that Péguy did know the Old Testament (although knowing the Old Testament would not in itself constitute being familiar with the Jewish tradition). The issue becomes relevant when one tries to understand what it was that Péguy saw when he saw the Jewish spirit of his nonobservant Jewish friends. Did he see the Jewish tradition in one of the ways in which it sees itself? I believe he saw the Jewish tradition in one of the ways in which the Christian tradition sees it. That does not mean, however, that he did not grasp anything real in it.

37. The recent consensus among scholars seems to be that the close personal relationship between Péguy and Bernard-Lazare dated back to 1901, although Péguy had begun to read Bernard-Lazare as early as 1897. See Péguy, *Notre jeunesse*, ed. Bastaire, pp. 27–28. See also Nelly Wilson, "L'Amitié de Péguy et de Bernard-Lazare," pp. 5–6.

38. Bernard-Lazare, *Fumier*, p. 39; id., *Contre l'antisémitisme* (1983), p. 43.

39. Bernard-Lazare, *Fumier*, p. 45.

40. Bernard-Lazare, *Antisemitism*, pp. 141–62.

41. Ibid., pp. 172–74; Bernard-Lazare, *Contre l'antisémitisme* (1983), p. 58.

42. That Péguy is standing within the Christian tradition in "Notre jeunesse" is evident from the text as a whole. But he also makes one specific explicit reference to speaking as a Christian, worth reproducing here, as it occurs later in the essay and thus is not part of the portrait of Bernard-Lazare proper: "It shall not be said that a Christian has not borne witness for them [the Jews]. It shall not be said that I have not borne witness for them. Just as it shall not be said that a Christian has not borne witness for Bernard-Lazare" (in *Oeuvres en prose complètes*, 3:134).

43. For a discussion of the changes in Christian perspectives on Judaism, see Manuel, *Broken Staff*, p. 181, who claims that in the seventeenth and eighteenth centuries, Christian apologetics switched to stressing the prophetic tradition, rather than miracles, as proofs of the authenticity of Christianity. Most of the Western Jews referred to as Liberal or Reformed expressed the essence of Judaism as universalism and messianism and derived it from prophetic teachings. See, e.g., Samuel Holdheim or Hermann Cohen in *Jew in the Modern World*, ed. Mendes-Flohr and Reinharz, pp. 184–87, 573–74.

44. One of Péguy's key rethinkings of his relation to Renan occurs in his essay "Zangwill." See also Winling, *Péguy et Renan*, and Fraisse, "Péguy et Renan."

45. Renan, *Identité originelle et séparation graduelle du judaïsme et du christianisme*, p. 12; id., *Le Judaïsme comme race et comme religion*, p. 7. Renan's classic work on the question was a five-volume study entitled *Histoire du peuple d'Israël* (1887–95).

46. James Darmesteter, *Les Prophètes d'Israël*, p. xiii.

47. "But among the Germans, there was never anyone who stood up for the misunderstood geniuses who were Jews. Nothing in German literature corresponds to those unforgettable pages, in which Charles Péguy, the French Catholic, portrayed Bernard-Lazare as a true prophet of Israel" (Scholem, *On Jews and Judaism in Crisis*, p. 87). Earlier in the same essay, he had said that no non-Jew had understood better than Péguy the Jews' desire to break away from their tradition (ibid., p. 82).

48. Finkielkraut, *Le Mécontemporain*.

49. Lévy, "Souvenirs," p. 5.

50. Duployé, *Religion de Péguy*, p. 56.

51. This is sometimes Jacques Petit's claim in his *Bernanos, Bloy, Claudel, Péguy*, pp. 197, 263.

52. Péguy, *Temporal and Eternal*, trans. Dru.

53. Ibid., p. 9.

54. Nearly every interpreter of Péguy struggles, at some point, with the meaning of this opposition, for which Péguy is famous. Some of the more interesting of these interpretive endeavors are those that attempt to place the terms *mystique* and *politique* historically. For instance, Gerbaud, "La reconstruction de l'affaire dans 'Notre jeunesse' de Charles Péguy," pp. 266, 269, attempts to place Péguy's usage within the context of the usage in the French language of Péguy's time. Duployé, in *Religion de Péguy*, pp. 228, 231, 240, 241–42, 430, 465, 513, attempts to place it in the context of the Christian usage of these terms.

55. See, e.g., Robert Burac, "Notre jeunesse," in Péguy's *Oeuvres en prose complètes*, 3:1492–93, which catalogues some of the contemporary reactions to the publication of "Notre jeunesse."

56. Péguy, "Un poète l'a dit," in *Oeuvres en prose complètes*, 2:877.

57. Péguy's portrait of Bernard-Lazare in "Notre jeunesse" was his third attempt to do homage to him. In 1903, the year of Bernard-Lazare's death, he wrote about 50 pages to this end, which were published posthumously; see "Bernard-Lazare" in *Oeuvres en prose complètes*, 2:1207–45. A second fragment of approximately 15 pages dates from 1907 and appeared as part of "Un poète l'a dit," in ibid., roughly

pp. 872–87. Nelly Wilson makes the point that the description we have in "Notre jeunesse" is only the precursor of a further portrait that Péguy in the end never wrote, because his attitude toward Jews changed (*Bernard Lazare* [French ed., 1985], pp. 370, 375–80).

58. See, e.g., Leroy, *Péguy entre l'ordre et la révolution*, pp. 124–25; Burac, "Notre jeunesse," p. 1492.

59. Péguy, "Notre jeunesse," in *Oeuvres en prose complètes*, 3:35–36.

60. For a much longer meditation on the difference between mystique and politique in "Notre jeunesse," see Aronowicz, "Reagan, Weizsäcker et la visite au cimetière de Bitburg."

61. Drumont, *France juive*, p. 9.

62. Leroy-Beaulieu, *Israel Among the Nations*, p. 194. While most of the comments in my analysis of this book show the similarity between Leroy-Beaulieu's position and that of the antisemites with whom he argued, his work did not necessarily make this impression on the Jews of his epoch. Edmond-Maurice Lévy, Péguy's observant friend mentioned earlier, claimed to have been brought back to the Jewish community through the reading of Leroy-Beaulieu's book ("Souvenirs," p. 7). It is not clear, however, whether Lévy was brought back to the Jewish tradition because he sympathized with Leroy-Beaulieu's views or because he reacted against them. Bernard-Lazare, on the other hand, did detect a veiled antisemitism in Leroy-Beaulieu's philosemitism. Such philosemites, he said, strove to prove "that the Jew is in all things similar to those surrounding him and that in every respect you can even detect in him a certain inferiority, which is one way for the philo-Semites to show their anti-Semitism. It must be admitted that the Jews are delighted by this and nothing could prevent them from believing in the genius of Anatole Leroy-Beaulieu" (*Job's Dungheap*, p. 81).

63. For one expression of this accusation, see Lasserre, "Logique de l'Action française," pp. 13, 16.

64. See Chapter 2, n. 30, below.

65. Péguy, "Notre jeunesse," p. 95.

66. Leroy Beaulieu was quite adamant about the Jews' need to assimilate, and to divest themselves of the rabbinic tradition, if they wished to be full-fledged citizens of the state. See *Israel Among the Nations*, pp. 134–35, 137–38, 142. Bernard-Lazare, in his earlier work (see *Antisemitism*, pp. 178–81), had argued in a similar vein. Péguy not only did not want Jews to lose their separate identity but also at times thought that that separate identity was essential to his own identity as a Catholic: "Je marche avec les Juifs, parce qu'avec les Juifs, je peux être catholique comme je veux l'être, avec les catholiques je ne le pourrais pas" ("I side with the Jews, because with the Jews, I can be Catholic in the way that I want; with Catholics, I couldn't be") (quoted in Rabi, "Israël," p. 334).

67. Péguy, "Notre jeunesse," p. 137. In this evaluation of what lies at the heart of antisemitism—a desire to obliterate difference as the only condition of acceptance—Péguy seems to share the understanding of some observant Jews of the nineteenth century. Reacting to his liberal co-religionists' conviction that embracing a Western style of liturgy would help make Jews full-fledged members of their states, Rabbi Solomon Jehuda Leib Rappoport retorted: "The intention and aim

of the gentiles . . . is not to reform our religion but to have us embrace their religion. As long as we do not do so, we are contemptible in their eyes" (*Jew in the Modern World*, ed. Mendes-Flohr and Reinharz, p. 189). Péguy's statement, coming as it does over 65 years later, takes into account that even conversion would not do it. Any perceptible difference, whether religious or not, evokes a desire to annihilate the Jews as Jews. They can adopt Western ways all they want, but it will not help, as long as in some dimension they remain Jews.

68. Drumont, *France juive*, p. 34.

69. Duployé draws attention in *Religion de Péguy*, p. 56, to this time frame for Péguy's public stands.

70. There were occasional physical threats from members of various antisemitic leagues; see Nelly Wilson, *Bernard Lazare*, p. 230. There was also generalized violence in 1898, most especially in the French colony of Algeria, where the police did little or nothing to check a riot against Jews; see Marrus, *Politics*, p. 163, and Stephen Wilson, "Anti-Semitism and Jewish Response in France During the Dreyfus Affair," pp. 227–28.

71. For a description of this contest, which involved Bernard-Lazare, since he agreed to serve as a judge to determine the winner, see his own description of it in *Contre l'antisémitisme*, pp. 64–75. He eventually fought a duel with Drumont because the latter accused him of making public confidential information about the contest.

72. One of the commentators on "Notre jeunesse" made an allusion to his portrait of Bernard-Lazare as a monument that, unlike the one defaced in Nîmes, was hewn of a stone that could not be harmed: "And today, who is being offered up to us so that we should admire him as a Dreyfusist par excellence? Not only Charles Péguy, but that other Jew, Bernard-Lazare, that last of the prophets of Israel, poured into the bronze of a splendid and savage prose whose nose cannot be broken by any iconoclast" (Burac, "Notre jeunesse," p. 1494; my translation).

73. While most commentators agree that the period from roughly 1880 to World War I witnessed an unprecedented rise of antisemitism in France, this opinion is not fully shared by Eugene Weber, who argues that hatred of foreigners in general was much more prevalent than hatred of Jews as such. See his *France fin de siècle*, p. 133.

74. See, e.g., *National Review* 43, no. 24 (Dec. 30, 1991), which was entirely devoted to reflections on antisemitism. Each of the essays argues that people like Patrick Buchanan are *not* antisemitic, even if they have made uncomplimentary comments about Jews. For a review of a change in attitude to the term *antisemitism*, see Lewis, *Semites and Anti-Semites*, pp. 26–34.

75. For example, the important French socialist leader Jean Jaurès, whom Péguy first greatly admired and then denounced (in fact, part of "Notre jeunesse" is a virulent diatribe against him for having betrayed the mystique of the Dreyfus Affair), although he was a staunch defender of Dreyfus, in a speech of 1898 to a crowd of 6,000 people, spoke of the Jews as forever consumed by the fever of profit (quoted in Nelly Wilson, *Bernard Lazare*, p. 233). Bernard-Lazare took him to task for this conception about Jews, claiming that the notion was based on blind acceptance of Karl Marx's *On the Jewish Question* and total ignorance of both Jewish texts and Jewish history; see *Job's Dungheap*, pp. 108–28.

76. Halévy, "Apologie pour notre passé," p. 92. Halévy, a close collaborator of Péguy's on the *Cahiers,* came from a distinguished family of musicians and writers and was himself a historian and essayist. Péguy seriously considered him as his successor when he was contemplating leaving the editorship in 1909. In the secondary literature about Péguy, he is often referred to as one of the many Jews in the latter's circle. Like his father before him, however, Halévy had converted to Catholicism, and his mother was Protestant. His sentiments toward Jews were not sympathetic, and he did not consider himself to be one.

77. Bloy, *Salut par les Juifs,* p. 15.

78. Leroy-Beaulieu, *Israel Among the Nations,* p. 147.

79. Milosz, *Native Realm,* pp. 128–47.

80. Ibid., pp. 146–47.

81. This blithe ability to make generalizations about groups was characteristic of the times. "Academics and politicians spoke unblushingly of 'The French Spirit' or 'the Jewish soul.'" Marrus remarks. "Scientific research, moreover, was generally considered not to be breaking down such concepts, but to be strengthening them, making characteristics more clear and identifiable, and providing increasing evidence for the differentiation of peoples" (*Politics,* p. 87).

82. Petit, *Bernanos, Bloy, Claudel, Péguy,* p. 67 n. 1, p. 260. See also Bernard-Henri Lévy, *L'Idéologie française,* pp. 115–17, although he charges Péguy with being a certain kind of racist rather than an antisemite per se.

83. The voice of the speaker changes midway through this passage. The first sentence is spoken by Jews. From the second sentence onward, it is Péguy himself, speaking as a Christian.

84. Prajs, *Péguy et Israël,* p. 133.

85. Péguy's opposition to antisemitism much predates "Notre jeunesse," as his involvement on behalf of Dreyfus and his many Jewish friends and contributors to the *Cahiers* make clear. During World War II, a group of French Catholics opposed to Nazism published excerpts from Péguy's texts against antisemitism dating back to 1898. See *Cahiers du témoignage chrétien* (1941–44; facsimile reprint, Paris, n.p., 1980), pp. 178–83.

86. Péguy refers here to Jørgen Peter Müller, a Dane, whose books on how to improve one's health enjoyed great success in France up to World War II.

87. Péguy, "Notre jeunesse," p. 138.

88. Ibid., p. 137.

89. Leroy, *Péguy entre l'ordre et la révolution,* pp. 124–25; Wilson, *Bernard Lazare,* p. 254. A law had been passed by the government of René Waldeck-Rousseau in 1901 decreeing that religious associations could only be created by government order. Combes, Waldeck-Rousseau's successor, closed down 3,000 parochial schools by applying the law retroactively. See Chapter 2, nn. 22–25, 28.

90. Burac, "Notre jeunesse," p. 1500.

91. Péguy is referring here to the military exercises he periodically engaged in as a reservist. The other person addressed in the passage is Claude Casimir-Périer, a good friend of Péguy's, who was also a reservist, with the same rank as Péguy (lieutenant). Cercottes was the military camp near Orléans they had both attended. See Chapter 2, n. 36.

92. See n. 36 above on the controversy over what Péguy knew about the Jewish tradition.

93. Leroy-Beaulieu, *Israel Among the Nations*, p. 225.

94. Ibid., p. 228.

95. Drumont, *France juive*, p. 5.

96. Ibid., p. 35.

97. Péguy, "Notre jeunesse," p. 145.

98. Num. 24:5 is in itself, of course, highly relevant to Péguy's point. It reverberates with many meanings at once, given his opposition to antisemitism and his efforts to locate a universal always in tension with the particular. The words in that verse are those of the prophet Balaam, a non-Israelite. He had been asked by Balak, king of the Moabites, to curse the Israelites so that he could defeat them in battle. Balaam, being a prophet, could speak only the word of God, however, and, to Balak's discomfiture, he uttered praise for the Israelites instead of curses.

If we transpose this to turn-of-the-century France, the very thing antisemites (like the Action française) curse and want to have cursed—the Jews' not being from one place—elicits praise from someone who remains within the prophetic tradition. The antisemitism spouted by the Church of the turn of the century was in conflict with its own tradition. It is noteworthy that this tradition requires, not only just toleration of, but admiration for that very quality of "being elsewhere." It is also noteworthy that the prophet here is a non-Jew, pointing simultaneously to one truth for both Jew and non-Jew and yet to irreducible difference. After all, Balaam does not become Jewish. Neither does Péguy.

99. The melancholy permeating Péguy's writings has impressed many of his readers. It is interesting to note that this was the feature that struck Walter Benjamin when he first read Péguy's essays in the late 1910's. Benjamin referred to it as that "fantastic controlled melancholy" (Bensaïd, *Walter Benjamin*, p. 75).

100. Péguy, *Oeuvres en prose complètes*, 3:20.

101. See Chapter 2, n. 37.

102. Péguy, *Oeuvres en prose complètes*, 3:10–12.

103. For some of Péguy's reasons for writing "Notre jeunesse," see Burac, "Notre jeunesse," pp. 1484–92, who claims that Péguy was also eager to mark his difference from the Right, whose adherents seemed to think that he had turned away from Dreyfusard and socialist causes since the publication of his long poem *The Mystery of the Charity of Joan of Arc* in that same year (1910). The obviously Christian commitment in that poem made them conclude that Péguy had adopted the Church's current political positions. This, as we know, was far from the case. In "Notre jeunesse," pp. 41–44, Péguy himself refers explicitly only to his differences with Halévy as the impulse for his essay.

104. Péguy's most extensive writing on hope is the long poem *The Portico of the Mystery of the Second Virtue*. The importance hope played in his theology as a whole is underlined by Jacques Ellul (quoted in Bastaire, *Péguy l'inchrétien*, p. 136): "The final great theological discovery of Péguy was, of course, hope. It is true that for centuries Christians argued about faith, about the content of faith, about dogma, etc. . . . but of the three theological virtues, hope has always been neglected. It was vaguely understood as an adjunct of faith. There is no theology of

hope before Péguy. I am not saying that he himself built a theory of hope in the manner of Moltmann, but that he succeeded in seeing and understanding that Christian hope [*Espérance*], which is the very opposite of hope [*Espoir*], is a decisive truth of Revelation, a unique dimension of Christianity, and here too, no doubt, is one of the consequences of his socialism" (my translation).

105. The two Clios referred to here are long dialogues on history, both of which were published posthumously (see Preface, n. 2, above). The first, often referred to by scholars as Clio 1, is the most explicit of Péguy's essays on the topic of incarnation. Clio 2, the essay referred to here, is most centrally preoccupied with the classical Greek heritage.

106. See Aronowicz, "Secret of the Man of Forty," for a much longer analysis of these pages. The passage itself can be found in Péguy's *Oeuvres en prose complètes*, 3:1132–34, and in Appendix A.

107. Péguy, *Oeuvres en prose complètes*, 3:1133: "Il sait que *l'on* n'est pas heureux. Il sait que depuis qu'il y a l'homme nul homme jamais n'a été heureux."

108. Ibid., p. 1134: "Or, je dis, dit l'histoire, que rien n'est aussi touchant que cette perpétuelle, que cette éternellement renaissante inconséquence; et que rien n'est aussi beau; et que rien n'est aussi désarmant devant Dieu; et c'est ici la commune merveille de votre jeune Espérance."

109. Many authors have insisted on the centrality of incarnation in Péguy's thought. See, e.g., Duployé, *Religion de Péguy*, p. xiii, and Bastaire, *Péguy l'inchrétien*, esp. pp. 85–109.

110. Péguy, "Notre jeunesse," pp. 98–104.

111. Ibid., p. 98.

112. Ibid., p. 101.

113. See Leroi, *Péguy entre l'ordre et la révolution*, p. 216; Duployé, *Religion de Péguy*, p. 120.

114. Ibid., pp. 84–85. See Appendix C for fuller text on the socialist mystique.

115. See n. 89 above and Chapter 2, nn. 22–25, 28, below, on Combes and Waldeck-Rousseau. Péguy had at first greatly admired Jean Jaurès (1859–1914), the great leader of the French Socialist Party. In the early years of the *Cahiers*, Jaurès was a frequent contributor. When Jaurès threw his support behind the Waldeck-Rousseau and Combes legislation against the Church, however, Péguy began to distance himself from him. Jaurès's pacifist policy in the face of mounting danger from Germany further angered Péguy. Many pages in "Notre jeunesse" are nothing but an outpouring of rage against Jaurès, done in the pamphleteering style for which Péguy was also well known. For some of the more violent of his attacks, see *Oeuvres en prose complètes*, 3:110–20.

116. Péguy, *Oeuvres en prose complètes*, 3:123.

117. Ibid., pp. 124–25.

118. Ibid., p. 124.

119. "Péguy does not proceed by abstraction, according to the usual philosophical method but rather, more practically, through *concretions*—that is, through accumulation, juxtaposition, *agglomeration*, addition of concrete values" (Dadoun, *Eros de Péguy*, p. 25; my translation).

120. In "Notre jeunesse," p. 14, Péguy himself makes a distinction between

idée and *pensée*, the latter being the deeper, all-pervasive, taken-for-granted framework, the former a consciously held theme or ideology for which one argues. See Gerbaud, "Reconstruction de l'affaire . . . ," p. 288. In *Historical Reason*, pp. 19–21, Ortega y Gasset comes up with a very similar distinction, although he labels the two *belief* and *idea*.

> Beliefs are all those things that we absolutely take for granted even though we don't think about them. We are so certain that they exist and that they are just as we take them to be, that we never question them, but instead take them automatically into account in our behavior. When we go down the street we never try to walk through the walls of buildings; we automatically avoid bumping into them without ever having to think: "walls are impenetrable."
>
> At each moment, our life is supported by a vast repertoire of such beliefs. But there are also things and situations regarding which we find ourselves without a firm belief: we sometimes wonder whether certain things exist or not, whether they are one way or another. When this happens we have no alternative but to formulate an idea, an opinion regarding them. Ideas, then, are those "things" we consciously construct or elaborate, precisely because we *do not believe* in them.
>
> I think this is the best, the most precise, articulation of a possible answer to the momentous question of the peculiar and extremely subtle role ideas play in our lives. Notice that all ideas are thus described: commonplace ideas and scientific ones, religious ideas, as well as all other kinds. Because a reality is only complete and real to us when we believe in it. But ideas are born of doubt, that is to say, born in the empty space or hole vacated by a belief. This means that whatever evolves from an idea seems less than a complete and authentic reality to us. Then what are they? The orthopedic nature of ideas is easily perceived: they become useful when a belief has given way or weakened. I express this dual fact by saying that we have *ideas*, but we inhabit *beliefs*. Man always lives in the belief of *this* or *that*, and on the basis of these beliefs—which to him are reality itself—he exists, behaves, and thinks. Thus even the most skeptical of men is a believer, and profoundly credulous.

121. Péguy, "Notre jeunesse," p. 156.

122. Bernard-Henri Lévy, *Idéologie française*, pp. 115–17.

123. See n. 89 above and Chapter 2, nn. 22–25, below. The Court of Appeals ruled in favor of the Combes decree. That is, it declared the retroactive application of the Waldeck-Rousseau law requiring parochial schools to seek state permits in order to operate to be legal.

124. "That entire nations have a price, a value of their own, [and] are singled out for history . . . and that the immense majority of nations . . . are singled out for silence and darkness . . . is a mystery we do not see, like all the greatest mysteries, precisely because we are bathing in it" ("Notre jeunesse," p. 34). Some events acquire world-historical significance. Others do not. Everyone is aware of this uneven weight of both events and people, and yet no one notices it.

125. Péguy, Clio 2, pp. 1158–68.

126. Ibid., p. 1168.

127. Péguy, "Zangwill," pp. 1433, 1434.

128. Péguy, "Bar-Cochebas," in *Oeuvres en prose complètes*, 2:642–73.

129. I do not mean to say that there are no arguments and no logical sequence in "Notre jeunesse." Rather, I simply mean that the essay is not constructed as one long, developing line of reasoning.

Chapter 2

1. The association of Israel with the carnal or the flesh is a constant motif in Christian writings about Jews, going back at least to St. Augustine, who himself derived these categories from St. Paul. The contrast is always between an Israel of the flesh, which lives by its own righteousness, its own works, and an Israel of the spirit, which lives by God's righteousness, by grace. The former was most often identified with the Jews, the latter with Christians. Other associations also commonly cluster around the carnality of Israel—its literal-mindedness, its inability to aspire to any but the goods of this world.

In "Notre jeunesse," carnal Israel carries with it another family of meanings than these. To be the "carnal voice and the temporal body" has to do with being the bearers of God, as the sentence immediately following these expressions makes clear. The carnality of Israel is tied to prophecy, and also to suffering, in the body, as the consequence of prophecy.

Thus, Péguy's usage of terms such as *carnal* in reference to the Jews does not seem to follow in the Augustinian line, although it does perpetuate the Pauline tradition of Rom. 9–11 in seeing Jews' *separate* spirituality as of continuing importance in salvation history.

The positive connotations of the phrase "carnal Israel" in "Notre jeunesse" bear little relation, however, to its use in some recent Jewish studies of this theme. In a work such as *Carnal Israel* (1993), the author, Daniel Boyarin, speaks primarily of the rabbinic affirmation of the body and, most specifically, of sexuality. This is not what Péguy intends by *carnal* either, although in essays such as Clio 1, he does meditate on the significance of the body as such. See Péguy, *Oeuvres III*, pp. 723–57. But the body, for Péguy, is not so much the locus of sexuality as it is the locus of aging, disease, and death. Thus, since human beings can rise to greatness only in the confrontation with these realities, the spirit is inseparable from these transformations of the flesh. In "Notre jeunesse," the terms *carnal, incarnation*, and *embodiment* have a broader sense yet, which I have tried to delineate throughout my commentary.

2. The 131st regiment was the infantry unit in which Péguy enlisted in 1892, when he began his military service. Originally named the Walcheren regiment, it had earned glory in the Russian and German campaigns of 1812–13. The names listed refer to those campaigns.

3. The provinces of Alsace and Lorraine were one of the great centers of Jewish population in France. Many Jews chose to emigrate after their annexation following the Franco-Prussian war of 1870–71, mostly to Paris, thus proclaiming their desire to be French rather than German citizens. Because of their German-accented

French, however, many of them were perceived as Germans and as foreigners by the French themselves. See Hyman, *From Dreyfus to Vichy*, p. 4; Marrus, *Politics*, p. 33. "He [Dreyfus] hates the French as a Jew and as a German. . . . German by taste and education, Jew by race, he did the job of a Jew and a German, nothing else," the antisemitic paper *La Libre Parole* pronounced. "The hideous Jews, vomited into France by the German ghettoes, are scarcely able to splutter out words in our language," fumed *La Croix* (both quoted in Bredin, *Bernard Lazare*, p. 142; my translations).

4. What Péguy means by the victory against the anti-Dreyfusist anti-Dreyfusists is the short time following Colonel Henry's suicide in 1898, which seemed undeniable evidence of the Army's manufacture of documents against Dreyfus. Péguy even claims that there was a 48-hour period around Henry's admission to forging the *petit bleu* in which everyone, including the leaders of the anti-Dreyfus movement, believed in Dreyfus's innocence. See "Notre jeunesse," p. 88. The defeat at the hands of the anti-Dreyfusist Dreyfusists probably refers to the loss of credibility of Dreyfus's defenders ensuing from their politicking against the Church. See ibid., pp. 88–89, 110–19.

5. "Israel" here, of course, refers to the Jewish people and not to the state, which needless to say did not yet exist.

6. James Darmesteter (1849–94), a Jew from Lorraine, was a professor at the Collège de France, renowned for his studies of the languages and religions of ancient Persia. He was the author of *Les Prophètes d'Israël* (cited in Chapter 1, n. 46). For a more extensive discussion of Darmesteter's views on Judaism and the French, see Marrus, *Politics*, pp. 100–110.

7. See Chapter 1, n. 57, above.

8. The École pratique des hautes études had three divisions: the natural sciences, the historical and philological sciences, and the religious sciences. There is a not very concealed jab here at the positivism of the era, proudly proclaiming the objective "scientific" status of the study of religion.

9. This is the Latin title of a work by Aristotle, *De generatione et corruptione*.

10. Charles Baudelaire, *Les fleurs du mal*, LXXXIX, "The Swan," ll. 7–8.

11. The archeologist and philologist Salomon Reinach (1858–1932) was an early supporter of Dreyfus and cofounder of the League of the Rights of Man, along with his brothers Joseph and Theodore Reinach. The League of the Rights of Man was founded in 1898, in the heat of the Dreyfus Affair. It consisted of various factions of the Left—intellectuals, writers, professors—with an antimilitarist and anticlerical agenda.

12. The great French writer Émile Zola (1840–1902) is renowned for novels such as *Nana* and *Germinal*, but the reference to him here is to his role in the Dreyfus Affair. On January 13, 1898, he published a letter entitled "J'accuse" in the newspaper *L'Aurore*, addressed to Félix Faure, the president of the Republic, which charged members of the General Staff with having covered up the truth about the Dreyfus trial. "J'accuse" was written shortly after the acquittal of Commandant Charles Walsin-Esterhazy on the charge of treason by a military tribunal. The original note, which was the sole piece of evidence alleged against Alfred Dreyfus in the 1894 court-martial, turned out to be in Esterhazy's handwriting. Zola was tried

for libel shortly after the publication of his letter and fled to England temporarily to escape possible imprisonment. "J'accuse" was very instrumental in forcing a retrial of Dreyfus's case and in making the affair a matter of national proportions.

13. Ludovic Halévy (1834–1908) was the father of Péguy's friend Daniel Halévy, who contributed the essay on the Dreyfus Affair, "Apologie pour notre passé," in response to which Péguy wrote "Notre jeunesse." Ludovic Halévy, together with Henri Meilhac, was renowned as the author of the librettos of numerous operettas by Offenbach. He had converted to Catholicism but apparently still retained a loyalty to the Jewish community. See Nochlin, "Degas and the Dreyfus Affair," p. 103.

14. Fernand Labori (1860–1917) was the second lawyer hired by the Dreyfus family to assist in Alfred Dreyfus's defense. He was also Émile Zola's lawyer when the latter was tried for libel as a result of his letter "J'accuse."

15. "Des amis qui tutoient"—those who say *tu* rather than *vous*. The *tu* form signals familiarity as opposed to the *vous* form, which denotes a formal relationship.

16. On Thursday of every week, Péguy received visitors at the bookstore (*la boutique*, "the shop"), in which he ran the *Cahiers* and sold issues both of it and of other publications. The bookstore faced the Sorbonne.

17. The French philosopher and social theorist Georges Sorel (1847–1922) served as an engineer with the Roads and Bridges Department for 25 years before retiring to devote himself to philosophy. One of the best known of his works is *Reflections on Violence* (1908). It is from him that we get the term *general strike*. He argued for the importance of mythology as a propeller of social action, and of the justifiability of violence in certain revolutionary situations. An ardent Dreyfusard associated with the Left (the Syndicalists), he took a turn in 1909 toward Action française, the ultrarightist organization founded by Charles Maurras. He had been closely associated with Péguy's *Cahiers* in its earlier years and a frequent visitor to the boutique on Thursdays. In 1912, Péguy broke with him, suspecting him of having prevented the French Jewish philosopher and novelist Julien Benda from receiving the Goncourt Prize, since Sorel had allied himself with the antisemitic faction. In the earlier part of 1912, Sorel had also written some articles very hostile to Bernard-Lazare.

18. The socialist newspaper *L'Humanité*, founded by Jean Jaurès, had been financed with a good deal of Jewish support. See Hyman, *From Dreyfus to Vichy*, p. 49.

19. Louis-Louis Dreyfus (1867–1940), banker, commercial shipowner, shareholder in *L'Humanité*, and one of the richest men in France, was elected as socialist deputy from the Department of Lozère from 1905 to 1910.

20. This line, while ultimately a reference to Isa. 6:6–7, quotes the nineteenth-century French poet Charles Leconte de Lisle's *Poèmes antiques*, "Dies Irae," l. 61.

21. "Apologie pour notre passé" is the title of the essay by Daniel Halévy that Péguy published in *Cahiers* 11, no. 10 (Apr. 10, 1910). Péguy's response to it in "Notre jeunesse" offended Halévy, and Péguy apologized for having unwittingly offended his friend and contributor in a later essay, "Victor-Marie, Comte Hugo or Solvuntur Objecta" (*Cahiers* 12, no. 1). See also Chapter 1, n. 76.

22. Émile Combes (1835–1921) headed the Council of State from 1902 to 1905. It was under his government that the previous Waldeck-Rousseau legislation mak-

ing it illegal for members of the Catholic Church to congregate without government authorization was made retroactive. See Chapter 1, nn. 89, 123.

23. Jean Deck was the pseudonym of Jean Poirot (1873–1924). The article in question, "Pour la Finlande: Mémoire et documents," appeared in *Cahiers* 3, no. 21 (Aug. 16, 1902), which concluded with Bernard-Lazare's "La Loi et les congrégations."

24. In July–August 1902, the Combes government closed 2,500 parochial schools established before the law of 1901, and that therefore had not sought government authorization to remain open, since that law stipulated that only those established after 1901 needed to do so. The law of assemblies referred to here is the *loi des congrégations* passed on July 1, 1901, under the government of René Waldeck-Rousseau (1899–1902), which required legal authorization for religious congregations to come into being. The original legislation had made the seeking of legal authorization necessary only for future religious assemblies. The Combes government made this retroactive, thus forcing all religious congregations to seek legal authorization. Particularly at stake were religious schools. The virulently anticlerical Combes government wanted the state to control education. On July 7, 1904, a law was in fact passed withdrawing the right to teach from all religious orders. The controversy surrounding the original Waldeck-Rousseau legislation and the debate regarding the subsequent Combes legislation are reported in Bernard-Lazare's "La Loi et les congrégations."

25. In 1904, a debate in the Chamber of Deputies revealed that Combes had "delegates" placed in communes whose mayors were suspected of not being sufficiently republican. These delegates acted as informants to Combes, proposing rewards and punishments for the mayors in question. See Péguy, "Chronologie," in *Oeuvres en prose complètes*, 1:lxxv.

26. Lieutenant Colonel Georges Picquart (1854–1914) eventually made public his discovery that a document that had been used to convict Dreyfus was a forgery. As a result, his military career suffered and he was imprisoned for over a year. He was later rehabilitated, rose to the rank of general, and became minister of war in the government of Georges Clemenceau.

27. I have translated *Cour de cassation* as Court of Appeals, since it reviewed convictions of lower courts. It is the highest judicial authority in France.

28. Péguy seems to be collapsing two events into each other. The first is the Combes legislation that applied the Waldeck-Rousseau legislation ("the law of assemblies") retroactively. To this, we know, Bernard-Lazare was completely opposed. The second is the Court of Appeals judgment of 1906 declaring Dreyfus innocent without sending the case back to a military tribunal for retrial. But by then Bernard-Lazare had been dead three years. As of 1899, according to a piece about Dreyfus's second trial (of 1899) that Bernard-Lazare published in an American journal, he seemed to favor the position that the Court of Appeals did have the legal authority to change a verdict without sending the case back to another court. He may have changed his mind about this, but there does not seem to be any written record of it. See Nelly Wilson, "L'Amitié de Péguy et de Bernard-Lazare," pp. 12–14, and Robert Burac, "Notices, notes et variantes," in *Oeuvres en prose complètes*, 3:1512–13, for some discussion of this issue.

29. Article 445 was the article in the criminal law code upon which the Court of Appeals based its decision to declare Dreyfus innocent without demanding a retrial. The controversy was about whether the Court of Appeals had the authority to do more than demand a retrial in a military tribunal. That is, many claimed that the Court of Appeals did not have the power to declare innocence or guilt. It only had the power to send a case back to the court in which it had originally been tried if it found new evidence or illegal procedure. For an elaboration of the nature of Article 445, see Martin, "Dreyfus Affair and the Corruption of the French Legal System," pp. 46–48. Arguing much the same way as Péguy, Martin claims that the decision of the Cour de cassation "was as surely an example of raison d'état as the first conviction of Dreyfus had been. . . . The decision rendered 'justice'—innocence was duly acknowledged—but it was not through sound jurisprudence." The Court of Appeals could decide a case itself only under two circumstances, neither of which applied to the situation at hand. The first was if the appellant was dead, and the second was if no punishable crime would exist after the judgment. There had in fact been a crime in 1894, but it had been committed by Esterhazy, not Dreyfus.

Georges Clemenceau (1841–1929), mentioned here, was a prominent statesman and journalist in the French Republic. He became premier of France from 1917 to 1920 and contributed greatly to the Allied victory in World War I. A Dreyfusard from 1897 onward, he also contributed an article to the *Cahiers*.

30. On the persecution of the Jews in Romania, see Bredin, *Bernard Lazare*, pp. 320–24. When Romania became independent in 1878, it did not grant Jews equal rights under the law. Various decrees excluded them from a wide variety of occupations and forbade them rights of residence in the countryside and the right to congregate, resulting in enormous economic deprivation and dislocation. This was completely ignored by the European powers. Westerners who did publicize injustices committed in this part of the world focused on the persecutions perpetrated by the Ottoman Empire against the Armenians. Bernard-Lazare himself was very concerned about the fate of the Armenians. He participated in the Pro-Armenia Congress held in Brussels in June 1902 and was elected a member of its propaganda committee. He nonetheless did not want the suffering of the Armenians to obscure the sufferings undergone by Jews.

31. Of the dying and the dead.

32. Victor Hugo, *La Légende des siècles*, "La conscience," l. 50.

33. Edmond-Maurice Lévy (1878–1971), librarian at the Sorbonne, furnished Péguy with bibliographical information, especially on Jewish matters. He was one of the few observant Jews in Péguy's circle. Péguy referred to him as his "Jewish chaplain." Lévy wrote some reminiscences about Péguy, published shortly after his (Lévy's) death. See Chapter 1, n. 36, above.

34. Cercottes was a military camp near Orléans where Péguy did part of his military service.

35. Num. 24:5.

36. Claude Casimir-Périer (1880–1915) was the son of a former president of the French Republic, Jean Casimir-Périer. He and Péguy became friends initially through their reserve service in the same infantry regiment. Claude Casimir-Périer

took over the command of Péguy's unit after the latter's death and was himself killed a year later. See Chapter 1, n. 91.

37. Romain Rolland's best-known novel, *Jean Christophe*, was first published in installments in the *Cahiers* from 1903 on. It presents the successive crises confronting a creative genius, partially based on Beethoven and partially based on Rolland himself. Rolland received the Nobel Prize for literature in 1915. He also contributed various political reflections and literary essays to the *Cahiers*. His last published work before his death was a two-volume study entitled *Péguy*.

38. By "the Dreyfus Affair itself," Péguy no doubt means the events that culminated in Dreyfus's retrial by a military tribunal in 1899. He was found guilty but was granted a pardon by the president of the Republic in September of that year. By "the second Dreyfus Affair," he no doubt means the events that led to the reversal by the Court of Appeals of his conviction in 1906, declaring him innocent. Jean Jaurès made a first move in this direction in 1903. Thus there seems to have been a four-year lull. In that period, an amnesty law covering all criminal acts and lawsuits arising out of the affair was passed by the Senate (December 1900). This is probably the "hollow peace" Péguy refers to a few sentences later.

39. Reference to the decision of the Court of Appeals in 1906 to declare Dreyfus innocent without a retrial by a military tribunal.

40. I have skipped eight pages of text here, a diatribe against Jean Jaurès, who, Péguy felt, had dishonored the Dreyfusard mystique. There are no references to Bernard-Lazare in these pages.

41. See Edmond Bernus, "Polonais et Prussiens: De la résistance du peuple Polonais aux exactions de la germanisation prussienne," *Cahiers* 8, nos. 11, 12, and 14 (Jan.–Mar. 1907).

42. That is to say, incorporate all of Bernard-Lazare's "La Loi et les congrégations" into "Notre jeunesse."

Chapter 3

1. Emmanuel Levinas's main philosophical works are *Totalité et infini* (1961) and *Autrement qu'être ou au delà de l'essence* (1974) His essays on the Jewish tradition, including the Talmudic commentaries, have been published under the titles *Difficile liberté* (1963, 1976), *Quatre lectures talmudiques* (1968), and *Du sacré au saint: Cinq nouvelles lectures talmudiques* (1977). Other writings of his include *L'Au-delà du verset* (1982) and *A l'Heure des nations* (1988). In "The Philosopher of Selfless Love," *New York Review of Books* 43, no. 5 (Mar. 21, 1996), p. 37, Denis Donoghue depicts Levinas as a Talmudic scholar. It would have surprised Levinas to be referred to in this way. He was not engaged in Talmudic scholarship at any point in his life, although he regularly studied Talmud with friends. Whatever came out of those study sessions, he always referred to as the work of an amateur. His reputation, established in Paris philosophical circles even before the publication of some of his most famous works, was always that of a philosopher.

2. The Talmudic text Levinas is interpreting in "The Temptation of Temptation" is from the tractate *Shabbath*, pp. 88a–b. It is reproduced in its entirety in Appendix B.

3. All specific citations to tractate *Shabbath*, pp. 88a–b, are from Levinas, *Nine Talmudic Readings*, trans. Aronowicz, pp. 30–31. They can also be found in Appendix B.

4. The prayer is "Sim Shalom": "Bless us, O Our Father, all of us as if one, in the light of your face, because in the light of your face, you gave us, O Lord Our God, the Torah of life, loving kindness and righteousness, blessing and mercy, life and peace."

5. Levinas, *Nine Talmudic Readings*, p. 47.

6. Ibid., p. 48.

7. For an expanded discussion of the meaning of the contrast between temptation and temptation of temptation, see Aronowicz, "Emmanuel Levinas's Talmudic Commentaries."

8. Levinas, *Nine Talmudic Readings*, p. 32.

9. Ibid., p. 37.

10. Ibid., p. 47.

11. Ibid., p. 99.

12. Ibid., p. 75.

13. When I visited Professor Levinas's home in July 1991, he asked me what I was currently working on. When I informed him it was Péguy, he expressed pleasure and said that Péguy represented French openness. He had been asked to write a few words on Péguy himself, he said, on the occasion of a conference on the latter in Italy. I asked him for a copy, but he never located it. In the course of the conversation, he made it clear that although he admired Péguy, he did not think of him as a philosopher of consequence. My hunch is that Levinas, like most Frenchmen, had mostly read Péguy's poetry and a few snippets from his essays. Some of Péguy's most interesting work did not come to light until after World War II, by which time he had been so appropriated by the Right that many people not of that camp dismissed him without reading him.

14. Levinas, *Difficult Freedom*, pp. 405–12.

15. Although Levinas does not mention Bergson in his brief intellectual autobiography in *Difficile liberté*, he does mention him elsewhere, e.g., in *Face to Face with Levinas*, ed. Cohen, p. 13, where he claims him as a significant early influence. There is confluence, then, at some point. But the influence of Bergson on both thinkers cannot account for the specificity of the echoes in the two thinkers' works.

16. I do not mean to suggest that for either Péguy or Levinas the responsibility one feels toward the other involves the hierarchy inherent in the parent-child relationship, with all authority vested in the one who is obligated. The only aspect both Levinas and Péguy are underscoring in the parent-child relationship is the unchosenness of the responsibility incurred by the parent.

17. On a responsibility enacted before a reasoned consent and its relationship to God, see Cohen, *Elevations*, ch. 8, "G–d in Levinas," esp. pp. 179–94.

18. "And the unlimited responsibility, which justifies this concern for justice and for self and for philosophy can be forgotten. In this forgetfulness egoism is born. But egoism is neither first nor ultimate. The impossibility of escaping from God—which in this at least is not a value among others—is the 'mystery of angels,' the 'We will do and we will hear.'" Levinas, *Nine Talmudic Readings*, p. 50.

19. Péguy, Clio 2, p. 1020 (my translation).

20. The passage about the contract between author and reader is, in fact, part of Péguy's polemic against positivistic approaches to the humanities and social sciences. For a more comprehensive interpretation of this polemic and for his own philosophy of history, see Aronowicz, "Secret of the Man of Forty."

21. The first of Levinas's essays about Rosenzweig appeared as "Entre deux mondes" in *La Conscience juive*, pp. 121–37. It was later reproduced in the second edition of *Difficile liberté* (1976), was first translated by Richard A. Cohen in *Midstream* 29, no. 9 (Nov. 1983): 33–40, and subsequently figures in another English translation, in *Difficult Freedom*, pp. 181–97. The second essay, "Franz Rosenzweig: Une Pensée juive moderne," appeared in *Les Cahiers de la Nuit Surveillée*, no. 1:65–78. There are currently two books on the relationship between the thought of Rosenzweig and that of Levinas: Gibbs, *Correlations in Rosenzweig and Levinas*, and Cohen, *Elevations*. Handleman, *Fragments of Redemption*, devotes a very long chapter to the thought of Levinas, interspersed with comparisons to Rosenzweig. The sentence about Rosenzweig appears in Levinas, *Totality and Infinity*, p. 28.

22. It is commonly known that he began this work while still in the trenches, sending it bit by bit by postcard or letter to his home address. He finished the work upon returning from the front.

23. *Franz Rosenzweig*, ed. Glatzer, pp. 128–29.

24. Rosenzweig's thinking about the role of both Jews and Christians occupies the bulk of bk. 3, "Redemption or the Eternal Future of the Kingdom," which comprises over half of the entire work. See Rosenzweig, *Star of Redemption*, pp. 265–424.

25. The road to assimilation began, it seems, with Rosenzweig's great-grandfather, Samuel Meir Ehrenberg, who headed an institution of Jewish learning in Germany in the first half of the nineteenth century, which was "originally a Talmudic school in which a few general disciplines were tolerated, later a scholarly institution in which Talmud was tolerated, and finally a high school without Talmud instruction," according to the Jewish historian Leopold Zunz, who had been one of its pupils (quoted in *Rosenzweig*, ed. Glatzer, p. xii).

26. The technical name for the disease is amyotrophic lateral sclerosis with progressive paralysis of the bulba.

27. Here is a partial description of the system that was devised, from *Rosenzweig*, ed. Glatzer, p. 140: "In the spring of 1923 a typewriter was bought to facilitate communication, a special model manufactured by the General Electric Company; the construction of this machine was such that the person working it had only to move a simple lever over a disk containing all the characters, until the point indicated the desired character, and at the same time one pressed a single key to make the imprint. At first F.R. was able to operate the machine by himself, but later on he had to point out the characters with his left hand. Arm and hand were supported in a sling hanging from a bar next to the sick man. The key was operated by someone else, usually Mrs. Rosenzweig. Eventually his ability to indicate the characters lessened, so that they had to be ascertained by guesswork. Again, Mrs. Rosenzweig was the only person who could do this, for friends who tried to

relieve her in the summer of 1923, and who only three months earlier had been able to do so, failed."

28. Rosenzweig, *On Jewish Learning*, pp. 55–71.

29. Ibid., p. 58.

30. Ibid., p. 66.

31. *Rosenzweig*, ed. Glatzer, p. 50.

32. The curriculum of the Lehrhaus focused on the Hebrew language, since it was the key to penetrating classical Jewish texts, both the Bible and its commentaries. Some of the offerings and the relation Rosenzweig perceived they had to each other can be gleaned from his description of it in Rosenzweig, *On Jewish Learning*, pp. 100–101.

33. Ibid., pp. 69–70.

34. In a letter to his successor as director of the Lehrhaus, Rudolf Hallo, he states: "For those who are still Jewish, or once again Jewish, the Lehrhaus is only qualifiedly necessary, that is, as introduction and stimulation. There is even a real and typical danger of restricting their Jewish activities and studies to attendance at the Lehrhaus, since their work there readily bears fruit. It is one of the tasks of the director to help those who have really gone through the Lehrhaus to get out of it again and to stand on their own Jewish legs in doing and learning." *Rosenzweig*, ed. Glatzer, p. 118.

35. Rosenzweig, *On Jewish Learning*, p. 65.

36. Ibid., pp. 66–67.

37. Ibid., p. 65.

38. It was with Buber that Rosenzweig undertook a new translation of the Hebrew Bible into German. He also enlisted him as a teacher in the Freies Jüdisches Lehrhaus. In 1933, seven years after the Lehrhaus ceased functioning regularly, it was Buber who reopened it and directed it, in an effort to help German Jews react as Jews to the current realities. All this and more notwithstanding, Buber and Rosenzweig had profound philosophical differences. One of these is adumbrated in the exchange of letters about Jewish Law, reprinted in *On Jewish Learning*, pp. 109–18.

39. Ibid., p. 82.

40. Ibid., p. 122.

41. Ibid., pp. 122, 121.

42. *Rosenzweig*, ed. Glatzer, p. 135. It must be emphasized that Rosenzweig himself became fully observant, coinciding in practice, if not in general philosophical understanding, with the Orthodox.

43. Ibid., p. 357.

44. It is clear from an essay like "The Builders" that Rosenzweig wanted a Jewish life suffused with commandments, with *mitzvot*. These commandments, in order to be fulfilled as such, could not merely be obeyed as prohibitions but had to be responded to as if the commandment had been uttered today, instituting a living relation to God. Part of keeping the commandment alive was to see its ramifications beyond the prohibition, in its positive aspect. That is, keeping the Sabbath is not just refraining from work. It is a commandment to rest. Keeping kosher is not just refraining from certain foods. It is recognizing one's Jewishness in the very mun-

dane acts of life. For Rosenzweig, Jewish observance should not be a matter of permitted and forbidden deeds but a matter of living the commandments as though there were no area that was unaffected by them. See *On Jewish Learning*, pp. 82–92.

45. Ibid., p. 98.

46. The neo-Orthodox referred to here and above were the Jews who reacted against the Reform movement in Germany in the mid nineteenth century. Their opposition to the changes proposed by the Reformers was given expression by Rabbi Samson Raphael Hirsch (1808–88), the leader of that opposition. The neo-Orthodox insisted on the centrality of Jewish Law, its continuing practice, against those who felt that it had become obsolete in the course of history. Unlike the traditional Jews of eastern Europe, however, the neo-Orthodox wanted to pursue secular learning as well as Jewish observance. The formula Samson Raphael Hirsch often used was "Torah im Derekh Eretz" ("Torah and the way of the land"), by which he meant, unlike the previous usage of this Talmudic phrase, a thorough acquaintance with and participation in Western culture.

In many respects, it would seem that Rosenzweig's position followed closely upon that of Hirsch. However, both in these essays and elsewhere, Rosenzweig insists on keeping his distance. One of his objections, stated already, was to what he felt was the neo-Orthodox pigeonholing of Judaism into a set of observances, leaving thought and life outside the home substantially untouched. That is, one could keep all the commandments and yet borrow all one's arguments for keeping those very commandments from current historicist controversies, even if one were to oppose them. For instance, grounding the obligation to perform the commandments in historical fact (it is attested that 600,000 Israelites accepted the Torah at Mount Sinai, and therefore it was indeed revealed) is to borrow the mode of reasoning of the secular world. It is to miss the *religious* dimension of being obligated to the mitzvot altogether. See *Rosenzweig*, ed. Glatzer, p. 240.

Rosenzweig also frequently objected to what he felt was the neo-Orthodox sanctimoniousness about Jewish Law. "Wherever the Law is still kept among Western Jewry, it is no longer a living 'Jewishness,' one that while largely based on legal paragraphs, was taken naturally and as a matter of course. This sort of Judaism has acquired a polemical point that quite contrary to any original intent—is turned not against the outsider, but mainly against the large majority of those within Jewry who no longer keep the Law. Today the Law brings out more conspicuously the difference between Jew and Jew than between Jew and Gentile" (ibid., p. 219). He expressed a similar sentiment in a letter to his future wife, Edith Hahn. "Just see the emotional sclerosis of many orthodox Jews, especially the sclerosis of their Jewish feelings! How they are unable to accept any Jew who does not live by the Shulhan Arukh [sixteenth-century code of Jewish Law]" (ibid., p. 91). On the other hand, he could be surprisingly sympathetic to the neo-Orthodox, recognizing, for instance, the closeness of Hirsch's translation of the Torah into German to his and Buber's (ibid., p. 158). Rosenzweig, in short, despite his differences with the neo-Orthodox (differences that, mutatis mutandis, he also had with the Reformers and the Zionists), did not have a particular axe to grind with them. He simply insisted on including them among the rest of Western Jewry—that is, as alienated from a fully Jewish life.

47. Ibid., p. 80.

48. Ibid., pp. 81–82.

49. Jean Bastaire in his edition of *Notre jeunesse*, p. 17, points out that Péguy, in making this choice, was anticipating the *Annales* school of the historians Lucien Fèbvre and Marc Bloch. His statements here thus also have affinities with contemporary social history, in its desire to look not at the elite but rather at the daily life of social groups usually not represented in the great texts.

50. Péguy, *Oeuvres en prose complètes*, 3:6–7.

51. Ibid., p. 9.

52. It is clear in this context that *race* is not a biological term in Péguy's vocabulary. Eugene Weber, in commenting on how it was used at the turn of the century, remarks, "We must not make too much of the term 'race.' At that time people used it loosely to describe groupings of family, profession, psychological type, and the like, not just to designate an ethnic group" (*Dreyfus Affair*, ed. Kleeblatt, p. xxvii).

53. Péguy, *Oeuvres en prose complètes*, 3:14.

54. A *politique* in this context, then, would not just be a public action for the sake of wealth, power or glory. It would also be *idée* instead of *pensée*, a certain kind of knowing. For an analysis of the difference between *pensée* and *idée* in "Notre jeunesse," see Gerbaud, cited in Chapter 1, nn. 54, 120. And for a similar distinction between modes of knowing, see Ortega y Gasset, *Historical Reason*, pp. 19–22.

55. *Rosenzweig*, ed. Glatzer, p. 157.

56. Rosenzweig consecrates bk. 2 of *Star* to the topic of revelation, pp. 156–204. For an in-depth analysis of the notion of revelation in Rosenzweig's thought, see Moses, *System and Revelation*, pp. 97–149.

57. For a more detailed description of the way love impels the human being toward his or her neighbor, see Cohen, *Elevations*, pp. 58–66.

58. Rosenzweig, *Star*, p. 215; my emphasis.

59. Robert Gibbs devotes two chapters to an analysis of the way eternity interrupts time in ch. 3 of *Star* (*Correlations*, pp. 105–54).

60. Rosenzweig, *Star*, pp. 383–84.

61. Ibid., p. 381.

62. *Rosenzweig*, ed. Glatzer, p. 92.

63. For a discussion of this section of *Star*, see Gibbs, *Correlations*, pp. 140–44. It must be emphasized here that by *sermon*, Rosenzweig specifically has in mind the "Davar Torah," a reading of the Bible passage of the week through a series of prior rabbinic interpretations.

64. Rosenzweig, *Star*, pp. 309–10.

65. Ibid., p. 322.

66. Ibid., p. 325.

67. For a description of Rosenzweig's own reflections on the name of God, particularly in relation to how to translate the biblical appellation into German, see Galli, "Rosenzweig and the Name of God."

68. Rosenzweig, *Star*, p. 323.

69. I have tried to point to this religious current in an earlier work, *Freedom from Ideology*.

70. I turn the reader's attention, as concerns hope, to Péguy's long poem in verse *The Portico of the Mystery of the Second Virtue*, and, as concerns incarnation, to Clio 1 (cited in Preface, n. 2, above).

71. Charles Péguy, "Par ce demi-clair matin," in *Oeuvres en prose complètes*, 2: 209.

72. I am referring to the positions of Pie Duployé, Edmond-Maurice Lévy, and Wladimir Rabi.

73. Duployé, *Religion de Péguy*, pp. 429, 470.

74. See ibid., pp. 57, 451, 613, and 673, and Rabi, "Israël," pp. 339 and 341.

75. Péguy made this statement to his friend Daniel Halévy, a man whose family had converted to Protestantism and Catholicism from Judaism. Quoted in Rabi, "Israël," p. 334.

76. Rosenzweig does mention other traditions in *Star*, but only to dismiss them.

77. Levinas, in his essay, "Franz Rosenzweig," p. 76, comments that the three traditions, rather than just referring to specific historical peoples, also, in Rosenzweig's thought, become types for the three modes of being human to be found anywhere: "(If other planets besides the Earth were to be inhabited, should one not seek pagans, Christians and Jews there?)"

78. See pp. 87–88 above.

79. Péguy, *Oeuvres en prose complètes*, 3:1164.

80. "It is a metaphysical thesis, and among the greatest, that the universe, I mean the physical universe, is a language that God speaks to man's intellect, a sign language, a figurative language, in other words, in specifically Christian terms, that creation is a language that God the creator speaks to man his creature. Itself included in this creation. But made in the image and likeness of its Creator. . . . Reciprocally, great philosophies, great metaphysics are only the responses. . . . Great metaphysics are the languages of creation. And, by virtue of this, they are irreplaceable. They cannot move into each other's space, replace each other, take each other's place, do each other's duty. . . . And least of all are they interchangeable. For they are each of them, all, eternal languages. Spoken once and for all, when they are spoken, with no other being able to speak in their stead." Péguy, "Bar Cochebas," in *Oeuvres en prose complètes*, 2:657; my translation.

81. Ibid., pp. 659–60. There is a variation on this theme in the later essay Clio 2, p. 1157: "Israel brought God, the blood of David, the long line of prophets. Rome brought Rome, the Roman arch, the legion, the emperor, the sword, temporal power. Rome brought the sword, Israel brought revulsion for the sword. *Converte gladium tuum in locum suum*. Rome brought space, Israel having brought time. Rome brought the habitat(acle), Israel having brought the Tabernacle. Rome brought the living space, the climate, the prefects, Israel having brought the race and revulsion for prefects. But Homer and Plato brought precisely what you will try to explain in your *Essay on the Purity of the Ancients* [an essay Péguy himself intended to write]" (my translation). The change in this passage from "Bar-Cochebas" is that Rome is now included along with Greece. The image used here is that of a cradle. That is, these three traditions were the cradle within which Christianity was nurtured ("le triple berceau temporel"). This image would seem to indicate a different relation between Christianity and the other traditions, since

it would seem that it eventually outgrew them, or grew beyond them. Given the close proximity of these sentences to the previous ones quoted about Christianity having invented nothing, I think, however, that they are, in fact, meant to be read in the same way. Christianity contains all of these voices within itself and assigns to each its full significance.

82. Levinas, *Nine Talmudic Readings*, p. 78.

83. An English translation of Rosenzweig's translation and commentaries on Yehuda Halevy has appeared in Galli, *Franz Rosenzweig and Jehuda Halevy*.

84. *Rosenzweig*, ed. Glatzer, p. 254.

85. Ibid.

86. Cf. e.g., the juggling in the following sentence (see p. 30 above): "Such is eternally, temporally (eternally temporally, and temporally eternally), the mysterious subjugation of even the eternal to the temporal."

87. See, e.g., Denise Hamilton, "What's Your Diversity IQ? Take this Quiz on Office Manners and Find Out," pp. 22–24 of a special 44-page segment of the business section of the *Los Angeles Times*, May 16, 1994, pt. 2, entitled "Work Force Diversity: Getting Along and Getting Ahead," which invites the reader to select the appropriate answers to various questions from a number of alternatives. The following is a sample:

> You work with a person of color. You like this person and want to become more friendly but feel awkward in conversation. You're not sure how to refer to him or her. As a black? African-American? Nor are you sure how to refer to Mexican Americans. By that term or Hispanic? Chicano? Latino? What is the appropriate and sensitive way to proceed?
> A. You play it safe and avoid the topic.
> B. You float a trial balloon and wait for the person's reaction.
> C. You ask the person what he or she would like to be called.
> The answer is C. The reason you feel uncomfortable is because in our society we think it's inappropriate to introduce and discuss such topics. You might tell your colleague that while you feel awkward about being so blunt, you are bringing up the subject so you can learn. This sets the tone for further communication and dialogue.

The answers to the questions were formulated by a group of experts in different fields, two of whom presented themselves as diversity experts. I mention this article, indeed the whole section, because it seems to me to offer proof, if any were needed, that the vocabulary of and concerns with diversity are not a matter of interest only on college campuses. They have become mainstream.

Chapter 4

1. Jaff Schatz, *The Generation: The Rise and Fall of the Jewish Communists of Poland* (Berkeley: University of California Press, 1991).

2. Ibid., p. 124.

3. Ibid., p. 48.

4. Der Algemayner Yiddisher Arbeiterbund in Russland un Poyln was a Jewish

socialist party founded in Russia in 1897. Several years after the Revolution, the Bund in the Soviet Union joined the Communist Party. In Poland, however, the Bund remained independent and played a major role in Jewish life (claiming 100,000 members on the eve of the Nazi invasion in 1939). The Bund differed from the communists in that it wanted to retain Jewish nationality, in the form of cultural autonomy, within the larger struggle for a socialist revolution. This Jewish nationality was to be expressed in Yiddish and, it goes without saying, to be completely secular. The Bund differed from the Zionists in that it did not want either political or territorial autonomy for the Jewish people. The great struggle remained, not for a Jewish state, but for the Jewish proletariat. For both primary documents and historical background on the Bund, see *Jew in the Modern World*, ed. Mendes-Flohr and Reinharz, pp. 417–23. See also Minczeles, *Histoire générale du Bund*, which in some ways does for the Bund what Schatz does for Polish Jewish communists, presenting the movement from within and attempting to sort out what its positive legacy was, despite its failure.

5. Schatz, *Generation*, p. 46.

6. The expression "non-Jewish Jew" is taken from the Jewish Marxist historian Isaac Deutscher, originally from Poland, who lived in Britain from 1939 until his death in 1967. He spoke of a particular sort of Jew, whose presence he already detected in the Talmud, who, while leaving the Jewish tradition behind, nonetheless still brings with him some eminently Jewish characteristics. See Deutscher, *The Non-Jewish Jew and Other Essays*, pp. 25–27.

7. Schatz, *Generation*, p. 121.

8. Ibid., pp. 137, 138, 140, 142.

9. Ibid., p. 239.

10. Ibid., pp. 127, 142.

11. Ibid., p. 274.

12. Ibid., p. 127.

13. *Dawkie* in this context means something like "for this very reason." It is a notoriously untranslatable expression.

14. Ibid., p. 356 n. 6, quoting Hanna Krall, *Sublokatorka* (Paris: Libella, 1985), p. 53. Krall's novel has since been translated by Jaroslaw Anders as *The Subtenant* (Evanston, Ill.: Northwestern University Press, 1992).

15. Schatz, *Generation*, pp. 241, 296.

16. Ibid., p. 11. Moreover, Schatz's ch. 16 is entitled "The Defeat," and the word *defeat* occurs innumerable times in the course of the book.

17. Ibid., p. 311. The Jews who emigrated were forced to renounce their Polish citizenship. "In renouncing their citizenship, they also had to state that they felt bound to Israel rather than to Poland, disavow all claims to pensions or compensation of any kind, and pay to the state's treasury the estimated equivalent of the costs of their children's studies. . . . Most probably, nearly 20,000 Jewish refugees left Poland, leaving some 5,000, mostly aged, behind."

18. There are apparently a growing number of Jews in Poland today, as well as a revival of Judaism. Quite a few people who were raised as Poles are now discovering that they have some Jewish ancestry and are becoming interested in Jewish learning and practice. The estimated figure for the current Jewish population of Poland

is 15,000, counting only those who acknowledge themselves as such. See Dan Caslez, "Yehudim Hadashim b Polin," *Haaretz*, Jan. 10, 1997, p. 6b.

19. Schatz, *Generation*, p. 2.

20. Ibid., pp. 1–2.

21. Ibid., pp. 2–3. Emphasis added.

22. Ibid., p. 314.

23. Ibid., p. 315.

24. Ibid., p. 1.

25. Ibid., p. x.

26. Philip Hallie, *Lest Innocent Blood Be Shed* (New York: Harper & Row, 1979). Since my essay was written before the publication in 1994 of a paperback edition with a new preface, I base my remarks on the preface to the first edition.

27. Ibid., p. 4.

28. Ibid., pp. 152–53.

29. Ibid., p. 260. Hallie mentions that Magda Trochmé was always at some distance from seeing herself as a believer. She claimed to have lost whatever faith she had possessed at the time of the death of her 14-year-old son, even resenting her husband's work as pastor, thus creating grave tensions in their marriage. Her notion of responsibility seems to have operated completely independently of these beliefs.

30. Ibid., p. 155.

31. Ibid., pp. 20, 154, 233, 285.

32. Le Chambon's two pastors, André Trochmé and Edouard Théis, had both studied theology at the University of Paris. Later, Trochmé attended Union Theological Seminary in New York. He met Madga Grilli in New York, where she was then studying to be a social worker.

33. Ibid., p. 128.

34. Ibid., pp. 132–33. Burns Chalmers was responsible for many of the Quakers' activities on behalf of the inmates of the camps in southern France. He was influential in helping to set up children's shelters in Le Chambon.

35. Ibid., pp. 182–83.

36. Ibid., p. 173.

37. Ibid., p. 285.

38. Ibid., p. 61.

39. Ibid., p. 4.

40. Ibid., p. 284.

41. Ibid., pp. 277–81.

42. Ibid., p. 281.

43. Ibid., p. 282.

44. Ibid., pp. 291–92.

45. Ibid., p. 291.

46. Ibid.

47. Ibid., p. 293. Quoted from *Pirkei Avot*, ch. 1:14.

48. I may be mistaken here, but the way Hallie quotes Jewish texts suggests this. When he quotes the Baal-Shem Tov to the effect that "the secret of redemption lies in remembering" (p. 6), he adds soon thereafter that he was not sufficiently religious to understand what the Baal Shem meant by "redemption." His interpre-

tation of the Shema, although quite beautiful, universalizes its meaning without any reference to the particularity of the Jews as a people. This also is an indication of a certain distance.

49. Hallie tells the story of the deportation of the children and the head of the schools, Daniel Trochmé, a cousin of the pastor's, on pp. 203–17.

50. Ibid., p. 2.

51. Ibid.

52. Ibid., pp. 292–93.

53. Ibid., p. 293.

54. Ibid., p. 7.

55. Ibid., p. 293.

Bibliography

Arendt, Hannah. "The Jew as Pariah: A Hidden Tradition." *Jewish Social Studies* 6, no. 2 (Apr. 1944): 99–122.

Aronowicz, Annette. "Emmanuel Levinas's Talmudic Commentaries: The Relation of the Jewish Tradition to the Non-Jewish World." In *Contemporary Jewish Ethics and Morality*, ed. Elliot N. Dorff and Louis E. Newman, 212–18. London: Oxford University Press, 1995.

———. *Freedom from Ideology: Secrecy in Modern Expression*. New York: Garland Press, 1987.

———. "Reagan, Weizsäcker et la visite au cimetière de Bitburg." *Esprit* 123, no. 2 (Feb. 1987): 87–101.

———. "The Secret of the Man of Forty." *History and Theory* 32, no. 2 (1993): 101–18.

Bastaire, Jean. *Péguy l'inchrétien*. Paris: Desclée, 1991.

Bensaïd, Daniel. *Walter Benjamin: Sentinelle messianique à la gauche du possible*. Paris: Plon, 1990.

Bernard-Lazare [Lazare Marcus Manassé Bernard]. *Antisemitism: Its History and Its Causes*. London: Britons Publishing Co., 1967. Lincoln: University of Nebraska Press, 1995. Translation of *L'Antisémitisme: Son histoire et son causes*. Paris: Léon Chailley, 1894. 2d ed., with an introduction by André Fontainas. Paris: Crès, 1934 with additional material, 1969. Paris: Editions de la Différence, 1982, re-edited.

———. *Contre l'antisémitisme: Histoire d'une polémique*. 1896. Paris: Le Sphinx, 1983.

————. *Job's Dungheap: Essays on Jewish Nationalism*. With a preface by Hannah Arendt. New York: Schocken Books, 1948. Translation of *Le Fumier de Job*. Edited by Edmond Fleg. Paris: Rieder, 1928. Reprint, with an introduction by Carole Sandrel. Strasbourg: Circé, 1990.

————. "La Loi et les congrégations." *Cahiers de la Quinzaine* 3, no. 21 (Aug. 16, 1902): 207–31.

Bloy, Léon. *Le Salut par les Juifs*. Paris: Joseph Victorian, 1906.

Boyarin, Daniel. *Carnal Israel*. Berkeley: University of California Press, 1993.

Bredin, Jean-Denis. *Bernard Lazare*. Paris: Fallois, 1992. 2d ed., 1994.

Burac, Robert. "Avertissement." In Péguy, *Oeuvres en prose complètes*, 1:ix–xxxvi. Tours: Gallimard, 1987.

————. Charles Péguy: La révolution et la grâce. Paris: Robert Laffont, 1994.

————. "Notices, notes et variantes." In Péguy, *Oeuvres en prose complètes*, 3: 1481–1813. Bruges: Gallimard, 1992.

————. "Notre jeunesse." In Péguy, *Oeuvres en prose complètes*, 3:1484–1503. Bruges: Gallimard, 1992.

Chouraqui, Léon. "Contribution à la connaissance de la pensée littéraire, morale et politique de Bernard Lazare." 2 vols. Ph.D. diss., Université de Aix-en-Provence, 1991.

Cohen, Richard A. *Elevations: The Height of the Good in Rosenzweig and Levinas*. Chicago: University of Chicago Press, 1994.

————, ed. *Face to Face with Levinas*. Albany: State University of New York Press, 1986.

Dadoun, Roger. *Éros de Péguy: La Guerre, l'écriture, la durée*. Paris: Presses Universitaires de France, 1988.

Darmesteter, James. *Les Prophètes d'Israël*. Paris: Calmann-Lévy, 1892.

Deleuze, Gilles. *Différence et répétition*. Paris: Presses Universitaires de France, 1968.

Deutscher, Isaac. *The Non-Jewish Jew and Other Essays*. London: Oxford University Press, 1968.

Donoghue, Denis. "The Philosopher of Selfless Love." *New York Review of Books* 43, no. 5 (Mar. 21, 1996): 37–40.

Drumont, Edouard. *La France juive*. Paris: C. Marpon and E. Flammarion, 1886.

Duployé, Pie. *La Religion de Péguy*. Paris: Klincksieck, 1960.

Finkielkraut, Alain. *Le Mécontemporain*. Paris: Gallimard, 1991.

Fraisse, Simone. "Péguy et Renan." *Revue d'Histoire Littéraire de la France* 73, nos. 2–3 (Mar.–June 1973).

————, ed. *Charles Péguy 2: Les Cahiers de la Quinzaine*. Special issue of the *Revue des Lettres Modernes*. Paris: Lettres Modernes Minard, 1983.

————, ed. *Charles Péguy 3: Un Romantique malgré lui*. Special issue of the *Revue des Lettres Modernes*. Paris: Lettres Modernes Minard, 1985.

————, ed. *Charles Péguy 5: L'Écrivain*. Special issue of the *Revue des Lettres Modernes*. Paris: Lettres Modernes Minard, 1990.

Galli, Barbara. *Franz Rosenzweig and Jehuda Halevy: Translating, Translations and Translators*. Montreal: McGill-Queens University Press, 1995.

————. "Rosenzweig and the Name of God." *Modern Judaism* 14, no. 1 (Feb. 1994): 63–86.

Gerbaud, Françoise. "La Reconstruction de l'affaire dans 'Notre jeunesse' de Charles Péguy." In *Les Écrivains et l'affaire Dreyfus*. Orléans: Presses Universitaires Françaises, 1983.

Gibbs, Robert. *Correlations in Rosenzweig and Levinas*. Princeton: Princeton University Press, 1992.

Guillon, Jean. "Bernard Lazare." Ph.D. diss., Université de Nice, 1967.

Hagani, Baruch. *Bernard-Lazare*. Paris: Les Forgerons, 1919.

Halévy, Daniel. "Apologie pour notre passé." *Cahiers de la quinzaine* 11, no. 10 (Apr. 10, 1910).

Hallie, Philip. *Lest Innocent Blood Be Shed: The Story of the Village of Le Chambon, and How Goodness Happened There*. New York: Harper & Row, 1979. 2d ed., 1994.

Handleman, Susan A. *Fragments of Redemption*. Bloomington: Indiana University Press, 1991.

Hertzberg, Arthur. "Is Anti-Semitism Dying Out?" *New York Review of Books* 40, no. 12 (June 24, 1993).

Hollinger, David A. "Post-Ethnic America." *Contention* 2, no. 1 (Fall 1992).

Hyman, Paula. *From Dreyfus to Vichy*. New York: Columbia University Press, 1979.

Itterboek, Eugène van. *Socialisme et poésie chez Péguy*. Paris: L'Amitié Charles Péguy, 1966.

Lasserre, Pierre. "La Logique de l'Action française." *Action Française* [Paris] 33 (Jan.–June 1910).

Lazare, Bernard. See Bernard-Lazare.

Leroy, Géraldi. *Péguy entre l'ordre et la révolution*. Paris: Presses de la Fondation nationale des sciences politiques, 1981.

Leroy-Beaulieu, Anatole. *Israel Among the Nations: A Study of the Jews and Anti-semitism*. Translated by Frances Hellman. New York: G. P. Putnam, 1896.

Levinas, Emmanuel. *Beyond the Verse*. Translation by Gary Mole of *L'Au-delà du verset* (1982). Bloomington: Indiana University Press, 1994.

———. *Difficult Freedom: Essays on Judaism*. Translation by Séan Hand of *Difficile liberté* (1963, 1976). Baltimore: Johns Hopkins University Press, 1990.

———. "Entre deux mondes," *La Conscience juive: Données et débats*. Paris: Presses Universitaires de France, 1963.

———. "Franz Rosenzweig: Une Pensée juive moderne." *Cahiers de la Nuit Surveillée*, no. 1 (1982): 65–78. Quétigny, France: La Nuit Surveillée et les auteurs.

———. *In the Time of the Nations*. Translation by Michael B. Smith of *A l'heure des nations* (1988). Bloomington: Indiana University Press, 1994.

———. *Nine Talmudic Readings by Emmanuel Levinas*. Translation by Annette Aronowicz of *Quatre lectures talmudiques* (1968) and *Du sacré au saint: Cinq nouvelles lectures talmudiques* (1977). Bloomington: Indiana University Press, 1990.

———. *Otherwise Than Being or Beyond Essence*. Translation by Alphonso Lingis of *Autrement qu'être ou au delà de l'essence* (1974). Hingham, Mass.: Kluwer, Boston, 1981.

———. *Totality and Infinity*. Translation by Alphonso Lingis of *Totalité et infini* (1961). Pittsburgh: Duquesne University Press, 1969.

Lévy, Bernard-Henri. *L'Idéologie française*. Paris: Bernard Grasset, 1981.

Lévy, Edmond-Maurice. "Mes souvenirs de Charles Péguy." *L'Amitié Charles Péguy: Feuillets mensuels*, no. 175 (Mar. 1972).

Lewis, Bernard. *Semites and Anti-Semites*. New York: W. W. Norton, 1985.

Manuel, Frank E. *The Broken Staff: Judaism Through Christian Eyes*. Cambridge, Mass.: Harvard University Press, 1992.

Marrus, Michael. *The Politics of Assimilation*. Oxford: Oxford University Press, 1971.

Martin, Benjamin F. "The Dreyfus Affair and the Corruption of the French Legal System." In *The Dreyfus Affair: Art, Truth and Justice*, edited by Norman L. Kleeblatt. Berkeley: University of California Press, 1987.

Mendes-Flohr, Paul, and Jehuda Reinharz, eds. *The Jew in the Modern World*. New York: Oxford University Press, 1995.

Miłosz, Czesław. *Native Realm*. Garden City, N.Y.: Doubleday, 1968.

Minczeles, Henri. *Histoire générale du Bund: Un Mouvement révolutionnaire juif*. Paris: Austral, 1995.

Moses, Stéphane. *System and Revelation: The Philosophy of Franz Rosenzweig*. Detroit: Wayne State University Press, 1987.

Nochlin, Linda. "Degas and the Dreyfus Affair: A Portrait of the Artist as an Anti-Semite," In *The Dreyfus Affair: Art, Truth and Justice*, edited by Norman L. Kleeblatt. Berkeley: University of California Press, 1987.

Ortega y Gasset, José. *Historical Reason*. New York: W. W. Norton, 1984.

Péguy, Charles. *Notre jeunesse, précédé par De la raison*. Edited by Jean Bastaire. Paris: Gallimard, 1993.

———. *Oeuvres en prose complètes*, vol. 1. Edited by Robert Burac. Tours: Gallimard, 1987.

———. *Oeuvres en prose complètes*, vol. 2. Edited by Robert Burac. Tours: Gallimard, 1988.

———. *Oeuvres en prose complètes*, vol. 3. Edited by Robert Burac. Bruges: Gallimard, 1992.

———. *Oeuvres poétiques complètes de Charles Péguy*. Paris: Gallimard, 1957.

———. *The Portal of the Mystery of Hope*. Grand Rapids, Mich.: W. B. Eerdmans, 1996.

———. *The Portico of the Mystery of the Second Virtue*. Translated by Dorothy Brown Aspinwall. Metuchen, N.J.: Scarecrow Press, 1970.

———. *Temporal and Eternal*. Translated by Alexander Dru. London: Harvill Press, 1958.

Petit, Jacques. *Bernanos, Bloy, Claudel, Péguy: Quatre écrivains catholiques face à Israël*. Paris: Calmann-Lévy, 1972.

Prajs, Lazare. *Péguy et Israël*. Paris: A. G. Nizet, 1970.

Rabi, Wladimir. "Israël." *Esprit* 330, nos. 8–9 (Aug.–Sept. 1964): 331–42.

Renan, Ernest. *Identité originelle et séparation graduelle du judaïsme et du christianisme*. New York: Rand School of Social Science, 1943.

———. *Le Judaïsme comme race et comme religion*. Paris: Calmann-Lévy, 1983.

Robinet, André. *Péguy entre Jaurès, Bergson et l'église*. Vichy: Seghers, 1968.

Rondeau, Daniel. "Péguy, la colère." *Le Nouvel Observateur*, no. 1497 (July 15–21, 1993).

Rosenzweig, Franz. *Franz Rosenzweig: His Life and Thought*. Edited by Nahum Glatzer. New York: Schocken Books, 1961.

———. *On Jewish Learning*. Edited by Nahum Glatzer. New York: Schocken Books, 1955.

———. *The Star of Redemption*. Notre Dame, Ind.: University of Notre Dame Press, 1985.

Sabiani, Julie. *La Ballade du coeur*. Paris: Klincksieck, 1973.

Schatz, Jaff. *The Generation: The Rise and Fall of the Jewish Communists of Poland*. Berkeley: University of California Press, 1991.

Scholem, Gershom. *On Jews and Judaism in Crisis*. New York: Schocken Books, 1976.

Steiner, George. "Drumming on the Doors." *Times Literary Supplement*, Dec. 25, 1992.

Viard, Jacques. "Prophètes d'Israël et annonciateur chrétien." *Revue d'Histoire Littéraire de la France* 73, nos. 2–3 (Mar.–June 1973).

Villiers, Marjorie. *Charles Péguy: A Study in Integrity*. London: Collins, 1965.

Weber, Eugene. Foreword to *The Dreyfus Affair: Art, Truth, and Justice*, edited by Norman L. Kleeblatt, xxv–xxviii. Berkeley: University of California Press, 1987.

———. *France fin de siècle*. Cambridge, Mass.: Harvard University Press, 1986.

Wilson, Nelly. *Bernard Lazare*. Translated by Christiane and Douglas Gallagher. Paris: Albin Michel, 1985. Translation, with additions, of *Bernard Lazare*. New York: Cambridge University Press, 1978.

———. "L'Amitié de Péguy et de Bernard-Lazare." *Bulletin de l'Amitié Charles Péguy*, no. 13 (Jan.–Mar. 1981): 3–26.

Wilson, Stephen. "Anti-Semitism and Jewish Response in France During the Dreyfus Affair." *European Studies Review* 6, no. 2 (1976): 225–48.

Winling, Raymond. *Péguy et Renan*. Lille: Ateliers reproductions de thèses, Université de Lille III, 1975.

Index

In this index an "f" after a number indicates a separate reference on the next page, and an "ff" indicates separate references on the next two pages. A continuous discussion over two or more pages is indicated by a span of page numbers, e.g., "57–59."

Library of Congress Cataloging-in-Publication Data

Aronowicz, Annette
    Jews and Christians on time and eternity : Charles Péguy's portrait of
Bernard-Lazare / Annette Aronowicz.
       p.   cm. — (Stanford studies in Jewish history and culture)
    Includes bibliographical references and index.
    ISBN 0-8047-3005-9 (alk. paper)
    1. Péguy, Charles-Pierre, 1915– Notre jeunesse. 2. Lazare, Bernard,
1865–1903—In literature. I. Title. II. Series.
PQ2631.E25Z5312   1998
844'.912—dc21   97-19076

Original printing 1997

Last figure below indicates year of this printing:

06 05 04 03 02 01 00 99 98 97

DATE DUE